A

PASTOR'S PERSPECTIVE...

Abram Cotton III

A 365-Day Devotional

ISBN-13: 978-1722838928
ISBN-10: 1722838922

First Edition

Printing in the United States

Editing: Wandah Gibbs, Ed. D.

Cover Art: Mari Smith

Cover Photo: Philip Thesing

WGW Publishing Inc., Rochester, NY

DEDICATION

I would like to dedicate this book to the origin of its content, the Holy Spirit! This inspired work confirmed my calling by transforming past dilemma into present day devotion. It is because of the power that embodies this work that I believe every "whosoever" will be inspired and empowered to resist temptation, challenge unsettling choices, and press towards the mark of the high calling in Christ Jesus!

Spirit of the Most-High God, thank you so much for your comfort, your guidance, and your compassion. May those you touch, in turn touch the lives of others.

"Let the words of my mouth and the meditation of my heart, be acceptable in thy sight, O Lord, my strength, and my redeemer." (Psalms 19:14).

FOREWARD

Don't let your past define your future. Dwelling on the past can be like walking around with a metal ball chained to your ankle. The bible tells us, "He whom the Son sets free is free indeed." (John 8:36). That means free from our past…indeed!

Abram "Bo" Cotton III is a free man though that wasn't always the case. I met Bo in jail. He was *doing time* again. He had a pretty thick rap sheet and Rochester, NY knew his name. He hurt people. Drugs and alcohol imprison you long before you are physically incarcerated. At the time, I was a Chaplain for the New York State Department of Corrections. I knew the "new Bo," the "new and improved Bo." His most recent bid had worked for him as he had made a quality decision to give himself totally over to Jesus. He got his head screwed on straight and in the words of another Christian brother, "I wasn't arrested, I was rescued."

Living for Jesus has its challenges and obstacles which can be amplified in the context of prison. Why? Because everybody knows your business. A thousand eyes and ears in close proximity means that who you really are can't be hidden for long. Abram's faith was solid however, and he had the respect of inmates and staff alike.

Bo did double duty for the Lord and served as both Choir Director and Chaplain's clerk. He is an accomplished vocalist and organizer. Obviously, a prison choir is not full of *Choir Boys* so to speak, yet Bo exhibited considerable wisdom and skill in handling the choir, picking up good insight from the Holy Spirit along the way. All these experiences proved valuable in becoming a pastor. His musical talent actually comes through in his writings. Note the prolific use of alliteration, his cadence in rhyme, and the balance of hard tones and soft ones in his words. His messages are like, "Hey, because I love you: take that!" It's really good stuff.

Because Abram served as my Clerk it meant we had extra time together, thus I got to know the mind and heart of the man. I observed devotion to God above all else! His was and is a dedication to become a quality disciple of Jesus. "I tell you her sins---and there are many, have been forgiven, so she has shown me much love." (Luke 7:47). Just put Bo's name in there. Of whom much has been forgiven, the same will love much. Bo's love for Jesus is seen in his service to Him. *A Pastor's Perspective* is a product of the love and service Bo has for his Savior.

Some are content to be forgiven of their past and coast into heaven. Not Bo! He was always probing, seeking, asking, wanting to know more, and wanting to grow more. He was always evaluating, assessing, refining and wanting to become the best he could be for the Glory of God. He's still that way. Read each Holy Spirit guided insight from *A Pastor's Perspective* and you will find each message worthy of reflection. Meditate on them, chew them over some more, refer back to them again, and then again. You will find deep stuff helpful for correcting, inspiring, motivating, comforting, faith building, and more. Good stuff! Dig in!

You'll note I've referred to him as Bo, which Is who I knew him as for four years. Ten years later, he is Pastor Abram Cotton III. He was my "son in the faith" while in prison and like any father who wants his son to achieve a better life than his own, I have seen Pastor Cotton do just that! He has been faithful to his calling and is an effective messenger for the King. And…he is really just getting started. I am certain you will see more and hear more about Pastor Abram Cotton III. Before Jesus comes or Abram lays his head in final repose, many will rise up and call him their "Spiritual Father."

-Chaplain Wayne Hampton

ACKNOWLEDGMENTS

I'd like to acknowledge my greatest supporters: my wife, Evangelist Rosa M. Cotton and the entire King of Glory Ministries family. Your love and encouragement have nurtured my purpose and helped shaped my understanding of unconditional love.

And all those who sowed advice, time, finances, and fellowship into my vision. You know who you are and God has promised to never forget your labor of love...

Special thanks to my mentors in the faith: Reverend Wayne Hampton (Prison Ministry), Pastor Abram Cotton Jr. (Christian Love Bible Church), and a whole host of contributing clergy throughout my life, of which there is not enough space to record all I've received from them. And most of all, my Lord and Savior Jesus Christ!

INTRODUCTION

*There are times when God will use bondage as a
bandage, to show forth His love to those who have
been bruised and to those who have been broken.
Although each state is different in its severity, God is
the same, in His sovereignty. When acceptance,
repentance, and submission enter a Man's heart, they
lovingly allow the position of prostration to enter his
will..."*

-Pastor A. Cotton III

Having grown up in the inner city of
Rochester, NY, I marvel and am humbled by
God's constant covering over my life. It is
God's relentless love, in pursuit of my
troubled heart, that continues to stir in my
soul a tenacity to touch the lives of others
with the same relentless love.

So much of my youth and young adult life
was obscured by past pain, peer pressure, and
spiritual promiscuity. But God's love proved
far more compelling than my confusion. He
graciously and gracefully showed me that my
future was brighter than the tinted obscurity
of my flawed past, in His love.

After being so true to His promise, He loved
me through my confusion, all the way to His
kingdom. It was in the midst of incarceration
that I received Jesus into my heart. I then
embraced deliverance from the bondage of

11

drugs, larcenous behavior, and the imprisonment caused by ill-conceived thinking.

The word of God gave my purpose perspective! And now, almost 27 years later I *serve* as pastor, husband, father, grandfather, and more importantly as a humbled and grateful child of the Most-High God! It was because of God's Amazing Grace and undaunting love, that I am not just free, I am FREE INDEED! (John 8:36).

JANUARY 1

Hallelujah and thank you Jesus for another Year! Some will start this New Year, the same way they ended last year; hangovers, hard times, and an obscured understanding of ALL things heavenly! But Jesus said, "Verily, verily, I say unto you, except a grain of wheat fall into the ground and die, it abideth ALONE! But, if it dies, it bringeth forth much fruit. If any man SERVE me, let him FOLLOW me! (John 12:24-26). My question to you this New Year is this...Who will YOU follow? Some of the toughest lessons we learn, are best absorbed when we accept responsibility for the direction we chose to go in! Sure, we want to blame people, circumstances, situations, and even God, but none of these things are to blame if the road YOU chose was NOT along the path of your destination! When you got behind the wheel of your WILL, you told everybody, including God...I got this! Jesus said, "I am the WAY, the TRUTH, and the LIFE!" (John 14:6). Jesus is at the next exit saying FOLLOW ME. Today is the perfect opportunity to start moving in the right direction...Follow the ONE, who will safely lead you home. Have a Blessed day, and thanks for allowing me to share the word from a *Pastor's Perspective*...

JANUARY 2

When God presented the PROMISE of
eternal life, He was revealing the only HOPE
for this world's heaviness. We can all quote
John 3:16…"For God so Loved the world
that He gave His only begotten Son, that
whosoever shall believe in Him shall not
perish but have eternal life." This is
foundational to our faith, an absolute truth in
our sanctification, and the core of our HOPE!
However, the crux of that which we know so
well (John 3:16), sadly overshadows the
purpose of that which is clearly overlooked
and hardly ever mentioned. God gave us His
Son because of this TRUTH…."For God sent
not His Son into the world to condemn the
world, but that the world through Him might
be SAVED! He that BELIEVETH on Him is
not condemned, but he that believeth not is
condemned ALREADY!!" (John 3:17-18).
Life without Jesus, is life on death row! The
true purpose of the SON, was to overturn the
sentence for SIN! From now on, don't just
quote John 3:16, remember the TRUTH of
your former life sentence: Condemned
ALREADY!! But Glory to God, His plan
came with the promise, that plugged our
Hope, into His heart, and we were acquitted
by the majesty of Heaven! Have a Blessed day,
and thanks for allowing me to share the word
from a *Pastor's Perspective*…

JANUARY 3

When God gave us GRACE, He knew everything we could be in Him! WOW, what omniscience! We can look at Grace like this: Grace is God's forethought of ME! The Apostle Paul was so incredibly grateful for the covering of Grace he wrote..."To the praise of the glory of His GRACE, through which He hath made US accepted in the beloved, in whom WE have redemption through His blood, the Forgiveness of sins, according to the riches in GRACE!" (Ephesians 1:6-7). I don't know how you see GRACE, but God saw YOU, through it! And because God is rich in all His deity, He distributed His divinity amongst all humanity through Grace, that it might lead us to Salvation...."For by GRACE are you saved through faith, and that

RICHES IN GRACE

not of yourselves!" (Ephesians 2:8). We need to constantly remind ourselves, we owe God praise for every day, every hour, and every minute! Never lose sight of the fact that Grace, is God's permission to Grow! If God wasn't rich in GRACE, we'd still be overwhelmed by Grief! Have a Blessed day, and thanks for allowing me to share the word from a *Pastor's Perspective...*

JANUARY 4

Job was able to express extremely profound thoughts because of his experiences; "Man born of a woman is of FEW days, and FULL of trouble!" (Job 14:1). So then, the irony of life according to Job is this: our days on earth are so FEW, and yet, they are so FULL of all sorts of trouble! Some troubles are due to external opposition and things outside of our control. While others are self-inflicted, causing enormous internal turbulence! Either way, there will be troubles! However, the Prophet Jeremiah says...It is because of the Lord's MERCIES that we are not consumed!!" (Lamentations 3:22). Some of us would not be alive today, if the Lord was not MERCIFUL! It is a blessing when you can look back over your life and see how God has kept, covered, and protected you from the world, and yourself! He is worthy to be praised, because He's been better to you, than you've been to yourself! Hence, not withstanding, God wants you to know that in spite of everything life throws your way, "Surely GOODNESS and MERCY shall follow you ALL the days of your life, so you can dwell in the house of the Lord FOREVER!" (Psalms 23:6). God gives MERCY, so we don't give in to Misery! Have a Blessed day, and thanks for allowing me to share the word from a *Pastor's Perspective...*

JANUARY 5

There is a sense of security in being
BLESSED that you can't find in being
wealthy, successful, or talented. But you say,
aren't all those things the result of being
BLESSED? Yes, to a certain degree, but being
BLESSED is more than what you possess
(Luke 12:15). Being blessed is not God
Satisfying your needs, but rather about God
Sanctifying you to complete your divine
assignment! If you don't have wealth, success,
or talent...but still have Jesus, you're
BLESSED! I particularly like the Prophet
David's outlook on this; BLESSED is the
man whom thou hast CHOSEN and cause to
approach thee, that he may dwell in thy
courts!!"(Psalms 65:4). Because the real beauty
of being BLESSED is this: it's not what I
prayed for, it's what GOD wanted for me!!
"BLESSED be the God and Father of our
Lord Jesus Christ, who hath BLESSED us
with all spiritual blessings in heavenly places
in Christ! According as he hath CHOSEN us
in Him BEFORE the foundation of the
world, that we should be HOLY and without
blame before Him in love!!"(Ephesians 1:3-4).
So then, being BLESSED is not about what I
have, it's more about the ONE who has me!
Have a Blessed day, and thanks for allowing
me to share the word from a *Pastor's
Perspective*...

JANUARY 6

"O God, you are my God! Early will I seek you! My flesh longs for you! In a dry and thirsty land, where no water is. So, have I looked for you in the sanctuary, to see your POWER and your GLORY! Because your LOVING KINDNESS is better than life!!" (Psalms 63:1-3). As I read this Psalm, I clearly detect that David believes everything he's discovered about God, far exceeds anything he has acquired in this life!

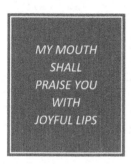

MY MOUTH SHALL PRAISE YOU WITH JOYFUL LIPS

David found out that there is more to life and that Salvation is more than sin's solution! Salvation is also our current satisfaction! God is BIGGER than life! And better than anything in it! Today, take a moment to reflect on the fact that if God wasn't God, you wouldn't be Saved! But because He is God, you can declare, "Thus will I bless you while I live, I will lift up my hands in your name! My soul is SATISFIED as with marrow and fatness, and my mouth shall PRAISE you with joyful lips!" (Psalms 63:4-5). Praise him now, so He will praise you on that day! Have a Blessed day, and thanks for allowing me to share the word from a *Pastor's Perspective...*

JANUARY 7

Do you realize that PAIN has just as much purpose as JOY? The Apostle Paul wrote, "For we know that the whole creation groaneth and travaileth in PAIN together until now. And not only they, but ourselves also, who have the first fruits of the Spirit, even we ourselves groan within ourselves, waiting for the adoption, that is, the REDEMPTION of our body!!"(Romans 8:22-23). But earlier, in the same text Paul expresses that PAIN is oftentimes the gateway to glory! "For I reckon that the sufferings of this present time are not worthy to be compared with the GLORY that shall be revealed in us!" (Romans 8:19). It's important that we not reduce, the lessons of PAIN! Had it not been for the painful lessons in life, we would still be confusing poison with passion! Like salt and sugar, they may look alike, but they don't taste the same!! The scripture says, "Looking unto Jesus, the Author and Finisher of our faith, who for the JOY that was set before Him, endured the cross!" (Hebrews 12:2). Allow yourselves to see PAIN as the weight of your glory! The world says, No Pain, No Gain! But we declare, where there's Pain, there's Purpose! Have a Blessed day, and thanks for allowing me to share the word from a *Pastor's Perspective*...

JANUARY 8

Being a believer is no bed of roses, but it's
certainly no bed of thorns either! Believers are
tried, tested, and sometimes trampled by the
world! But they are also true, triumphant, and
treasured by God! For those who truly believe
in the power of God, the bible says, "We are
not of them who draw back unto perdition,
but of them that BELIEVE to the saving of
the soul!"(Hebrews 10:39). Believers are
champions by FAITH, and God's elect by
CHOICE! (John 15:15). When we accepted
the call to believe, we were freed from the
thing that destroys people's faith: the world!
Your belief is not like a badge displayed on an
officer's chest, your belief is more like a
banner held high, so others will know, "For I
am not ashamed of the gospel of Christ, for it
is the power of God unto Salvation to
everyone that BELIEVES!!" (Romans 1:16).
Therefore, those who firmly BELIEVE in the
power of God, have come to understand,
there is no need to worry about what COMES
OUT of the world, instead WE truly
BELIEVE in the OUTCOME! Blessed are
those who BELIEVE! Have a Blessed day,
and thanks for allowing me to share the word
from a *Pastor's Perspective…*

"But they that wait upon the Lord shall RENEW their strength, they shall MOUNT up with wings like eagles, they shall RUN, and not be weary, they shall WALK, and not faint!!" (Isaiah 40:31). What a spiritual awakening for those determined to reach their destiny! Let's take a moment to break this down. God is telling US...If we wait on His guidance, His presence, and His permission, He will RENEW our strength to fulfill our calling! His strength in YOU will help you MOUNT up or rise up as though you have wings like an eagle! Wings that are strong and durable! You will have the ability to fly above storms, but you will also be able to RUN away from the floods! And when all that GOD IS,

HE WILL RENEW OUR STRENGTH

becomes all that YOU ARE, He said you can now WALK with him, and never grow faint! Good God Almighty!

God wants you to know that those who WAIT on the Lord, will have what it takes, to leave the world behind! Have a Blessed day, and thanks for allowing me to share the word from a *Pastor's Perspective*...

JANUARY 10

When you know God has called you with a HOLY calling, (II Timothy 1:9), you don't have time to respond to negative labels acquired in your past. Instead, God calls you BELOVED! (I John 4:7). They may call you names associated with your former weaknesses, but God calls you DELIVERED! (Jeremiah 1:8). They may call you names that define former recklessness, but God now calls you his RIGHTEOUSNESS! (II Corinthians 5:21). They may even call you names that associate you with the darkness you once lived in, but God has brought you out of darkness and calls you a child of LIGHT!
(I Thessalonians 5:5). Today, God wants to remind you that it doesn't matter what people call you, so long as YOU know, who you ARE! Jesus said, "And when he putteth forth HIS own sheep, He goes before them, and the sheep follow HIM, for they know HIS voice! And a stranger will they not follow, but will FLEE from him, for they know not his voice!!" (John 10:4-5). If you only Respond, to what people Remember, they'll never Receive, what God has Restored! Have a Blessed day, and thanks for allowing me to share the word from a *Pastor's Perspective...*

There are many examples where people only call on God out of NECESSITY! Otherwise, calling ON God or hearing FROM Him is unimportant! But God inspired the Apostle Paul to ask four questions to those who had his attention: "How, then, shall they call on Him in whom they have NOT believed? And how shall they believe in Him of whom they have NOT heard? And how shall they hear WITHOUT a preacher? And how shall they preach, EXCEPT they be sent? (Romans 10:14-15). Yes, God gave every man A measure of faith (Romans 12:3), but did you know that same measure is the first MINISTER to come in contact with your misery! How? Because, "Faith comes by HEARING, and HEARING by the WORD of God!!" (Romans 10:17). This is why people call on God, and it sometimes seems as though He's not there or He just doesn't want to be bothered. God knows when you're calling Him out of FEAR! Instead, when you call on God, call Him because He's ABLE, not just because He's AVAILABLE! Remember, FEAR accepted, is FAITH contaminated! Have a Blessed day, and thanks for allowing me to share the word from a *Pastor's Perspective...*

JANUARY 12

When you were Born Again, washed in the cleansing Blood of Jesus Christ, and the Holy Spirit took residence in your heart, you entered a COVENANT that COVERED it!! Whatever "it" was, was paid in full!! "If the Son, therefore, shall make you free, you shall be free indeed!!" (John 8:36). God wants you to walk in the TRUTH of how He turned your MESS into a MINISTRY! No longer do you have to cave in to the call of your past! The Prophet David, after all he had done, from adultery to murder asked of God from a pure heart: "Purge me with hyssop, and I shall be clean! Wash me, and I shall be whiter than snow! Create in me a clean heart, O God, and renew a right Spirit within me!!" (Psalms 51:7, 10). But look what God already knew about David, before David knew about God: "The Lord hath sought Him a man after His own heart." (I Samuel 13:14, Acts 13:22). People oftentimes judge the part of you that's prone to sin and totally forget it's the part of you Jesus died to Save! When your life is hidden in Christ, it's also Covered in the Blood! Have a Blessed day, and thanks for allowing me to share the word from a *Pastor's Perspective*...

People often talk about FAITH, RIGHTEOUSNESS, and HOLY living. Ironically spoken of by saints and sinners alike, who live ON, grow IN, and try to cultivate the FALLOW ground of their own lives. Mere spiritual conversation will leave one wondering why they haven't experienced a true spiritual conversion! If you keep doing what you're doing, you'll keep getting what you're getting! However, God tells us to, "Sow to yourselves in RIGHTEOUSNESS, reap in MERCY, break up your FALLOW ground!" Why? "For it is time to seek the Lord, till He come and rain RIGHTEOUSNESS upon you!" (Hosea 10:12). When the ONE who is Righteous shows up, only those who are Righteous, will go up! We need to break up the FALLOW ground in our lives, to avoid the destruction coming to those who continue to FALL away! Let us be reminded that it's better to break up the unseeded ground now and find rest than to FAIL like the wicked and have no eternal peace at all! (Isaiah 57:21). Have a Blessed day, and thanks for allowing me to share the word from a *Pastor's Perspective*...

JANUARY 14

The Psalmist David declared, "The steps of a good man are ordered by the Lord, and He delights in His way." (Psalms 37:23). David was not using the word "Good" as though men are void of anything bad, no not at all! David used the word "Good" because that's the only way God orders the steps of those that walk to bring Him glory! When we walk to honor God, our paths may encounter a certain amount of rocky terrain, but not even the ups and downs of the JOURNEY can change the expected joy of the

DESTINATION! When your steps are ORDERED by the Lord, your PATH gets clearer with every mile! Just as there is no darkness in God at all! (I John 1:5). God doesn't make bad turns when He's ordering your steps! (Revelation 22:13). So then, our daily prayer should include the words of the Psalmist: "Order my steps in Thy WORD and let not ANY iniquity have dominion over me!!" (Psalms 119:133). As long as God is ordering your steps---keep walking and don't look back! Have a Blessed day, and thanks for allowing me to share the word from a *Pastor's Perspective...*

One of the things overlooked along the road to Ministry is that your Lifestyle, is the root of your Legacy! The Apostle Paul wrote, "All things are lawful unto me, but all things are not expedient or profitable! All things are lawful FOR me, but I will not be brought under the power of any!" (I Corinthians 6:12). In other words, just because you have the heart to do something, doesn't mean you should continue to do it, especially when the PROFIT, stifles the PROPHET! "For which of you, intending to build a tower, sitteth not down FIRST, and counts the cost, of whether he has sufficient resources to finish it?" (Luke 14:28). And so, the next question is...What are you allowing in your Life, your home, your marriage, even your church that is costing you more than you're able to give? In creating a lasting legacy, you have to know the importance of leading a disciplined lifestyle because people may forget how you leave, but they will never forget how you lived! Be careful what you do in FRONT of others, as poor examples do not make good role models. To leave a good Legacy for the glory of God, you need to be a good testimony on the pages of Life! Have a Blessed day, and thanks for allowing me to share the word from a *Pastor's Perspective…*

Jesus said something so profound to Nicodemus about being born again, that he was compelled to rethink birth altogether. "The wind bloweth where it willeth, and thou HEAREST the sound of it, but can't tell which direction it is coming from, and where it goes! So is every one that is born of the Spirit." (John 3:8). Jesus went on to ask Nicodemus: "Are you a TEACHER of Israel and don't know this?" (vs.10). Jesus warns us not to allow the intellect of men, disguised as wisdom, to destroy the WITNESS of God's Will in you! You don't need to SEE or UNDERSTAND how the wind works to know when it's blowing! But you do have to pay attention to what the wind blows in! Have a Blessed day, and thanks for allowing me to share the word from a *Pastor's Perspective...*

> THE WIND BLOWETH WHERE IT WILLETH, AND THOU HEAREST THE SOUND OF IT, BUT CAN'T TELL WHICH DIRECTION IT IS COMING FROM, AND WHERE IT GOES...SO IS EVERYONE THAT IS BORN OF THE SPIRIT

It feels good to be alive! Although life is happening all around us, we still have life in us! Once and again God has given us another opportunity to give Him a *Perfected Praise!* You may be wondering what it means to give God a praise that is PERFECT. When Jesus ran all the money changers and all those who sold doves out of the temple and began to heal the blind and the lame, the chief priests and the scribes didn't have too much of a problem with that. However, when the children present began to cry aloud, "Hosanna, to the Son of David!" Only then did the Pharisees became very displeased! Then they asked Jesus: do you hear what they are saying? Jesus simply replied...Yea, have you never read, "Out of the mouths of babes and sucklings thou hast Perfected Praise!" (Matthew 21:12-16). A Perfect Praise comes from the same place our Perfect God dwells...in the completed work of Christ in You! Scriptures reveal that YOU are COMPLETE in HIM! (Colossians 2:10). So then, your PRAISE is made PERFECT because the work of Christ in you is COMPLETE! Though your journey CONTINUES! Remember that Perfect Praise is part of your continued work. Have a Blessed day, and thanks for allowing me to share the word from a *Pastor's Perspective...*

JANUARY 18

Here is a question for you to ponder: What are you BELIEVING God for? We've all been taught: "Now unto him who is ABLE to do exceedingly, abundantly above all that we could ASK or THINK, according to the power that worketh in us..." (Ephesians 3:20). We have all probably read..."No GOOD thing will He withhold from them that walk uprightly." (Psalms 84:11). And we know, "Be anxious for nothing, but in everything, by PRAYER and supplication with thanksgiving, let your requests be made known unto God." (Philippians 4:6). But you would be shocked to know how many professing saints there are who: "Having a FORM of godliness, continue to deny the POWER thereof!" (II Timothy 3:5). And it is all due to...UNBELIEF! Jesus said..."You BELIEVE in God, BELIEVE also in me!"(John 14:1). BELIEF is not just knowing GOD is able, BELIEF is also trusting God to be God, even in your Unbelief! Remember what Jesus said..."If thou can BELIEVE, all things are possible..." and then, humble yourself enough to simply say... "Lord, I BELIEVE, but help my UNBELIEF." (Mark 9:23-24). Have a Blessed day, and thanks for allowing me to share the word from a *Pastor's Perspective*...

There is so much being said about this generation and the subcultures in which they exist! However, God is waiting to Refine, Restore, and then Receive His CHURCH! Using the analogy of a Husband's love for his wife, the Apostle Paul reminds us of the Church's purpose: "Husbands love your wives, even as Christ loved the Church, and gave Himself for it! That He might sanctify and cleanse it with the washing of water by the word!" (Ephesians 5:25-26). But He really nails down the core cause of this analogy when he pens, "That He might present it to HIMSELF a glorious CHURCH, not having spot or wrinkle, or any such thing, but that it should be HOLY and without BLEMISH! (vs.27). Before we can Restore the path of this generation, we must Refine the course of the Church! The breach is NOT the problem, instead, the problems in our churches have become the breach! This generation will NEVER experience the Spirit of the Lord if we, the Church, don't work towards being spotless before God! To close the breach between this generation and the Church, we must raise the standard IN the Church! Have a Blessed day, and thanks for allowing me to share the word from a *Pastor's Perspective*...

JANUARY 20

The Prophet Solomon was inspired to write, "Without Counsel, PURPOSES are disappointed! But in the multitude of counselors, they are established." (Proverbs 15:22). This profound truth reveals the necessity of surrounding ourselves with people that not only have Spiritual PURPOSE, but who also possess the seed of Spiritual PROGRESS! It is vital to understand that victims don't become spiritually victorious, without first, learning their spiritual VALUE! People of God, if you learn the PURPOSE of PROGRESS, you'll see the VALUE! This value is usually acquired when the counsel of God, shows the misery of men, that you are MORE THAN OVERCOMERS!! (Romans 8:37). To have purpose apart from potential, is like having a praise conversation, with a defeated attitude! Solomon said..."Where no Counsel is, the people fall! But in the multitude of counselors, there is safety!" (Proverbs 11:14). Guide your soul to safety by surrounding yourself with those who are counseled by God! The world says you need a degree to BE a counselor, Jesus says you need only to AGREE that I AM the Counselor! Have a Blessed day, and thanks for allowing me to share the word from a *Pastor's Perspective...*

JANUARY 21

Sometimes we must remind ourselves that God's purpose came long before our presence. When God called the Prophet Jeremiah, He said to him, "Before I formed thee in the womb, I KNEW thee, and before thou camest forth out of the womb, I SANCTIFIED thee, and I ORDAINED thee a Prophet unto the nations." (Jeremiah 1:5). However, instead of being in awe because of WHO was speaking to him, Jeremiah began to flirt with fear and apprehension because of the state HE was in. "Then said I, ah Lord, God! Behold, I cannot speak, for I am a child!" (vs.6). So often, when God's calling comes, we respond with all manner of reserve! We fail to realize that when He calls, He only wants to hear your ACCEPTANCE, not your EXCUSES! Why? Because God didn't just throw you together! "YOU are FEARFULLY and WONDERFULLY made! Your SUBSTANCE was not hidden from Him, when you were made in SECRET! And His eyes saw your SUBSTANCE, before YOU were ever FORMED!" (Psalms 139:14-16). Ponder this, God's CALLING never needs CORRECTION! But you're COMING does need COURAGE! Have a Blessed day, and thanks for allowing me to share the word from a *Pastor's Perspective*...

35

JANUARY 22

Jesus said: "My PEACE I leave with you, My PEACE I give unto you." (John 14:27). Why then are so many believers living in PIECES!!? I believe the answer to this question is found in the following verse: "Thou shalt Love the Lord thy God with ALL thy heart, and with ALL thy soul, and with ALL thy strength, and with ALL thy mind!" (Luke 10:27). You can't expect to give God bits and pieces of you, and then be made WHOLE in Him! If you don't give Him ALL your life, you'll live in PIECES! God wants ALL of you, because your enemy only needs a piece of you to STEAL, KILL, and DESTROY you! (John 10:10). Your life is not a puzzle whereby God must get all the corners correct before he can build. In fact, He prefers to start building in the middle, at your HEART! If your life is in pieces, and you've had enough, gather ALL the broken pieces together, give them ALL to the Lord. FREELY receive the PEACE He gives and begin to live where the world and everything in it, can't do you any harm. To live in God's PEACE, is to live in God's PROTECTION! Have a Blessed day, and thanks for allowing me to share the word from a *Pastor's Perspective...*

JANUARY 23

Sometimes to prove where your heart is, God will allow a TRIAL to stand between you and your TREASURE! Why? "For where your treasure is, there will your HEART be also!" (Luke 12:34). God allows this to see if you are a FAN or a FOLLOWER. The bible provides a great illustration of both in the book of Ruth. When Naomi lost her husband, her two sons, and even her position in society, she was left with two daughters-in-law, Orpah and Ruth. Each of them proved who they were to God, by accepting His will! Even though Naomi was old, broken, and truly hurt, God still expected her to FOLLOW His lead! Orpah had enough faith to be a FAN, but not enough trust to continue to FOLLOW! But RUTH had enough faith, not only to stand during the opposition, she was steadfast enough to sincerely FOLLOW despite the intensity of the trial and its fire! Thus proving, to be the real blessing of God! (RUTH 1:11-18). FANS in the faith will carry the banner! But only a true FOLLOWER will endure the burden! FANS are often swayed by fear, but FOLLOWERS are determined by FAITH, to FINISH! Today, purpose to FOLLOW Jesus, because it's not enough, to just be a FAN! Have a Blessed day, and thanks for allowing me to share the word from a *Pastor's Perspective*...

JANUARY 24

The Apostle James wrote, "Every good GIFT and every perfect GIFT is from above, and cometh down from the Father of lights, with whom is no VARIABLNESS, neither shadow of turning!" (James 1:17). Every Good and Perfect gift comes from God, and the Apostle Paul eloquently reminds Us, "The Gifts and Calling of God are without repentance!!" (Romans 11:29). We really need to understand that Gifts from God, are separate from the innate talents and abilities we possess! The difference is this: talent and ability are the result of a skill set and expression. Whereas, gifts from God are the result of a predestined calling. "Moreover, whom he did predestinate, them he also called!" (Romans 8:30). You see, while talent is the expression of an ability, being gifted is the work of the Anointing! Talents show the world around you, *I have what it takes to get there!* But when your Gift is predestined by the call of God, *you have what it takes to stay there!* Today, ask God to reveal HIS gift, in you. And whatever it may be, if you use it for His glory, because it is GOOD and PERFECT, He'll also glorify you with it!!...Have a Blessed day, and thanks for allowing me to share the word from a *Pastor's Perspective...*

When your WORSHIP and your WILL unite to bring God the glory, your PRAISE is unstoppable! When you have the mindset that you're not going to allow anything or anyone to stand between God's LOVE and your LIFE, you are more than a conqueror!! (Romans 8:37). You are fully persuaded that what God has promised, He is ABLE to perform! (Romans 4:21). Those who don't know God, don't know HE'S able! And so, while the WORSHIP in your WILL is giving God glory, your bold CONFIDENCE is telling your circumstance..."For I am persuaded that neither death, nor life, nor angels, nor principalities, nor powers, nor things present, nor things to come, nor height, nor depth, nor any other creature shall BE ABLE to separate ME from the LOVE of GOD in CHRIST JESUS!!" (Romans 8:38-39). When the WORSHIP in your WILL is stronger than the war in your way...No weapon that has been formed against you, can EVER prosper, and every tongue that shall rise against thee in judgement, YOU shall condemn! Knowing that God is able is ALL you need!! HALLELUJAH!! Have a Blessed day, and thanks for allowing me to share the word from a *Pastor's Perspective...*

JANUARY 26

When Jesus was preparing the minds of the disciples for His ascension, He first had to address their understanding: "I have many things to say unto you, but you cannot bear them NOW." (John 16:12). At times God wants this or that said or done, but He knows it's something too much to bear, and could be too much to comprehend! Therefore, He simply told them, "When the spirit of truth, is come, HE will guide you into all truth." (vs.13). Though they needed to know, He knew they would have more than they could handle in trying to understand HIS ascension. This is one of the greatest examples where God does not put on us, more than we can bear. (I Corinthians 10:13). However, God is faithful to reveal all you need to know, when His knowledge will be clearly understood. When the Apostle Paul got the go ahead to preach, he never tried to validate what he knew! He let his preaching reach those who were within reach, and let the Holy Spirit draw the rest! In other words, you don't have to validate NOW, what is reserved for others LATER! God doesn't take things out of scripture because we're not there yet, He sends the Holy Spirit to guide us, until we get there! Have a Blessed day, and thanks for allowing me to share the word from a *Pastor's Perspective...*

There are two significant, pertinent truths about FAITH that must never be forgotten; We are SAVED through it (Ephesians 2:8), and we are SANCTIFIED by it (Acts 26:18). Our Faith in God's love, is what ushers our faults unto God's forgiveness! A soul devoid of Faith, is equivalent to a sinner overwhelmed by faults! When Jesus told Peter that Satan desired to sift him as wheat, He also told him, "But I have prayed for you, that your FAITH should not fail!" (Luke 22:31-32). So often we subject ourselves to situations and emotions that Jesus has not only prayed for, but also delivered us from. However, in our humanity we continue to allow the insanity of imperfection to blind us from the reality of God's favor! (Hebrews 8:7-8). God's plan for our failures, is kept by our faith in God's plan! You'll never win a war through WORSHIP, if you never really WALK by FAITH! Just think about it, if we need FAITH to please HIM (Hebrews 11:6), we certainly can't comfort one another without it! Hence, the last thing Jesus told Peter in this context was: "And when thou art converted, strengthen your brethren!" (Luke 22:32). It's time we let the enemy know, those who walk by FAITH, don't walk alone! Have a Blessed day, and thanks for allowing me to share the word from a *Pastor's Perspective*...

JANUARY 28

The Spirit of God informed the Prophet Jeremiah of His plans for all Israel after Babylon. He warned that it was a place of bondage and that even amongst the believers there would be false prophets and diviners speaking in God's name, but lacking God's authority, because He had not sent them! (Jeremiah 29:4-9). However, He told Jeremiah that although there would be a time of trial, there would also come a time when He would visit them again to reveal His purpose. He would perform the good intended towards them and give them the EXPECTED end designated for them. (vs.10-11). For every soul God created, His expectation is high! The question is however, what do you EXPECT at the end of your life? Therefore, the Prophet David wrote...."My soul, waits silently for God alone. For my EXPECTATION is from Him!"(Psalms 62:5). True satisfaction is only found in that which God has for You! Jesus IS the expected end the Spirit of God was speaking to Jeremiah of! And He's the same expected end the Spirit of God is speaking to you today! If you don't get what you expect in the end, it's undoubtedly because God isn't getting what He expected from you now! Have a Blessed day, and thanks for allowing me to share the word from a *Pastor's Perspective...*

I've been saved long enough to know the difference between a fleshly WANT and a spiritual DESIRE. God has taught me that fleshly Wants can lead to spiritual Wars! How? Because when the Lord is your shepherd, your spirit should not be wanting things that are already in His will for You! (Psalms 23:1). However, all throughout scripture God encourages us to DESIRE the things of the Spirit. As we all know, the Prophet David had many wants and all his WANTS created all of his WARS! So much so, that by the time the wars within him were over, David himself was left with the PROMISE of God's presence, but not the permission to move in it! And because of all the things David had done, I believe he learned to be content simply to be in the presence of God. The ability to move in Him would have been great, but he learned that being still in Him was even better! Consequently, he was inspired to write: "One thing have I DESIRED of the Lord, that will I seek, that I may DWELL in the house of the Lord all the days of my life. To behold the beauty of the Lord and inquire in His temple!"(Psalms 27:4). Today let your DESIRE for the Lord trump the agenda of your flesh. Have a Blessed day, and thanks for allowing me to share the word from a *Pastor's Perspective...*

There are many people who still don't realize that the RIGHTEOUSNESS of God is the only recourse for the WILDERNESS within! The Apostle Paul was inspired to write this absolute truth, to help groom our hearts to receive God's grace. "For he hath made Him, who knew NO sin, to be sin for us, that we might be MADE the RIGHTEOUSNESS of God!" (II Corinthians 5:21). From generation to generation it seems to get harder and harder for man to embrace the reality of RIGHTEOUSNESS, which simply means being in right standing with God. It is a trick of the enemy to keep your mind trapped in the penalty box of SIN! Because, "Whom the SON sets free, is free indeed!" (John 8:36). However, because God's RIGHTEOUSNESS is exhibited through simple compassion, many question the authenticity of its work! The righteousness of God, releases the reality of His love. People of God, it is through this belief, we are MADE the RIGHTEOUSNESS of Him, who is NEVER wrong! Today is a good day to settle all accounts with God. The best way to keep things right with Him, is to keep Him right next to you! Have a Blessed day, and thanks for allowing me to share the word from a *Pastor's Perspective…*

We are so blessed to have God's amazing Grace. We are extremely blessed to have God's unconditional Love. But how often do we stop and think about the blessing of God's longsuffering? The bible tells us, "But the fruit of the Spirit is Love, Joy, Peace, LONGSUFFERING, Gentleness, Goodness, Faith, Meekness, and Self-Control." (Galatians 5:22). It takes this combination of fruit, to establish spiritual character, that is useful to God. The fruit we talk about the least is Longsuffering, because it reveals the TRUTH of our intentions! Let me explain: Longsuffering is the purpose of patience! "The Lord is not slack concerning His promises as some men count slackness, but is LONGSUFFERING towards us, not willing that any should perish, but that all should come to repentance!" (II Peter 3:9). You see, God's Longsuffering is proof of His promise, but more than that, it reveals the intent behind the invitation of salvation. God suffers long with us now, because He knows, eternity is an even longer time to suffer for sin! Today, purpose to let your Patience have its perfect work, so that your Longsuffering can be proof of your perfected soul. Have a Blessed day, and thanks for allowing me to share the word from a *Pastor's Perspective...*

FEBRUARY 1

It's been said...."If you don't *STUDY*, you won't be *STURDY*!" With everything from bible commentaries to full length messages on line, it seems that studying God's word for oneself is no longer necessary. Scripture tells us to, "Study to show thyself APPROVED unto God, a WORKMAN that needeth not be ashamed, rightly DIVIDING THE WORD of truth!" (II Timothy 2:15). You can't expect to be an *Approved Workman that can truly Divide the Word* if all the word you've received was spoon fed to you, instead of through tenacious study! Now, don't misunderstand me, today's technology has its place in ministry, and is very helpful to the spreading of the gospel. Nonetheless, God

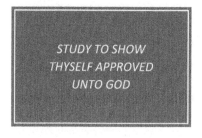

STUDY TO SHOW
THYSELF APPROVED
UNTO GOD

wants us to Study for ourselves. You can't expect to get on-line, that which is found only in His PRESENCE! Sometimes, God wants it to be, just YOU and HIM. We show God how much He means to us, when we spend time studying about Him...Have a Blessed day, and thanks for allowing me to share the word from a *Pastor's Perspective*...

The Apostle Paul wrote..."I thank God through Jesus Christ, our Lord. So then, with the MIND I myself serve the law of God, but with the FLESH, the law of sin!" (Romans 7:25). We all have the propensity to sin and cater to our flesh, but we also know, there is an enormous price to pay for doing So! "If we sin WILLFULLY after we have received the knowledge of the TRUTH, there remains no more sacrifice for sins! But a certain fearful looking for of judgement and a FIERY indignation which shall devour the adversaries!" (Hebrews 10:26-27). Therefore, the Apostle Paul had this to say about his adamant attitude towards God, and his fervent fight against his flesh: "But I keep my body (that is, his flesh) under subjection, lest that by any means, when I have preached to others, I myself should be a castaway!!" (I Corinthians 9:27). It would be sad to have helped many people get to the throne of God, though you yourself were not accepted because of the Sin within! Today, ask yourself, "Is my worship in vain? Are my prayers in vain? Is my life in vain? Is vanity, my version of victory?" You don't simply court Jesus! You're either in Love with Him, or you're not! Have a Blessed day, and thanks for allowing me to share the word from a *Pastor's Perspective...*

When your WORSHIP level only goes *TO* the roof, it could possibly mean the WAR is still *IN* the house! We must allow our WORSHIP to rip a hole in the roof in order to set the atmosphere for the PRAISE of God's people! The old saying goes, "When the Praises go up, the *BLESSINGS* come down!" God wants to send those blessings through the hole you made in the roof with your Worship!! Bear in mind that WORSHIP is our *Breakthrough* (Psalms 95:6-7), while PRAISE is the *Breakout* (Psalms 34:1, Psalms 71:14). When Praise and Worship work together, all

WORSHIP IS OUR BREAKTHROUGH

forms of carnality become casualties to the weapons of our warfare! (II Corinthians 10:4). It is through our Praise and Worship, that the journey through our struggles becomes the footstool of our JOY! Today and every day, let Praise and Worship rip a gaping hole in the place, or thing that won't let your Blessings flow freely! Have a Blessed day, and thanks for allowing me to share the word from a *Pastor's Perspective...*

An INCREDIBLE God, deserves INCREDIBLE praise! When we give God an INCREDIBLE praise, it's because we have in our spirits, an INCREDIBLE power! Jesus said, "Behold, I give you the authority to trample on serpents and scorpions, and over all the power of the enemy, and nothing shall by any means hurt you!"(Luke 10:19 NKJV). The same thing that happened on the Day of Pentecost, happened to you and I in our new birth experience..."But you shall receive POWER when the Holy Spirit has come upon you!!" (Acts 1:8). If we would dare to operate in the power we were given, we would stop declaring ourselves powerless, in situations where we mistakenly used less-power! To every born-again believer, "God has not given you the spirit of failure, deficiency, nor fear! But of Love, POWER, and a sound mind!"(II Timothy 1:7). When you operate in the spirit of Jesus, you operate with ALL POWER! There's no way you can't give God an INCREDIBLE praise this day, when He's given you ALL the POWER you need with which to do it! Have a Blessed day, and thanks for allowing me to share the word from a *Pastor's Perspective*...

FEBRUARY 5

Have you ever stopped to ponder the last three words of Jesus? Every time I think about those words my gratitude grows and my respect for Grace literally brings me to tears. Jesus, having been beaten beyond recognition, hanging on a cross, huge spikes in his hands and feet, a crown of thorns pressed into his head, life as His *body* knew it, slowly leaving and with one last breath He says: "IT IS FINISHED!" (John 19:30). No more pain, no more crowd, no more suffering, no more separation! All that He was sent to do, was done! He was finally on his way back to the Father, the only one who truly understood the sacrifice made for all creation. We must all realize, before we hear "WELL DONE," God would love to hear "IT IS FINISHED." Don't let the last breath you take be infiltrated with uncertainty, lack, and loss! Make full PROOF of your ministry! (II Timothy 4:5). Why? Because your REDEMPTION is getting closer and closer every day! (Luke 21:25-28). Today, purpose in your heart to work your faith until your work is finished! Going home to glory is so much sweeter, when you know for yourself, the work you were given; IS FINISHED! Have a Blessed day, and thanks for allowing me to share the word from a *Pastor's Perspective*...

FEBRUARY 6

I believe we must commit to ENCOURAGING one another and to becoming less JUDGEMENTAL of one another! We disappoint God, when we *diss* those who have a divine appointment with destiny! The Apostle Paul wrote..."Therefore, JUDGE nothing before the time, until the Lord come, who both will bring to light the hidden things of darkness and will make manifest the counsels of the heart!" (I Corinthians 4:5). The Apostle Paul later said, "ENCOURAGE one another and build each other up." (I Thessalonians 5:11 NIV). We spend far too much time trying to discredit what God has already consecrated! If I spend more time lifting you up by faith, and you spend just as much time doing the same for me, there's nothing either of us should be down about in spirit!! How can we be children of the Most-High yet speak so low of one another! These things ought not be! (James 1:10). Jesus said..."Judge not according to appearance but judge righteous judgement!" (John 7:24). If your judgement doesn't leave room for Grace, then it's highly probable your heart doesn't have room for Love! Have a Blessed day, and thanks for allowing me to share the word from a *Pastor's Perspective*...

God has three words that come with the sole purpose of strengthening, sustaining, and celebrating the substance of your soul! First, "Refreshing" your Faith through his presence has come! (Acts 16:14-18). Secondly, this is the day God will "Renew" what you thought was losing its worth! (Romans 12:2). Third, and lastly, God's purpose for all of this, is to "Restore" the JOY of your salvation, (Psalms 51:12) and the years that the locust and cankerworms in your life have eaten away! (Joel 2:25). God wants your soul to be completely saturated in these three things this morning. Why? Because these pillars support the infrastructure of the triangle of Faith! Wherever you are at this very moment, whether pondering the course of the day, or sitting quietly meditating, God wants to reaffirm that this is more than just a day that

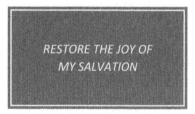

RESTORE THE JOY OF MY SALVATION

He has made! It is the day He has designated to Refresh, Renew, and Restore your JOY in the Lord...Have a Blessed day, and thanks for allowing me to share the word from a *Pastor's Perspective...*

King David said, "Happy is that people, that is in such a case, that people whose God is the Lord." (Psalms 144:15). When you KNOW God for yourself, you have all the confidence to FOLLOW Him all by yourself! Those who are truly HAPPY in the Lord have learned that the JOY of knowing Him, is the strength that moves them in the Him! (Nehemiah 8:10). Holy Happiness is not like the happiness that satisfies our flesh! Holy Happiness doesn't bring butterflies in the belly, or an overwhelming burst of uncontrolled enthusiasm. Holy Happiness comes from the fulfillment of a God purpose! David said, "Blessed be the Lord, my STRENGTH, who TEACHETH my hands to WAR, and my fingers to FIGHT!" (Psalms 144:1). David understood that before a man can truly be HAPPY in the Lord, he needs to be content with the work of his calling!! The work of David's calling was to wage WAR against anyone, who was against the work of God's people! Today as you walk with Him who has ALL power in His hands...Let Holy Happiness be the strength of your work! Those of you who are living Holy before God---don't WORRY, be HAPPY!! Have a Blessed day, and thanks for allowing me to share the word from a *Pastor's Perspective...*

FEBRUARY 9

Those who live to PLEASE God are constantly being shunned and ostracized because they refuse to embrace the ways of the world. Their character is often scrutinized by those who would rather compromise with sin, and not conform to the ways of righteousness. Pleasing God gives us home field advantage though it oftentimes brings out the worst in the other team! The Apostle Paul asked a question to the church when they questioned the church in him: "For do I now seek the favor of men or of God? or do I seek to PLEASE men?" He went on to affirm, "For if I yet pleased men, I should NOT be the servant of Christ!!" (Galatians 1:10). Jesus never allowed the flesh (that is, men) to dictate the course of the Father! In fact, even when the disciples didn't understand, He let them know..."He that sent me is with me. The Father hath not left me alone! For I do always those things that PLEASE Him." (John 8:29). Pleasing God will always bring persecution! But know this: God is using the persecutors as the set-up crew for your praise party! Continue striving to please God and watch God continue to be faithful and Bless you!! (Matthew 5:11). Have a Blessed day, and thanks for allowing me to share the word from a *Pastor's Perspective*...

FEBRUARY 10

Situations that take up most of our PRAYER time, are situations that effect our passions, our purpose, and our perspectives. We find ourselves asking over and over for those things that require patience! God wants you to come to him (Matthew 11:28, Philippians 4:6). Why? Because the things that concern you the most, are the same things that prompt your prayers! That's why Jesus said..."In your Patience possess ye your souls." (Luke 21:19). Prayer and Patience are the sustainers of the soul whenever there has been a war on ground reserved for worship! Prayer is more than just talking to God, prayer is God taking time to LISTEN to YOU! "What a friend we have in Jesus, all our sins and griefs to bear, what a privilege to carry, everything to God in prayer." (Charles Crozat Converse, 1968). God has many ways of reaching OUR heart, but he has designed only one specific way to reach HIS: Prayer. Always remember that no matter what you're going through, no matter how bad it seems, and no matter what anyone says; when you let Patience possess your soul, Prayer will provide Peace that surpasses your understanding. Have a Blessed day, and thanks for allowing me to share the word from a *Pastor's Perspective*...

FEBRUARY 11

Have you ever asked God a question that you already knew the answer to but were hoping He'd respond differently? God is so consistent at being God, that not even your most heartfelt, sincere, spiritually induced cry, will change the fact that He knows what's best for you. "For I know the thoughts that I think toward you, says the Lord. Thoughts of PEACE and not evil, to give YOU a FUTURE and a HOPE."(Jeremiah 29:11). There are many of us who seem dissatisfied with the way God lords our lives and orders our steps! Sure, we've endured losses, hard times, struggles, and even friction in the faith, but none of this compares to a FUTURE and a HOPE secure in Jesus! (Romans 8:18). We try and rationalize what God is saying, or what God is doing, because the truth of the matter is...sometimes, we really wish He would see things from our perspective and use a few of our ideas instead...after all, it's my life right? Wrong!!! God paid an enormous price for your life and it's high time you stopped griping about the emotionally challenging changes you face, and realize they are the building blocks of your devotion! Have a Blessed day, and thanks for allowing me to share the word from a *Pastor's Perspective...*

FEBRUARY 12

We've all had, "close calls!" But the closest call you'll ever have is...."Today if you hear His voice, and you harden your hearts!!" (Hebrews 3:15). God calling you, while you are rebellious, insubordinate, and disobedient in every way, is a very close call! Especially when your flesh, the prince of this world, and every demonic force around you is set on destroying you. You must understand the Sovereignty of God's call, He's trying to keep you from reaping the Severity of your own rebelliousness! The bible says...."Because thou hast rejected knowledge, I will also reject you!!"(Hosea 4:6). To clearly hear God's voice then blatantly disregard it, is a Call too Close to ignore!! Ignoring Close Calls, can lead to unexpected tragedy! So then, "Faith cometh by HEARING, and HEARING by the WORD of God!" (Romans 10:17). Those who refuse to Hear God's voice and receive His help, will assuredly, run a greater risk of experiencing Hell's heat! If God is that Close, and you can hear Him Calling you, that means He's that Close, trying to protect you! Have a Blessed day, and thanks for allowing me to share the word from a *Pastor's Perspective*...

FEBRUARY 13

Did you know that even Pain has Purpose? Pain in the general sense, always announces the problem, not the solution. The sole purpose of Pain is to reveal reality, not relevance! And so, for everything and everyone that ever hurt you, it was the PAIN of the circumstance, that revealed the PURPOSE of the problem! Scripture reveals that God causes the PAIN, the PURPOSE, and the PROBLEM to work together for good, for all those he has called! (Romans 8:28). Our confidence in God's PROTECTION during the process, should NEVER be threatened by the circumstances that surround our calling! "For the Gifts and Calling of God are without repentance!" (Romans 11:29). When God uses Pain to reveal Purpose, you can rest assured that the circumstances surrounding the situation are preparing you for Promotion! Just like giving birth, it's Painful until that last push! But afterwards, all the Pain and all the pushing, reveal the expected Purpose! If God is using your Hurt to Help you, it's only right that you use your purpose to promote Him! Have a Blessed day, and thanks for allowing me to share the word from a *Pastor's Perspective...*

King Solomon said, "For the perverse or wicked man is an abomination to the Lord, but His SECRET is with the righteous."(Proverbs 3:32). The SECRET of God, is the Private Counsel of God. It is the spiritual counsel that strangles confusion until it is no more! It would behoove us to seek this kind of counsel from God, for it is through this Private Counsel that the FAVOR in your life goes public! Solomon said, "Where no Counsel is, the people fall!" (Proverbs 11:14). Additionally, the Psalmist declared: "He who dwells in the SECRET place of the Most-High shall abide under the shadow of the Almighty!" (Psalms 91:1). Essentially, he was saying the Secret place, where the Secret is found, is the sacred place of my Private Counsel! When God wants a one-on-one with you, He will only host it in the SECRET place. The COUNSEL received in that place, is like no other word He's ever spoken to you. It's precise, it's effectual, but more than anything, it's PRIVATE! While a Secret from God may be just for you, as a testament to His omnipotence, He's expecting the context of the Counselling to go viral! Have a Blessed day, and thanks for allowing me to share the word from a *Pastor's Perspective...*

One of the most common clichés about LOVE is...LOVE is in the air! However, God wants LOVE to abide and remain in our heart, not in the air! Love in the air will never change a man like Love in the heart will! The Apostle Paul said: "Because the LOVE of God is shed abroad in our hearts by the Holy Spirit who is given unto us; Our LOVE is NOT for the air, but rather, for our tribulations, our patience, our experiences, and even our hope!" (Romans 5:4-5). If we could not feel the Love of God in our hearts, we would easily succumb to the shame that oftentimes follows rejection! Today, tell somebody that you LOVE them! Let them feel the comfort of the Father in you! (John 13:35). Circumstances such as; being booed off stage, tripping in public, or being told you're not good enough is shameful treatment, but Jesus was not just shamed, He was utterly rejected! And yet, from His manger to His majesty, His purpose was LOVE! When LOVE is in your HEART, you have the power to clear the air around you! Let's take LOVE and put it back where God intended it to dwell...in our heart! Have a Blessed day, and thanks for allowing me to share the word from a *Pastor's Perspective*...

FEBRUARY 16

Sometimes the solution to our circumstances rests in the SILENCE found in solitude! "Wherefore, my beloved brethren, be swift to hear, SLOW to SPEAK, slow to wrath!" (James 1:19). When we're not doing all the talking, we give ourselves a chance to hear what God has to say. Jesus concluded many parables with, "He that hath ears to hear, let him hear!" Listening to God is a command, not a privilege! "Keep thy foot when thou goest to the house of God, and be more willing to HEAR, than to give the sacrifice of fools! For they consider NOT that they do evil. Be NOT rash with thy mouth and let NOT your heart be hasty to utter just anything before God! For God is in heaven, and thou upon the earth! Therefore, let your words be FEW!!" (Ecclesiastes 5:1). Sometimes God must SHOUT: "SHUT UP," so you don't get yourself SHUT OUT!! Those who humble themselves and listen for God can HEAR His voice in the very midst of a crowd! Today, the LORD wants us to learn to listen more when HE speaks, so that when WE speak, those around us can still hear HIM! (Luke 10:16). Have a Blessed day, and thanks for allowing me to share the word from a *Pastor's Perspective...*

"Behold, how GOOD and PLEASANT it is for brethren to dwell together in UNITY." (Psalms 133:1). UNITY in the church, demands scrutiny in the church! Whenever we don't examine and inspect things in the church, the enemy is sure to weaken and infect things in the church! There has never been a greater need for church UNITY as now! With all the liberalism, and various denominations and spiritual agendas, there seems to be more self-gratification than spiritual unification! Where there is no Spiritual UNITY, there will be enormous spiritual casualties! The enemy is always seeking whom he can devour! (I Peter 5:8). Especially those, who would rather die in their spiritual independence, and not live in the UNITY of the spirit! The Apostle Paul said we should be: "Endeavoring to keep the UNITY of the Spirit in the bond of peace!" Why? "Till we all come to UNITY of the faith and of the knowledge of the Son of God, to a perfect man, to the measure of the stature of the fullness of CHRIST!"(Ephesians 4:3,13). Remember, "Therefore let him who thinks he stands take heed, lest he fall!"(I Corinthians 10:12). It's a beautiful thing to rise in UNITY, but it's a terrible thing, to fall ALONE! Have a Blessed day, and thanks for allowing me to share the word from a *Pastor's Perspective*…

"God so Loved the world that he gave..." (John 3:16). It must be heart-wrenching to God that he gave so much TO the world, and yet, he gets so little FROM the world. How do I know this to be true of God's heart? Just listen, "I am sought by those who asked NOT for me! I am found by those who sought me NOT! I said, behold me, behold me, unto a nation that was NOT called by my name! I have spread out my hands all-the-day, unto a rebellious people, that walketh in a way that was NOT good, after their own thoughts! A people that provoke me to anger continually to my face!" (Isaiah 65:1-3). As a born-again believer, I am so grateful that God reached out to the Gentile, after the Chosen rejected Him. He has given so many of us the opportunity to be eternally secured by GRACE through Faith! And yet, so many still reject Him unto Death! He inspired the Prophet David to write, "He will NOT chide (That is, keep scolding or rebuking), neither will he keep his anger, forever!"(Psalms 103:9). If God is speaking to you, harden Not your heart! Don't let a hard heart, be your ticket to an even harder HELL! Have a Blessed day, and thanks for allowing me to share the word from a *Pastor's Perspective...*

FEBRUARY 19

Waking up, clothed in my right mind, blood running warm in my veins, and in hot pursuit of that which is righteous is good enough for me this morning! So often we forget to give God praise for all that we HAVE, instead of focusing on the things we don't have! But the word says, "Your heavenly Father knows that you have need of all these things!" (Matthew 6:32). What things? The things that divert your attention from giving God the praise for everything you do Have! If we would truly follow God's word..."Seek ye first, the kingdom of God, and All these things shall be added unto you,"(Matthew 6:33) we would truly see how God's math has always ADDED to us! God wants us to get the WORD in our understanding, before we're taken in by the philosophy of the world! So that, "The man of God may be perfect, thoroughly furnished unto all good works!" (II Timothy 3:17). When you're not looking at life from a deficit perspective, you can appreciate life through the promise! If you praise Him for what you have, seek His direction in all things, and let patience have her perfect work, you'll soon discover...you're perfect and entire, and lacking NOTHING! (James 1:4). Have a Blessed day, and thanks for allowing me to share the word from a *Pastor's Perspective*...

Our prayer life is our lifeline to heaven. It is how our requests are made known unto God. Prayer is EVERYTHING when you have NOTHING else! But know this, PRAYER is all you need if PRAYER is all you've got! Sometimes, the only thing God needs from YOU regarding His divine plan for YOU, is your PRAYER! "Praying always with all prayer and supplication in the Spirit! And watching thereunto with all perseverance and supplication for all saints!" (Ephesians 6:18). It's been said that Prayer is the key, whereas Faith unlocks the door. However, it must be understood that PRAYER is not just *a* key, but *a* MASTER KEY, and has the power to open every door, not just certain doors! And the only door that prayer can't open is the door that God Himself has closed! When your Prayers start opening doors, that's the manifestation of your supplication! God is supplying in the natural what you're requesting in the spirit! "Be anxious for NOTHING! But in EVERYTHING, by PRAYER and supplication with thanksgiving, let your requests be made known unto God!" (Philippians 4:6). Have a Blessed day, and thanks for allowing me to share the word from a *Pastor's Perspective*...

FEBRUARY 21

The time is NOW, to declare to this world that the victory is WON! The Apostle Paul urges us to do this with a fervent and adamant attitude; "And that, knowing.the time, that NOW it is high time to awake out of sleep! For NOW, is our salvation nearer than we believed!" (Romans 13:11). We don't have time to waste wondering what God wants us to do, when we can see for ourselves, all that needs to be done! God is bellowing from the heavens: stop standing around doing NOTHING, start moving around, and do SOMETHING! Because He's coming sooner than you think! We have been given an explicit example from Christ himself concerning His return and His expectations upon His arrival...For the Son of man is like a man taking a far journey, who left his house, and gave authority to his servants, and to EVERY MAN his work, and COMMANDED him, the porter, to WATCH! Watch ye, therefore, for ye know not when the master of the house cometh!" (Mark 13:34). Don't allow *YOUR* work to be found undone on *YOUR* watch!! Have a Blessed day, and thanks for allowing me to share the word from a *Pastor's Perspective*...

To experience and then release true WORSHIP, you must have and abide in true FELLOWSHIP with Christ. Did you know that WORSHIP is the by-product of a right relationship with Christ? The Apostle John had such an amazing relationship with Jesus that his Fellowship in the spirit, became WORSHIP through his testimony! "That which we have SEEN, and HEARD declare we unto you, that ye may also have Fellowship with us! And truly our Fellowship is with the FATHER and with his SON, Jesus Christ." (I John 1:3). Every spiritual war you've ever won, was won through Worship! You may be thinking; but many of my victories came through Fasting, Praying, and just being strong in the Faith. And that very well may be true. In fact, they are the tools God uses to sculpt your WORSHIP! Your WORSHIP is a monument today, because your relationship with the Lord is for REAL! True FELLOWSHIP will always lead to Worship! Let your WORSHIP work in the Fellowship of your right relationship with Christ...You never have to wait to WORSHIP God, when your FELLOWSHIP and your RELATIONSHIP with Him are real! Have a Blessed day, and thanks for allowing me to share the word from a *Pastor's Perspective*...

FEBRUARY 23

The parable of the persistent widow, starts with: "Men ought to always pray," and ends with: "When the Son of man returns, will he really find Faith on the earth?" (Luke 18:1-8). The judge in the parable had power he wouldn't use, but the widow had persistence she wouldn't let be denied! Sometimes people won't respect your passion, until they experience the work of your persistence instead! Spiritual persistence is vital to the manifestation of your prayers! The bible says...the judge would not listen FOR A WHILE, however, AFTER A WHILE "position" gave way to "persistence" and "prayer" brought the widow "peace!" (vs. 4-5). When you know God is able, you must commit yourself to the strength of your faith! Your prayer may go unanswered FOR A WHILE, but the bible says..."After you have suffered A WHILE, the God of ALL grace shall PERFECT, ESTABLISH, STRENGTHEN, AND SETTLE YOU!!" (I Peter 5:10). Arriving at your Destiny is a marathon not a sprint! You need PERSISTENCE to go the DISTANCE! Those who do not cease to PRAY, God will not cease to AMAZE! Have a Blessed day, and thanks for allowing me to share the word from a *Pastor's Perspective*...

FEBRUARY 24

We need to understand that BONDAGE
starts in the mind, then it affects your
ministry. The Apostle Paul wrote, "Stand fast
therefore in the liberty by which Christ has
made us FREE, and do not be entangled
again, with a yoke of bondage!" (Galatians
5:1). Bondage on any level is a Burden on
every level! When we allow bondage to
restrain the works of the Spirit, it burglarizes
our soul, and steals our will to rejoice!
Bondage is oftentimes down-played because it
comes subtly. When the serpent coaxed Eve
to listen, Eve in turn introduced Adam to
bondage! (Genesis 3:1-6). But to keep things
in perspective, God did not become a part of
their blame game. Instead, He started
preparing OUR deliverance from inevitable
bondage! Sin never wins where God reigns!
God fulfilled His will through
Jesus...Therefore, when He came into the
world He said, "Sacrifice and Offering you
DO NOT desire! But a BODY you have
prepared for me!" (Hebrews 10:5). If your
BODY is a living sacrifice, there's no way
your mind should be in BONDAGE! The
enemy can't bind what he can't find! Anything
hidden in Christ is totally free from
BONDAGE! Have a Blessed day, and thanks
for allowing me to share the word from a
Pastor's Perspective...

When you don't allow PEACE to truly serve its purpose, you bury problems in the promised land of tomorrow! Many of us fail to realize the things that try to disrupt the Peace of today, come from the struggles of yesterday! I like to look at yesterday's struggles in Life, as today's motivation in the Lord!! The Apostle David gave us these words of encouragement to stay the course; "The Lord will give strength unto His people, the Lord will bless His people with PEACE!!" (Psalms 29:11). Do you know why Jesus left us HIS PEACE? (John 14:27). Because his PEACE today is the only thing that can silence

yesterday! The Spirit of the Lord instructs us to, "Mark the perfect man, that is, (those who are truly trying to live in peace), for the end of that man is PEACE." (Psalms 37:37). When you have PEACE in your Life, yesterday no longer prevents you from living! "For the eyes of the Lord are over the righteous, and His ears are open unto their prayers." (I Peter 3:10-12). You can have complete PEACE today, when you give God all the pieces of yesterday! Have a Blessed day, and thanks for allowing me to share the word from a *Pastor's Perspective*...

When we look at the lives of men called of God, we can clearly see how it had to be God Himself who ENCOURAGED them in their calling. From Moses to Jesus, the life of a prophet has never been without criticism. They endured much scrutiny, because they understood that God was the Lord of their destiny! And no matter what those around them said, God said what really needed to be heard..."Fear thou not, for I Am with thee! Be not dismayed, for I Am thy God! I will strengthen thee! Yea, I will help thee! Yea, I will uphold thee with the right hand of my righteousness!" (Isaiah 41:10). You'll notice the Spirit of the Lord encourages in this manner throughout scripture. (Joshua 1:6-7, Jeremiah 1:8, John 14: 27-31, Matthew 28:19-20). However, there are also times when God expects your Faith to soar above criticism, pessimism, and all other isms, so you can do as the Prophet David did..."But David ENCOURAGED himself in the Lord!" (I Samuel 30:6). Be careful not to waste too much time trying to explain to men what God is doing in you! Jesus said: "For they have not rejected thee, but they have rejected me!" (I Samuel 8:7) Have a Blessed day, and thanks for allowing me to share the word from a *Pastor's Perspective...*

FEBRUARY 27

King David declared..."I delight to do thy will, O my God! Yea, thy law is within my HEART!" (Psalms 40:8). When pleasing God becomes the focal point of your life, something deep within changes. It doesn't announce its presence and yet, a change occurs that doesn't go unnoticed! Your demeanor reveals a divine depth that displays a righteousness that cannot be denied! Your desire in the Spirit is compelled to overthrow and subdue the works of the flesh! So much so that your soul cries out in complete submission..."Thy WORD have I hid in mine HEART, that I might not sin against thee!" (Psalms 119:11). Those who truly desire to please God refuse to be DOMINATED by their flesh any longer! When thoughts of God consume you, not only is that a good thing, but it's evidence that YOU are allowing God to do His thing! When your desire for God, is greater than your desire to Sin, your prayer is always, "Let the words of my mouth, and the meditation of my heart, be acceptable in thy sight, O Lord, my strength, and my redeemer!" (Psalms 19:14) Have a Blessed day, and thanks for allowing me to share the word from a *Pastor's Perspective*...

In the Apostle Paul's last letter to the Corinthian church he admonished them to EXAMINE themselves! (II Corinthians 13:5), to see whether they were in fact in the FAITH! He wanted them to have an understanding about what it means to have a relationship with Christ! You see, you cannot be in Christ but live in folly! God's love may seem reckless because He even gives it to a world of sinners, but reckless He is not! And by no stretch of the imagination does this give any of us leeway to live recklessly before Him! However, this kind of LOVE is evidence that His RIGHTEOUSNESS is supreme, and that SALVATION has come! God knows that none of us are perfect, (Philippians 3:13), and that there is none righteous, no not one, in and of ourselves! (Romans 3:10). He wants us to line our lives up with the TRUTH. Today, reflect on whether you are in the faith or still in the world! Jesus said you cannot serve two masters (Matthew 6:24). The Apostle James wanted us to know that we can't be double minded! (James 1:8). So, EXAMINE yourself today, because EXCUSES will have NO place in the end! Have a Blessed day, and thanks for allowing me to share the word from a *Pastor's Perspective...*

MARCH 1

When Jesus shared the last supper with the disciples, He wanted them to realize that it was the last time He would drink the fruit of THIS vine with them. (Matthew 26:26-29 KJV). He specified THIS fruit because it represented His blood, and THIS shed blood is what put our sins in remission! So then, when He said...He will drink it NEW with us in His Father's kingdom, He was telling us we

FORGIVENESS:
YOUR RSVP TO
THE FOREVER
FEAST

would commune with Him in the fullness of the true, new fruit: that of FORGIVENESS! Communion on this side of Glory is for

our ACCEPTANCE of all that Jesus DID! But the communion we will have on the other side of glory is for our SECURITY of all that Jesus IS! Jesus let us know at the last supper that he was going to set up an eternal supper! Never forget, FORGIVENESS is bigger than accepting an apology, in fact, FORGIVENESS is your RSVP to the FOREVER FEAST. Have a Blessed day, and thanks for allowing me to share the word from a *Pastor's Perspective*...

God is a good God! He's a God of great compassion and unconditional love! He considers our hearts, minds, and motives when He addresses our sins and iniquities. God is so pure in Spirit that He distributes punishment according to HIS expectations, and NOT according to our transgressions! "While our transgressions are many, His PERFECT Love covers a multitude of Sins and casts out the fear that promotes its condemnation!" (I Peter 4:8, I John 4:18). God is sovereign and don't let anyone tell you differently!! After all King David had done, from adultery to murder, he humbled his heart to understand that God, "Has NOT dealt with US according to our Sins, nor punished US according to our Iniquities!!" (Psalms 103:9-10). And people of God, that's Just how GOOD God is to us still today! To know that you're FORGIVEN, is to LIVE in His LOVE, and to live in His LOVE is FREEDOM all by itself...Have a Blessed day, and thanks for allowing me to share the word from a *Pastor's Perspective*...

MARCH 3

When the Prophet Job said, "Though he slay me, yet will I TRUST Him," (Job 13:15) he was saying, no matter what God allows in my life, I know it's according to His plan, and will work out for my good! Job was inspired to pen, "Man that is born of a woman is of few days, and full of trouble!" (Job 14:1). Now let's look at this whole thing objectively. Life compared to eternity lasts only a few days. And ALL those days are filled with the TRIALS of life! So then, trusting God shouldn't be an option, it should be a no brainer! Why wouldn't you give ALL your circumstances to the one who can use them for your good? When God is behind the trial, the verdict always comes back NOT GUILTY!! Trusting God in the few days you have left to live is like having a good lawyer, during a speedy trial! Today, let ALL that God is, be ALL that you need! Those who really TRUST God, don't count days as they're too busy using their time to count BLESSINGS! Have a Blessed day, and thanks for allowing me to share the word from a *Pastor's Perspective...*

MARCH 4

Every time I read the Apostle Paul's testimony I am encouraged in God's Love, His Patience, and His Plan for MY life. "But when it pleased God, who separated me from my mother's womb, and called me by His GRACE, to reveal His Son IN me, that I might preach Him among the Gentiles, IMMEDIATELY I conferred NOT with flesh and blood!" (Galatians 1:15-16). The Apostle Paul is speaking to those who feel their life is beyond fixing, and their soul is beyond saving...that is NOT true! Before Paul was called to PREACH, he PERSECUTED believers! But when God revealed His Son IN him, Paul gave his life TO Him! And he didn't care what others knew about his past! He was totally convinced that the plan of GRACE, was more than sufficient! (II Corinthians 12:9). God wants you to know He has a plan for your life. God wants to REVEAL His Son in you, so he can REVERSE the curse ON you! Let His plan for your life, be the LIFE in your plans! Have a Blessed day, and thanks for allowing me to share the word from a *Pastor's Perspective...*

MARCH 5

"This is the day which the Lord hath made, we will rejoice and be glad in it!" (Psalms 118:24). When your soul rejoices because God is more than enough, you've reached the place in your heart that's reserved just for Him! The scripture calls it your "Secret Place" (Psalms 91:1). It's in the Secret Place, that the *more than enough God* presents the things, that make you rejoice! There are no hindrances, no hang-ups, no heartaches, not even a hard time! And it all starts with what He calls a new DAY! By declaring, "This is the DAY which the Lord hath made," The psalmist is telling everything connected to the agenda for this DAY is set by the One who created the DAY! And what He has planned for me today is more than enough and He has declared it Good! Therefore, allow yourself to appreciate all that God has planned for you in this DAY! God wants you to truly experience what it means to...Have Life and have it MORE abundantly! Have a Blessed day, and thanks for allowing me to share the word from a *Pastor's Perspective...*

MARCH 6

When you give your life to the Lord, there are those who will try to make you feel as if you're doing something wrong! They make remarks that challenge your independence or say things that go against your individuality! In addition, they act as if God is a foe, because now they must share you with Him! Remember the question He inspired the Apostle Paul to ask: "What fruit had ye then in those things of which ye are now ashamed? For the end of those things is death!" (Romans 6:21). Now that I've learned what righteousness IS, I can hardly bear to look at all the damage I did in my ignorance! Isn't it funny, that while you lived worldly, people never really questioned your choices, but as soon as you chose JESUS, they treated you like JUDAS! God knows you will be criticized for your faith, but He wants you to know, you will also be rewarded for it! Hallelujah!! "For the wages of SIN is death, but the GIFT of GOD is eternal life through Jesus Christ, OUR Lord!" (Romans 6:23) Have a Blessed day, and thanks for allowing me to share the word from a *Pastor's Perspective...*

MARCH 7

God freed the children of Israel from Egypt, so they could freely serve Him! (Exodus 12:31-41). They experienced pure joy when they were loosed from the grips of Pharaoh, but that quickly changed when bondage was no longer a burden! As soon as they got loose, they forgot God, not realizing that abandoning the Liberty of God is bondage all over again! The Apostle Paul wrote: "Stand fast therefore in the liberty wherewith Christ hath made us free and be NOT entangled AGAIN with the yoke of BONDAGE!" (Galatians 5:1). If God has delivered you from that which oppressed, depressed, and almost possessed you, why would you even try to live life without Him! We must not think for a moment that yesterday's deliverance, is the stage for today's disobedience! Do yourself a huge favor, look back on where God has brought you from, then think about where you might be if He hadn't freed you from bondage. Have a Blessed day, and thanks for allowing me to share the word from a *Pastor's Perspective*...

The Apostle Paul wrote, "For Christ is the END of the law for righteousness to everyone who believes!"(Romans 10:4). Pious acts validated by works, religiosity, and legalistic behavior are NOT righteousness! If you fail to understand that Christ is the END of the law FOR righteousness, you are victimizing yourself with wrong indoctrination and violating the repeal. "There is therefore NOW no condemnation to those who are in Christ Jesus, who do not walk according to the flesh, but according to the Spirit! For the law of the Spirit of life IN Christ Jesus has made us free from the law of sin and death!" (Romans 8:1-2 NKJV). When we try to connect kingdom work with earthly understanding, we fall short, instead of forward! If what you do, is not validated by what JESUS did, it may look right, but that doesn't make it righteousness! If it doesn't EDIFY Christ NOW, it may TESTIFY against you later! Have a Blessed day, and thanks for allowing me to share the word from a *Pastor's Perspective*...

MARCH 9

"Let the redeemed of the Lord say so!"
(Psalms 107:2). Those who are truly
REDEEMED shouldn't have to ask. "Say
what?" All who have experienced the
GOODNESS, the GRACE, the MERCY,
and the LOVINGKINDNESS of God, open
your mouth and give God a Holy Ghost
Praise which will put the enemy in flight! The
bible says God is the same Yesterday, Today,
and Forever! (Hebrews 13:8). What He did for

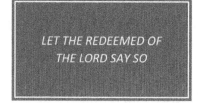

Israel in their
distress, He
has done for
us, in ours!!
"He sent His
WORD, and
HEALED them, and DELIVERED them
from their destruction!!" (Psalms 107:20). His
love towards us His people, is without a
doubt...UNCONDITIONAL! God has been
better to us, than we have ever been to
ourselves! And it is high time that the
REDEEMED of the LORD, say so! Have a
Blessed day, and thanks for allowing me to
share the word from a *Pastor's Perspective*...

According to the Apostle Paul, "The eyes of your understanding being enlightened that you may know what is the HOPE of His calling, and what is the RICHES of the GLORY of His inheritance in the saints, and what is the exceeding greatness of His POWER toward US who BELIEVE, according to the working of His POWER!" (Ephesians 1:18-19). When you have the word of God in you, you have POWER that is so gloriously rich that it changes your STATUS, no matter what your STANDARDS used to be! It won't allow anything to hinder your HOPE! The GLORY of this POWER is that it fuels and enlightens your understanding through your BELIEF! Making you an heir to an inheritance that cannot and will not fade! (I Peter 1:4). When you believe in GOD, you introduce your DESTINY to your GREATNESS! Allow the HOPE of His calling, to empower and enlighten the understanding that fuels your vision! Have a Blessed day, and thanks for allowing me to share the word from *A Pastor's Perspective...*

MARCH 11

Confidence is oftentimes mistaken for arrogance, but we should be operating in the spirit of CONFIDENCE, because the scripture indicates: "Cast not away, therefore your CONFIDENCE, which hath great recompense of reward!" (Hebrews 10:35). And because confidence isn't built-in, it must be built-up! We build and develop our confidence with the exact thing that builds our Faith...BELIEF! Every promise in God's word is first HEARD, then BELIEVED, and finally MANIFESTED! And when this happens enough times, oh HALLELUJAH somebody!! You'll begin to say from the depths of your belly: "Being CONFIDENT of this very thing, that he who hath begun a good work in me, is able to complete it!" (Philippians 1:6). You'll never be confused by what THEY say, as long as you're CONFIDENT in what GOD is able to do! CONFIDENCE in God is progress, in formal attire! Have a Blessed day, and thanks for allowing me to share the word from *A Pastor's Perspective...*

Waiting on God can be a burden or a blessing depending on how you WAIT! Those who worry, complain, and become weary while they WAIT are always disappointed in the end! Not because God wasn't ABLE, but because God wasn't TRUSTED! Even some of God's chosen deal with the issue of waiting with an improper outlook (II Kings 6:24-33). But those who WAIT with godly expectation, blessed assurance, and complete confidence have been BLESSED since the beginning of man's purpose (Isaiah 64:4). And God has always allowed WAITING to precede blessing! (Psalms 27:14, 46:10). Waiting is worship! Scripture says..."Be anxious for nothing!" (Philippians 4:6). God does things IN our lives, according to the things we do WITH our lives! Despite his circumstances, Job held on to the promises of God and said..."All the days of my appointed time will I WAIT till my change comes!" (Job 14:14). It's always worth it to WAIT on the Lord! Have a Blessed day, and thanks for allowing me to share the word from a *Pastor's Perspective*...

MARCH 13

Have you ever wondered how people expect the BEST from God, when they really don't BELIEVE in God! It's not disbelief as it relates to God's existence, it's disbelief in terms of God not meeting all their needs, when they want Him to! The bible tells us, "For He who COMES to God, must BELIEVE He is God!" (Hebrews 11:6). It's of no use to COME to where God is, then leave with the same DISBELIEF you arrived with! The Apostle James said it like this, "But let him ask in FAITH, with no DOUBTING, for he who doubts is like the wave of the sea DRIVEN and tossed by the wind! For let NOT that man suppose that He will receive anything from the Lord!!" (James 1:6-7). The Prophet Abraham received all God had for him, because he believed that God was completely able! (Romans 4:20-21). Why ask God for something you don't believe He will do! Ask in FAITH. Have a Blessed day, and thanks for allowing me to share the word from a *Pastor's Perspective*...

MARCH 14

As Jesus hung on the cross, the entire land was filled with darkness (Matthew 27:45). Can you imagine what was going through the minds of the Roman soldiers, the religious Jews, His mother, and brothers? It's bad enough to be crucifying an innocent man, but to have NIGHT where there should be DAY during the crucifixion! That alone was solid evidence that whom they crucified, was not only God of ALL, but also, ALL Of GOD!! And then to have the veil torn from top to bottom allowing us access to the throne of GRACE! He conquered death and brought back LIFE! When the spirit of life reached eternity, the LIGHT of day returned to man! God has given us everything we need to dispel the darkness in this land. The veil was torn, so victory could be yours! The more you experience LIFE in the LIGHT, you too will testify, "Truly this was the Son of God!" (Matthew 27:54). Have a Blessed day, and thanks for allowing me to share the word from a *Pastor's Perspective*...

MARCH 15

After everything KING David had to learn, go through, and be disciplined for, God knew his appointment to the PREISTHOOD would be nothing short of praiseworthy!! When David prayed the following words, he was praying from a place of strength that demons could no longer penetrate: "Vindicate me, O Lord, For I have WALKED in my integrity! I have TRUSTED in the Lord! I shall not slip! Examine me, O Lord, and PROVE me. Try my mind and my heart! (Psalms 26:1-2). David's prayer tells us that a soul sold out for God is stronger than the scrutiny of an oppressor! The three key elements David declared were; how he NOW walks, how he NOW trusts, and how his life will NOW prove that what comes out of his mouth is that which has taken over his heart! When we make up our minds to truly walk with God, we serve the devil notice that the sifting is over! Have a Blessed day, and thanks for allowing me to share the word from a *Pastor's Perspective*...

When God called the Prophet/Priest Samuel, the bible tells us..."And the WORD of the Lord was rare in those days, there was no frequent vision!" (I Samuel 3:1). You mean to tell me, there were times when God withheld his PRESENCE! Yes, that's exactly what I'm saying. Men were continually evil and had irreverent attitudes towards God. Even men who were said to be priests in the land were immensely corrupt! (I Samuel 2:12, 22-25). When God called Samuel, the bible tells us..."Now Samuel did NOT yet know the Lord, neither was the WORD revealed unto him!" (I Samuel 3:7). And yet, the scripture also reveals, "And the Child Samuel MINISTERED unto the Lord before Eli!"(I Samuel 3:1). Look at our world today, school shootings, murders, disasters, bombings, etc. It appears that God is withholding His PRESENCE! We cry out to God, "Where are you"? But God in His silence is saying: "You left me, I didn't leave you!" Have a Blessed day, and thanks for allowing me to share the word from a *Pastor's Perspective*…

MARCH 17

"And YOU, that were once alienated and enemies in your mind by wicked works, yet NOW hath he RECONCILED! In the body of his flesh through death, to present you holy, unblameable, and unreproveable in his sight!" (Colossians 1:20-22). The reconciliation of us back to Himself is beyond selfless love, it is the powerful work of GRACE and the immutable wonder of MERCY refusing that none should perish! (II Peter 3:9). We were reconciled back to God, because God could never turn his back on us! We need to understand, Hell is a choice! Sin is a choice! Corruption is a choice! But to be reconciled, is also a choice! Choose you this day...Life or Death! (Deuteronomy 30:15). When you put on the mind of Christ (I

GRACE, MERCY, RECONCILIATION...

Corinthians 2:16), you also received the ministry of reconciliation (II Corinthians 5:18). Have a Blessed day, and thanks for allowing me to share the word from a *Pastor's Perspective*...

MARCH 18

Some spiritual wonders found IN scripture literally blow my mind! Like, "If ye abide IN me, and my word abide IN you, ye shall ask what ye will, and it shall be done unto you!" (John 15:7). It amazes me how He fills us with His Spirit, and yet, ONLY the part of us that is like Him, can abide IN Him! He's all IN us, but ALL of *us*, is not IN Him! The bible says, "There is no darkness in God, At All!" (I John 1:5). Doubt, Worry, Weakness, Pride, etc. these are all components of Darkness! And as much as God is IN you, none of these things can EVER be IN Him! In Christ Jesus we're not just IN the light! We ARE, the light! (Matthew 5:14). Our illumination, swallows up our opposition. To abide IN Christ, is to be void of darkness! And to be void of darkness, is the true meaning of abiding IN Him! You can only ask what you will, when you ask from the light! Abiding IN Christ, is the Lamp unto my feet, and the Light unto my path! (Psalms 119:105). Have a Blessed day, and thanks for allowing me to share the word from a *Pastor's Perspective*...

MARCH 19

Sometimes we are baffled by God's benevolence on earth. We question His will, His Compassion, and even His Sovereignty. We just can't seem to understand His Love for His creation! We look at acts of Men, then at the Love of God, and conclude that God is far too lenient as Men are far too evil! Contrary to what we believe, God is not lenient nor slack in His promises! (II Peter 3:9). God always leaves room for Repentance and Grace! Nonetheless, one principle remains misunderstood: "For to whosoever much is GIVEN, much is REQUIRED!" (Luke 12:48). If God has Favored you in situations where you should have fallen, protected you in situations that may have terminated your Faith, covered you in storms that could've blown your house AWAY! God has given you so much! His Son, Our Salvation, His Love, His Grace, and the list goes on! To Love God, is to treat HIM, like He treats you. Those who take God's Love for granted NOW, will surely give an account of it LATER! Have a Blessed day, and thanks for allowing me to share the word from a *Pastor's Perspective…*

King Solomon was inspired to write, "Good understanding giveth FAVOR, but the way of transgressors is HARD!" (Proverbs 13:15). If we love like Jesus loves, talk like Jesus talks, respond like Jesus responds, I believe we will receive what Jesus received---The Father's approval! "This is my beloved Son, in whom I am well pleased!" (Matthew 17:5). When you have GOOD understanding of God's ways, God's Goodness towards others won't be HARD to handle! The Apostle Paul wrote: "He said to Moses, I will have MERCY on whom I will have MERCY, I will have COMPASSION on whom I will have COMPASSION!" (Romans 9:15). Remember

we all have faults, but you will NEVER be anyone's failure, as long as God is your Father! So then, if anyone should question your TODAY in comparison to your YESTERDAY, simply tell them: "GOD FAVORED ME." Have a Blessed day, and thanks for allowing me to share the word from a *Pastor's Perspective*...

MARCH 21

Jesus said..."The harvest truly is plentiful, but the LABORERS are few." (Matthew 9:37). SALVATION was made free to us, FORGIVENESS was made free to us, REDEMPTION was made free to us, GRACE was even made free to us, but ALL of this was afforded through the sacrifice of God's only Son, Jesus Christ! Something that cost him EVERYTHING! He looked past our faults and attended unto our NEEDS and yet there remains a lack of the very LABORERS he sacrificed himself to save. If we won't labor, Jesus asks us to at least, "PRAY the Lord of the harvest to send out LABORERS into the harvest!?" (Matthew 10:38). What you do today may not be rewarded today! But God WILL make good on his promise (Hebrews 6:10). Therefore, my beloved brethren, be steadfast, immovable, always abounding in the work of the Lord! Knowing that your LABOR is not in vain in the Lord!" (I Corinthians 15:58). Have a Blessed day, and thanks for allowing me to share the word from a *Pastor's Perspective*...

MARCH 22

We often hear, "To God Be The GLORY! It's all for the GLORY of God! Lord we give you all the GLORY! And yet, when you feel something's NOT all about you, not only does your attitude change, it hinders your elevation! When the Spirit of God said to the Prophet Isaiah, "I am the Lord, that is MY name, and MY GLORY will I NOT give to another, neither MY praise to carved images!" (Isaiah 42:8). He was saying I Will NOT give to any man the very ESSENCE, PRESENCE, and COMPLETENESS of my existence, not because I don't desire them to have it, but because I know men would count themselves, greater than me! "Jesus did not commit himself unto men, because he knew ALL men!" (John 2:24). But when God made man in HIS image, he GLORIFIED the image, of those who believe in the NAME! "Father, GLORIFY thy NAME!" (John 12: 28). God will never give His GLORY to US, but He has blessed us, IN IT! Have a Blessed day, and thanks for allowing me to share the word from a *Pastor's Perspective...*

MARCH 23

It is God's desire, to care for us, in every way. Yet, there are things He allows us to do to test our character, build our faith, and prove our passion. But He cannot deny His own in any way, "Fear not, little flock, for it is your Father's good pleasure to give you the kingdom!" (Luke 12:32). If Jesus desires to give you..."Life and life more abundantly," (John 10:10), and the Father desires to give you the kingdom and everything in it, how can we NOT "Seek ye first the kingdom of God and His righteousness?" So that ALL this can be ours both NOW, and THEN!! (Matthew 6:33). Even when we think we

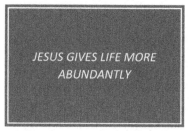

JESUS GIVES LIFE MORE ABUNDANTLY

know what we WANT, God knows exactly what we NEED! And in His perfect timing, according to His perfect will, He releases every GOOD and PERFECT gift! (James 1:17). Whatever God WILLS, is what WILL be!! Have a Blessed day, and thanks for allowing me to share the word from a *Pastor's Perspective...*

"All Scripture is given by inspiration of God, and is profitable for DOCTRINE, for REPROOF, for CORRECTION, for INSTRUCTION in righteousness, that the man of God may be thoroughly furnished unto ALL good works!" (II Timothy 3:16). When the Apostle David wrote..."Create in

...AND WE SHALL BE CHANGED

me a clean heart, O God, and renew a right Spirit within me" (Psalms 51:10), he was asking God to INSPIRE him with enough authority to renew the part of himself he no longer wanted to live with!! We must remind ourselves by FAITH that *I* am made whole, but not all of *me* is heaven bound, which is why the Apostle Paul was INSPIRED to write, "In a moment, in the twinkling of an eye, at the last trump, for the trumpet shall sound, and the dead shall be raised INCORRUPTIBLE, and we shall be CHANGED!" (I Corinthians 15:52). Have a Blessed day, and thanks for allowing me to share the word from a *Pastor's Perspective*...

MARCH 25

Sometimes we act as if we're taking God with us! No, it's the other way around: He's taking us with Him! "Ye have not chosen me, but I have chosen you, and ordained you, that ye shall go!!" (John 15:16). And in our finite thinking we fail to understand that no matter how great our purpose may appear, we must give God permission to develop the GIFT! The bible says, "Every good GIFT, and every perfect GIFT is FROM above!" (James 1:17). Please understand this, the Gifts and Calling of God are without repentance (Romans 11:29). But, if you don't give God permission to develop the GIFT, you're attempting the impossible without His help. We are unable to develop purpose, through imperfection!!! Every failure we've ever experienced, started with a single flaw!! Give God permission to develop your gift so He can infuse His PERFECTION with your PERMISSION and present your PURPOSE, to the world! Your Gift will never need a car seat if you give God permission to do the driving!!...Have a Blessed day, and thanks for allowing me to share the word from a *Pastor's Perspective*...

How many zeros are there in infinity? How long is eternity? Is forever the address of heaven? The answers to these questions cannot begin to describe who God is, how long He has existed, nor where He originated! Anticipating this, God tells us to just know that, "I AM, THAT I AM!" (Exodus 3:14). The Apostle Paul wrote: "According as HE hath chosen us IN HIM, HE IS before the foundation of the world!"(Ephesians 1:4). But Jesus wanted to reassure us even more as His beloved, so He said, "I am Alpha and Omega, the beginning and the ending!" (Revelation 1:8). God wants us to know that it was with His words that He framed the world!! (Hebrews 11:3). He has touched our understanding with His Spirit, so we can humbly embrace and rest in the following: "Beloved, now are we the children of God, and doth not yet appear what WE shall be, but WE KNOW that, when He shall appear, WE shall be LIKE HIM, for WE shall see Him as HE IS!" (I John 3:2). Have a Blessed day, and thanks for allowing me to share the word from a *Pastor's Perspective...*

Have you ever thought that what you do, what you say, and how you act could be impacting your relationship with God? The Apostle James wrote: "A DOUBLE-MINDED man, is unstable in all his ways." (James 1:8). You're probably thinking: "I may not have it all together, but I am definitely not unstable!" But spiritually speaking, Doubt is

DOUBT CORRUPTS THE HEART

one of the greatest tools our adversary uses to corrupt the heart! So then, being DOUBLE-MINDED is akin to being pulled in two different directions! You can't serve God if you Doubt Him, no more than you can stay married by being selfish! Nor be a witness, if you're wishy-washy! And you'll never be that voice of ministry if you always speak from a position of misery! However, real spiritual instability is this: thinking God's hand is all over your life, when you haven't even given him full reign of your heart! Have a Blessed day, and thanks for allowing me to share the word from a *Pastor's Perspective...*

MARCH 28

"This is the day the Lord has made, let us rejoice and be glad in it!" (Psalms 118:24). This day is another opportunity to give back to God with Praise and Worship, glory, and honor! Because He is so very worthy! The Prophet and Psalmist David said..."Bless the Lord, O my soul, and forget not ALL His benefits!" (Psalms 103:2). We must realize that the greatest benefit of this day is not our opportunity to Worship Him, but rather to be covered in His Omnipotence, His Omniscience, and His Omnipresence! This is a COVENANT that entirely COVERS it!! However today may turn out, let us be glad in it, because we have full coverage! Let me encourage you to dance on the neck of your circumstances! Shout Hallelujah down the hallways of your heartache! And praise God for ALL His benefits! He has blessed you to see another day, now you ought to bless him in the fellowship of his PRESENCE, His PURPOSE, and His POWER!! Have a Blessed day, and thanks for allowing me to share the word from a *Pastor's Perspective*...

MARCH 29

Mass tragedies, political pollution, unrest in our country's moral understanding, and constant compromise in the church's foundation may cause us to see things differently than the way God would have us them seen! All unrighteousness is SIN! (I John 5:17). Can we find PEACE, when God has declared, "There is no PEACE for the wicked!" (Isaiah 48:22). We sometimes fail to remember, "The earth is the Lord's and the FULLNESS thereof!!" (Psalms 24:1). We really need to get this in our spirits today, there will be no PEACE until we give God back His place of preeminence! Wickedness in the land is gaining strength because of our refusal to Worship the One and True Living God!! "If my people, who are called by my name, will HUMBLE themselves, and PRAY, and SEEK my face, and turn from their WICKED ways, then Will I HEAR from heaven, and will FORGIVE their SIN, and will HEAL their land!" (II Chronicles 7:14). Have a Blessed day, and thanks for allowing me to share the word from a *Pastor's Perspective*...

MARCH 30

There are six things God wants us to know about His theocracy. "The LAW of the Lord is PERFECT, converting the soul; the TESTIMONY of the Lord is SURE, making wise the simple; the STATUTES of the Lord are RIGHT, rejoicing the heart; the COMMANDMENTS of the Lord are PURE, enlightening the eyes; the FEAR of the Lord is CLEAN, enduring forever; and the JUDGEMENTS of the Lord are TRUE and RIGHTEOUS altogether!!" (Psalms 19:7-9). The Laws, Testimonies, Statutes, Commandments, Fear, and Judgements of God are the tenets of God's majestic Love! And it is His expectation that this preeminence will be the structure of our obedience! Everything about our will to obey, must be connected to the knowledge that He is God! Everything that He requires of us, are the things that keep us in Him! It is God's desire to be one with all that He has created. In Him, we LIVE, MOVE, and HAVE our being (Acts 17:28). Have a Blessed day, and thanks for allowing me to share the word from a *Pastor's Perspective*...

MARCH 31

The way we think, has a lot to do with how
we serve God, how we love one another, and
how we live our lives. The Apostle Paul
wrote...For to be carnally minded (that is, to
think like the world) is DEATH, but to be
spiritually minded is LIFE and PEACE!"
(Romans 8:6). Additionally, the Prophet
Solomon said: For as he THINKETH in his
heart, so is he!" (Proverbs 23:7). Jesus
said...For out of the abundance of the
HEART the MOUTH speaks!"(Matthew
12:34). People are quick to say...Don't judge
me! But the truth of the matter is, people
don't have to judge, what is evidenced from
YOUR mouth! It's only a matter of time, that
what's IN you, comes OUT! But if you follow
the scriptures and work towards changing
how you think (Philippians 4:8), what you say
will be like Honey to bees. Today, allow your
thoughts to be governed by God, so His
presence will be revealed in your
speech...Have a Blessed day, and thanks for
allowing me to share the word from a *Pastor's
Perspective*...

APRIL 1

Have you ever pondered the dialogue between Mary and the angel Gabriel concerning the birth of Jesus? (Luke 1:26-38). First, he told her she was HIGHLY FAVORED among women! (vs.28). Then, he told her she'd found FAVOR with GOD! (vs.30). He told her that her calling, consecration, and conception was a HOLY thing! (vs.35). And then he said: your cousin Elizabeth is six months pregnant too, I know you knew her to be too old, and on top of that BARREN, however, you need to understand this..."For with GOD, nothing shall be impossible!!" (vs.36-37). What am I saying? God doesn't need us to trust him in OUR plans, we need to trust Him, in HIS! He's the only one who can make the IMPOSSIBLE, POSSIBLE! Life can be so much bigger and brighter if we allow GOD to be in the center of it! Mary didn't ask to be the Mother of the Messiah, but God proved to us once again that He IS the GOD of the IMPOSSIBLE (vs.34). Have a Blessed day, and thanks for allowing me to share the word from a *Pastor's Perspective*...

When you have the mind of Christ, you have His compassion also. Of course, you want to see everyone saved, sanctified, and filled with the Holy Spirit, but there is one other thing you'll want for people: to see them CARED for! Jesus said..."The harvest truly is plenteous, but the laborers are few!" (Matthew 9:37). Not only is time winding up, but people are losing hope! We really need to adhere to what Jesus said to the disciples..."Pray ye therefore to the Lord of the harvest, that he shall send forth laborers into His harvest." (Matthew 9:38). And the Apostle Paul chimed in and said the following: "And how shall they preach, except they be SENT!!" (Romans 10:15). Listen how the Spirit of the Lord encourages us..."How beautiful upon the mountains are the feet of him that bringeth glad tidings, that publisheth peace, that bringeth good tidings of good, that publisheth salvation, that saith unto Zion, Thy God Reigneth!!" (Isaiah 52:7). Have a Blessed day, and thanks for allowing me to share the word from a *Pastor's Perspective*...

APRIL 3

The Psalmist said..."I will bless the Lord at all times, and His Praise shall continually be in my mouth!!" (Psalms 34:1). If we'd spend more time PRAISING God, and less time focusing on our problems, we would see for ourselves..."When the PRAISES go up, the blessings come down!" Or I like to look at it this way... When the PRAISES go up, the problems go away! When we build upon our most holy faith (Jude 1:20), we wage war on our most intimidating fears! We don't ever have the right to question God's ABILITY to be God, especially when we don't have the courage to address our own INSECURITIES! You can't BLESS the Lord at times, if you spend all your time BLAMING God for everything that's wrong! God wants you to know...it's your PRAISES that stop your PROBLEMS, NOT your complaints! If we put PRAISE on our PROBLEMS, God will manifest PROMISE to His people...Have a Blessed day, and thanks for allowing me to share the word from a *Pastor's Perspective*...

APRIL 4

When Jesus called Zaccheus down from the sycamore tree, he told Jesus the reason he had been up there, was so He could SEE Him. Jesus called him down from that HIGH place, so he could be seen! (Luke 19:1-10). You see, Zaccheus may have been small in stature, but he was big in pride. After answering the call from the tree, he immediately started telling Jesus all he does for the poor, and how he would gladly repay anyone for treating them unfair. If anyone knows how prideful you can be, it's YOU! Stop taking PRIDE in everything you do and start taking responsibility for not responding to His call for your life! We put so many things before God...our job, our spouse, our children, golf, favorite TV shows---you name it! And then, expect God to just wait His turn, in a life He owns! Something to consider: Perhaps God is calling you today from your HIGH PLACE, because your HIGH PLACE, is taking HIS PLACE! Have a Blessed day, and thanks for allowing me to share the word from a *Pastor's Perspective*...

APRIL 5

The Apostle Paul wrote: "For many walk of whom I have told you often, and now tell you even WEEPING, that they are the enemies of the cross!!" (Philippians 3:18). Here, Paul is emphasizing that it was painstakingly awful for him to watch those who oppose God and His work. It literally brought him to tears! With all that God affords man, the redeeming reconciliatory work at the cross, the gift of forgiveness through repentance, and the resurrection work of salvation, how does one become an ENEMY of God? The answer: "Ye adulterers and adulteresses, know ye not that the FRIENDSHIP of the WORLD is ENMITY with God? Whosoever, therefore, will be a FRIEND of the WORLD is the ENEMY of God!!" (James 4:4). Which is why God is calling you away from the world! Therefore, the Apostle John wrote: "Love NOT the world, neither the things in the world. If ANY man LOVE the world, the LOVE of the Father is NOT in him!" (I John 2:15). Have a Blessed day, and thanks for allowing me to share the word from a *Pastor's Perspective*...

APRIL 6

The Psalmist said..."As the deer panteth after the water brooks, so panteth my soul after thee, O God" (Psalms 42:1). I have heard it told that **GRACE** is...**G**od **R**unning **A**fter **C**hristian's **E**verywhere. But how many of you have heard this about **MERCY**: **M**y **E**ternal **R**ighteousness **C**arrying **Y**ou! We can't REPAY Him for what He did at the cross, so we certainly should be willing to REPENT for what we do while on this earth that he created! To not desire God, is the equivalent of not desiring to live! Listen to the question the Spirit of the Lord asked the Prophet Ezekiel: "Have I any pleasure AT ALL that the wicked should die? Saith the Lord God, and not that he should return from his ways, and live?" (Ezekiel 18:23). Now listen to God's answer: "For I have NO PLEASURE in the death of him that dieth, saith the Lord God, wherefore, turn yourselves and LIVE!!" (Ezekiel 18:32). So then, those who desire GOD, desire LIFE! And those who don't, are living beneath their privileges! Have a Blessed day, and thanks for allowing me to share the word from a *Pastor's Perspective*...

If you truly Love the Lord and understand that GRACE is...God's Righteousness at Christ's Expense, you will never, ever take his Grace for granted again! For it is by GRACE we are justified (Romans 3:24). By GRACE

BY GRACE WE ARE SAVED

we stand in the hope of God's glory (Romans 5:2). By GRACE we know that God is sufficient (II Corinthians 12:9). By GRACE we are called (Galatians 1:15), and it is by GRACE we are saved! (Ephesians 2:8). If it wasn't for GRACE, the gospel message would have been our death sentence! Because all have sinned and fallen short of the Glory of God (Romans 3:23). Today, stand in the liberty of GRACE and all that Christ did for you through it. For where sin once abounded, now GRACE does much more! (Romans 5:20). To understand GRACE is to know that, GRACE is the ONLY TRUE RELIEVER of GRIEF!! Have a Blessed day, and thanks for allowing me to share the word from a *Pastor's Perspective...*

When God does ANYTHING for you, it's not by accident, nor do you receive ANYTHING that wasn't meant for you! It was done according to His WILL, not your WANTS! Please understand that God's Will is connected to His PROMISES! And the scripture says...For ALL the PROMISES of GOD are *YES* and *AMEN*, unto the glory of GOD by US!!" (II Corinthians 1:20). And because we were made in HIS image, He delights in giving us everything according to HIS promise! All that we are or will ever be, is because HE is! The Prophet Solomon said..."The blessing of the Lord, maketh rich, and he addeth no sorrow with it! (Proverbs 10:22). You never have to apologize for the GOODNESS of God in your life! You have what God gave you, because you accepted what God was offering! God didn't bless you because you deserved it, He blessed you, because He PROMISED he would!!...Have a Blessed day, and thanks for allowing me to share the word from a *Pastor's Perspective*...

Jesus going to the cross for our sin is God's pre-approval for salvation! (John 3:16). God loved the world, and gave His Son, but it's up to you and I to BELIEVE in what He did! To be pre-approved for anything is like having hope...you HAVE it, until you stop believing IN it!! Now don't misunderstand what I'm saying, Salvation is not like rolling the dice. No, not at all! But Salvation does require that you BELIEVE in Christ to complete the work in you! (Hebrews 11:6). Being pre-

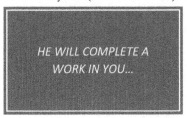

HE WILL COMPLETE A WORK IN YOU...

approved by God is Him revealing His desire to have you always. Pre-approval may be a worldly term, but it has astounding spiritual connotations! "But God demonstrates His own love towards us, in that while we were still sinners, Christ DIED for us!!" (Romans 5:8). Bad credit or No credit...Christ still did it!! When you BELIEVE in what He's done, there's nothing left to do, but BELIEVE! Have a Blessed day, and thanks for allowing me to share the word from a *Pastor's Perspective*...

APRIL 10

When I hear people say, "ALL I can do is pray," it sounds as if PRAYER is the last resort! Like there were better options! If only praying about everything was the worst habit you had! In fact, the bible says: "And He (Jesus) spoke a parable unto them to this end, that men ought ALWAYS PRAY, and not faint!!"(Luke 18:1). A strong prayer life is a life that's war ready!! Some believe prayer is telling God what we need, how we feel, what we think and so on. However, PRAYER is not simply what we tell God as he already knows everything (Matthew 6:32). He knows all about our internal and external wars! We don't have a clue how many times we've called our complaints PRAYER, and then feel as though God is not listening. It's not that He's not listening, it's just that sometimes...WE KNOW NOT, what to pray! (Romans 8:26). Develop your daily PRAYER life by doing it ALL the time. When PRAYER is a priority, it won't be ALL you CAN do, it will become ALL you NEED to do! Have a Blessed day, and thanks for allowing me to share the word from a *Pastor's Perspective*...

Whenever you are going through something in your mind, your heart, or with your health, listen to what the Prophet Solomon has to say about God's words: "For they are life unto those that find them, and health to all our flesh." (Proverbs 4:22). When afflictions occur---and they will occur, there is nothing more soothing to the soul than the word of God! He sees your suffering, He sees your perseverance, but He wants to see your confidence in His word! He knows you believe it is His word, however, do you TRUST what He says?" He's been watching your spirit break through self-effort, and today he wants the, "Joy of the Lord, to be your strength!" (Nehemiah 8:10). He wants us to understand..."A merry heart doeth good like a medicine, but a broken spirit drieth up the bones!" (Proverbs 17:22). God's word is our spiritual multivitamin that keeps us healthy in mind, body, and soul. Have a Blessed day, and thanks for allowing me to share the word from a *Pastor's Perspective...*

APRIL 12

The saying goes…"I can't see the forest, for the trees!" In other words, there are so many trees in the way that I can't even see what the forest looks like! Sometimes this is how we feel about certain obstacles though the bible tells us how blessed we are as a people. Not only do we know God, but we have a relationship with the Spirit that is so close to Him that, "Angels desire to look into it!!" (I Peter 1:12). The spiritual obstacles we experience are not to block OUR view, and we need not ever question the view WE have, we just have to follow the vision GOD has! Jesus said…."Thomas, because thou hast seen me, thou hath believed, but blessed are those who have not seen, and yet have believed!" (John 20:29). I understand, how natural it is, to want to know what God is doing in your life. But, when God takes your faith into a forest, it's because your enemy is tracking your steps! God is not blocking your view, He's losing your enemy! Have a Blessed day, and thanks for allowing me to share the word from a *Pastor's Perspective*…

APRIL 13

It has been said, "When life brings you lemons, make lemonade!" The only way to do that is to sweeten that which is sour! The Apostle David said, "Oh, taste and see that the Lord is good!" (Psalms 34:8). The Prophet David said, "My meditation of Him shall be SWEET!" (104:34). The Prophet Solomon said..."Every desire accomplished in the Lord is SWEET to the soul!" (Proverbs 13:19). The Prophet Isaiah warns us however, "Woe unto them who call evil, good, and good, evil! Who put darkness for light, and light for darkness! Who put bitter for SWEET, and SWEET for bitter! (Isaiah 5:20). Life is full of bitter moments, but if you say to yourself...Hold up, wait a minute, let me put some JESUS in it! I guarantee you'll sweeten the situation! If your situation is still bitter, you haven't added enough JESUS! Remember, David said, "Oh, TASTE and SEE..." Sometimes you must add more and more JESUS until the tough times taste SWEET! Have a Blessed day, and thanks for allowing me to share the word from a *Pastor's Perspective*...

When the Apostle David wrote, " Thou hast PROVED mine heart, thou hast VISITED me in the night, thou hast TESTED me, and shalt find NOTHING! I PURPOSE that my mouth shall NOT transgress! (Psalms 17:3). This adulterous, murdering, wayward King was coming to the end of himself, and into the knowledge of who he was in God! When David realized that he had ALL that God is, on the inside of him, he refused to let everything he once wasn't hinder his faith! There are two things you must understand about your PAST...you'll always have it, and you can't out live it! But there are two greater things about God's Grace and Mercy you need to understand; it's' free to all, and is from everlasting to everlasting! When God accepted your confession of FAITH, He changed your position from GRIEF to GRACE! God wants you to know, "You are more than a conqueror through Him who loves you and gave HIMSELF for you!" (Romans 8:37). Have a Blessed day, and thanks for allowing me to share the word from a *Pastor's Perspective*...

I would like to encourage you, to learn to encourage YOURSELF! And not necessarily because something is wrong, but rather, because God has made everything alright! When Jesus said..."Let not your heart be troubled, ye believe in God, believe also in me." (John 14:1). He was not only speaking of

MERCY TO COVER YOU ALWAYS

deliverance, He was speaking of destiny! He was setting in order our

hearts to receive Psalms 32 in its entirety! Take a moment and read Psalm 32 right now...Selah. Can you see why you should be encouraged? Your transgressions were forgiven, your iniquities were not imputed, your life in Christ has become a hiding place from evil, and your trust IN God, is the mandate of God that orders Mercy to cover you ALWAYS! This is the destiny God has always had for you. You may not have it all together, but together with God, you have it all! And no demon in Hell, can take that away! Have a Blessed day, and thanks for allowing me to share the word from a *Pastor's Perspective...*

APRIL 16

"Thou wilt show me the path of LIFE. In thy PRESENCE is fullness of JOY, at thy right hand there are PLEASURES for evermore!"(Psalms 16:11). Now let's look at this more closely. God orders our STEPS (Psalms 37:23), and those steps along the path of LIFE. Our lives are always filled with His PRESENCE, even when it doesn't feel like it. Mind you, because He is present, we are full of JOY knowing that every problem we will ever face is merely labor towards birthing our PURPOSE and the work of His PLEASURE! WOW!!

When God orders your steps, there's no need to watch where you're walking, you need to be paying extreme attention to what really pleases Him! Our finite understanding is always tainted by how we want things done! But if we let God order the steps, we can rest assured that we'll rejoice in the outcome! When God's PRESENCE is the architect of your PURPOSE, God's PLEASURE becomes the center of your JOY! Have a Blessed day, and thanks for allowing me to share the word from a *Pastor's Perspective...*

A HUMBLE heart will always receive heaven's help! God will send somebody, from somewhere, to do something, to help! Here's what happens when you HUMBLE yourself; First, "Better it is to be of a HUMBLE spirit than to DIVIDE the spoils with the proud!" (Proverbs 16:19). Secondly, "God RESISTS the proud, and gives GRACE to the Humble." (I Peter 5:5). Third, "Then God gives MORE GRACE to the HUMBLE!" (James 4:6). And last of all, you must, "HUMBLE yourselves, therefore, under the mighty hand of God, that He may EXALT YOU in due in time!"(I Peter 5:6).

I believe one of the saddest things God witnesses, is the wickedness of rebellion! Why? Because sooner or later, He must judge it! If you HUMBLE yourself under His mighty hand, you'll never experience the judgment of His mighty wrath! It is NEVER God's intent, to HURT what He's trying to HUMBLE!!...Have a Blessed day, and thanks for allowing me to share the word from a *Pastor's Perspective...*

Jesus said, "Be anxious for nothing," (Matthew 6:25), because your Heavenly Father knows exactly what you need and when you need it! (vs.32). We say God's timing is perfect, but the reality is, God doesn't operate WITHIN time! Our needs are met according to His purpose, and according to His will! Now, don't get me wrong, timing is instrumental in the realm in which WE exist, but only to help us understand and trust the process and promises of heaven. When the scripture says that..."God will never leave us, nor forsake us" (Hebrews 13:5), that promise is NOT connected to time, it's connected to covenant! This morning if your back is against the wall, circumstances are developing and it seems as though the walls are closing in; don't focus on how much TIME you have, but rather on how BIG of a God you have! He's an on-time God simply because He IS! When you know Him to be the Almighty God....it's not about our TIMING, it's about His AUTHORITY! Have a Blessed day, and thanks for allowing me to share the word from a *Pastor's Perspective*...

One of the hardest things believers deal with is their own nature. At times we all must address the PETER in us: a little hard of hearing, but always having something to say. The THOMAS in us: Attempting to mix doubt with devotion. The SAUL in us: Destined to be a PAUL but struggling to overcome the persecutor within. When disciples James and John wanted to call down fire from heaven to consume those who did not receive Jesus, the bible says He turned and rebuked them and said..."Ye know not what spirit ye are of!" (Luke 9:55). Jesus knew then that the disciples didn't have the compassion it would take to complete the mission in the village because they didn't know the spirit they were working with. And as they were leaving the village Jesus said..."For the Son of man is NOT come to destroy men's lives, but to SAVE them!" (Luke 9:56). We don't want to make the mistake of SLAYING, that which God intends on SAVING! Have a Blessed day, and thanks for allowing me to share the word from a *Pastor's Perspective*...

APRIL 20

Have you ever wondered why Jesus said..."And thou shalt love the Lord thy God with all thy HEART, and with all thy SOUL, and with all thy MIND, and with all thy STRENGTH, this is the FIRST commandment"(Mark 12:30)? I believe Jesus gave us these instructions to help us better understand how to live amongst one another! To LOVE God with all your HEART, SOUL, MIND, and STRENGTH is the exact same regimen it takes to LOVE your neighbor as yourself! (vs.31). Sometimes the idiosyncrasies

HEART, SOUL, MIND, AND STRENGTH

of humanity challenge the core makeup of the ministry within us.

But the truth of the matter is...it is through our Heart, our Soul, our Mind, and our Strength that God is revealed to our neighbors! Neighbors are not just people who live next door to us, neighbors are the people God uses to bring the best out in us! Have a Blessed day, and thanks for allowing me to share the word from a *Pastor's Perspective...*

Hope helps us envision God's goodness on earth, as it is in Heaven! And Hope helps us reject all that's awarded to those who are bound for Hell! When we rest in the HOPE of glory, we are accepting the Healing that delivers the heart from all manner of circumstance. The Apostle Paul wrote: "And HOPE maketh not ashamed, because the LOVE of God is shed abroad in our hearts by the Holy Spirit, who is given to us." (Romans 5:5). To Hope in the righteousness of God's love, is nothing to ever be ashamed of!! At times we wonder, what's the use?" But that's precisely when you must remind yourself that God is going to use your HOPE to help you see the purpose of a situation. This is NOT a waste of effort, and there is NOTHING for me to be ashamed of!! The devil is always mocking your HOPE, because he knows God's LOVE is making you Whole! Those who HOPE in God's LOVE, will always have God's help! Have a Blessed day, and thanks for allowing me to share the word from a *Pastor's Perspective...*

APRIL 22

Jesus said something so profound in one of his teachings that hundreds of years later, it still speaks volumes to our hearts! He said..."While you have light, BELIEVE in the light, that ye may be children of the light!" (John 12:36). Then we read: "These things spake Jesus, then departed, and did HIDE himself from them!" Sometimes the Lord will hide His light to see if you will ignite the light within YOU. When Jesus appears to be hidden, he isn't hidden to be evasive, He wants to see if those who are looking for HIM, can find him in YOU! Jesus tells us..."YOU are the LIGHT of the world!" (Matthew 5:14). Don't panic about temporary moments of darkness. A BELIEVER in this situation isn't on punishment and sometimes it's simply Him proving you! God is testing whether you're walking in the LIGHT! With Jesus, LIGHTS *out*, doesn't necessarily mean the LIGHT is *gone*! Sometimes He just wants to see, if you're letting YOUR light shine! Have a Blessed day, and thanks for allowing me to share the word from a *Pastor's Perspective...*

Sometimes we receive kindness from the most unlikely people as was the case for the Apostle Paul on the Island of Malta. (Acts 28:1-10). The natives were barbaric by nature, but indeed a blessing! They made Paul and all the men with him feel welcome and built a fire to warm them from the cold. When Paul tried to gather a bundle of sticks to help kindle the fire, a venomous snake latched onto his hand and bit him! The Apostle Paul then shook the viper off into the fire. As kind as the natives were, they NATURALLY watched and waited for Paul to die from this encounter with the snake, but the scriptures tell us: "After they had watched and waited for a LONG TIME, they CHANGED their minds and said that Paul was a god!" Remind yourself: "Your God PURPOSE has God POWER!" If you can shake into the fire anything that's trying to put you in a coffin, your onlookers will soon realize that worldly POISON is no match for a life driven by God's POWER and PURPOSE! Have a blessed day, and thanks for allowing me to share the word from a *Pastor's Perspective...*

The Prophet Solomon said..."The fruit of the righteous is a tree of LIFE, and He that winneth souls is WISE." (Proverbs 11:30). Please allow me to ask two questions: First, has your LIFE become fruitful enough that it provides sustenance for someone else's spiritual stability? And secondly, does your WISDOM bear record that your witness is winning souls for the glory of God? These two questions are not meant to validate your efforts, they are simply to encourage your works! The Apostle James said. "Faith without WORKS is dead." (James 2:17). Your works alone can't save anyone! They couldn't even save you! But your Faith mixed with your works have the power to be incredibly LIFE-changing! Remember, Solomon didn't say everyone would love your fruit, he said there will be some souls who are drawn by your FRUIT, but saved through your WISDOM...If you work on being WISE, you'll always have FRUIT fit to serve your guests...Have a Blessed day, and thanks for allowing me to share the word from a *Pastor's Perspective*...

When David prayed, "Let the WORDS of my mouth, and the MEDITATION of my heart, be acceptable in thy SIGHT, O Lord, my strength, and my REDEEMER" (Psalms 19:14), he was not just praying TO God, he was speaking FROM experience! David knew how vile and ungodly his heart could be, but he also knew what God could do with his heart, if he LET Him! When David came to the crossroad of his understanding, he desired a relationship with God that was BIGGER than the relationship he had with his flesh! Are you desiring God above all else or are you 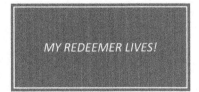 still in love with the temptations of the flesh? Truth be told, your flesh has been deceiving you, since the two of you met and has been flirting with the devil, all along! God on the other hand, is seeking a real relationship with you because He wants to give you TRUE Love. Have a Blessed day, and thanks for allowing me to share the word from a *Pastor's Perspective...*

Christ says GIVE and they won't! Christ says LOVE and they don't! Christ says have FAITH and they WORRY! Christ says HONOR Him, and instead they WORSHIP themselves! So then, Christ asks..."And why call ye me Lord, Lord, and do not the things which I say?" (Luke 6:46). The bible tells us that God inhabits the praises of HIS people (Psalms 22:3). But please take heed to this undeniable truth..."Nevertheless, the foundation of God is SURE, having this seal, THE LORD KNOWETH THEM THAT ARE HIS! And let everyone that name the name of Christ depart from iniquity!!" (II Timothy 2:19). We profess that Jesus is LORD and SAVIOR, but live lives that reflect the lost and sinful! To proclaim that Jesus is LORD, you need to honor that proclamation by LISTENING to Him! Jesus is telling us...you can't label me with your mouth, and then lose me in your Sin! If I'm not LORD of ALL, I'm not LORD at ALL! Have a Blessed day, and thanks for allowing me to share the word from a *Pastor's Perspective*...

Jesus wants us to love one another ALWAYS! He said, "A new commandment I give unto you, that ye LOVE one another, as I have LOVED you, that ye also LOVE one another. By this shall all men know that you are MY disciples, if ye have LOVE, one to another." (John 13:34-35). Jesus warned, "It is impossible that offenses will not come, but woe unto Him, through whom they come!" (Luke 17:1). In other words, it is virtually impossible for anyone to go their entire life and not be offended in some way. However, the LOVE a believer has for the Father and the LOVE the Father has for the believer makes all the difference! (Matthew 5:11-12, I Peter 4:12-16). Hence, Jesus strongly warns unbelievers and malicious people who might persecute His own, "It were better for him that a millstone were hanged about his neck, and he be cast into the sea, than that he should offend one of these little ones!!" (Luke 17:2). Today, and every day, consider how you treat those who LOVE Jesus! Have a Blessed day, and thanks for allowing me to share the word from a *Pastor's Perspective*...

APRIL 28

Spring is in the air, flowers will soon start to bloom, everything that was lying dormant through winter will rise with vigor, and the beauty of God's creation will manifest with each passing day. However, our adversary the devil, will undoubtedly change just like the seasons and the prince of the air will manifest as well! (Ephesians 2:2). Which is why the scriptures warn us, "For we wrestle NOT against flesh and blood, but against principalities, against powers, against the rulers of the darkness of this world, against SPIRITUAL WICKEDNESS in high places!!" (Ephesians 6:12). These "high places" are subject to CHANGE according to the season you're in! In the spiritual realm some things promote GROWTH while some promote GRIEF! And again, according to the season you're in, pay attention to what's trying to blossom in your life! It is your responsibility to know, when to weed your garden! Have a Blessed day, and thanks for allowing me to share the word from a *Pastor's Perspective*...

When the angel announced to the women, "He is not here, for HE IS RISEN!" (Matthew 28:6), those words became our hope of glory! We find refuge, peace, victory, and above all, Salvation in His rising! He conquered death, so we could be delivered from the fear of it! And thousands of years later His rising still brings the gospel to the poor, heals the brokenhearted, preaches deliverance to the captives, and gives sight to the blind! The angel said, "HE IS NOT HERE!" One day you and I will not to be here either! We are going to RISE with the Lord! (I Thessalonians 4:16-17). Those who die in Christ, will also RISE in Christ! We are victorious, even now! Jesus said..."I am the Resurrection, and the life, he that believeth in me, though he were dead, yet shall he live! And whosoever liveth and believeth in me shall NEVER DIE!!" (John 11:25-26) Aren't you glad that Christ conquered death, so you and I can enjoy FOREVER! Hallelujah, HE IS RISEN!!! Have a Blessed day, and thanks for allowing me to share the word from a *Pastor's Perspective*...

Every born-again believer has a season of Greatness awaiting them! (Mark 10:30). The "Eyes have not seen, nor ear heard, neither have entered into the heart of man, the things God hath prepared for them that love Him!!"(I Corinthians 2:9). GREATNESS does not come through WEAKNESS! Matter of fact, Paul said, "Now unto Him who is ABLE to do EXCEEDINGLY, ABUNDANTLY, ABOVE all we can ask or think!" (Ephesians 3:20). Nothing about that describes weakness! God wants you to be strong in the Lord and the power of His might! He wants your belief in Him, to start a rapid, spiritual growth increase in your GREATNESS! Jesus said..."Verily, verily, I say unto you, He that BELIEVETH on me, the works that I do, shall he do also! And GREATER works than these shall he do, because I go unto my Father!" (John 14:12). God wants you to understand, there is NO weakness in Him! And if you're in Him, there is NO weakness in you either! Meekness is NOT weakness, it is strength turned inside out! "Blessed are the Meek, for they shall inherit the Earth!!" (Matthew 5:5) Have a Blessed day, and thanks for allowing me to share the word from a *Pastor's Perspective...*

Though the Apostle Peter was inspired to write this word concerning LOVE in his time, God knew we would need it in ours!
"But the end of all things is at hand, be ye, therefore, sober minded, and watch unto prayer. And above all things have fervent LOVE among yourselves, for LOVE shall cover the multitude of sins." (I Peter 4:7-8). For GOD so LOVED that He GAVE...and JESUS so LOVED that He SAVES! Because God is LOVE (I John 4:8), Jesus must be LOVE also! Why? Because He and the father are ONE! (John 17:22). The Father gave in LOVE, the Son died in LOVE, and we are commanded to live in LOVE! When we Love like the Godhead, we become ambassadors of the Godhead's LOVE! When Jesus prayed to the Father on our behalf concerning LOVE, He concluded his prayer with these words...
"And I have declared unto them thy name, and will declare it, that the LOVE with which thou hast LOVED me may be in them, and I in them." (John 17:26). If you want all you do, to touch the Father's heart, do it for LOVE...Have a Blessed day, and thanks for allowing me to share the word from *a Pastor's Perspective...*

MAY 2

One of the most comforting scriptures in the bible is..."When the enemy shall come in like a flood, the Spirit of the Lord shall lift up a standard against him!" (Isaiah 59:19).
In other words; "No weapon formed against you shall prosper!" (Isaiah 54:17). God's PROTECTION is a PROMISE! And the promises of God are YES, and AMEN to his glory! (II Corinthians 1:20). We can't always stop an adversarial onslaught or attack, but we MUST always TRUST the protection of our God! "Because he hath set his love upon me, therefore will I DELIVER him, I will set him on high, because he hath known my name. He shall call upon me, and I WILL ANSWER HIM! I WILL BE WITH HIM IN TROUBLE! I WILL DELIVER HIM, AND HONOR HIM! With LONG LIFE I will SATISFY HIM and show him my salvation!" (Psalms 91:14-16). Sometimes all you need to do is remind yourself that VICTORY is MINE, in JESUS' NAME, AMEN! Have a Blessed day, and thanks for allowing me to share the word from *a Pastor's Perspective...*

MAY 3

Why does it sometimes take US so long to
answer God's call for our lives? As I look
back at my own life, there was NOTHING
going on back then that remotely compares to
what God has been doing since I was born
again! I mean think about it, He chose you
before the foundation of the earth (Ephesians
1:4). He knew you before He formed you in
your mother's womb (Jeremiah 1:5). And
because He foreknew you, He predestined
you to be conformed to the image of His Son,
that he might be the first born among many
brethren (Romans 8:29). And why was it so
important for God to do this in your life?
Because, when you finally said, "Yes Lord,"
and totally surrendered; it would please God,
who separated you from your mother's womb,
and called you by His grace, to reveal His Son
in you, that you might preach Him among the
fainthearted. (Galatians 1:15-16). If you're
wrestling with your calling this morning, cut it
out! It's high time you STOP with all your
apprehension and excuses! Life is too short to
take for granted, and eternal separation from
God is too long to suffer! Have a Blessed day,
and thanks for allowing me to share the word
from *a Pastor's Perspective...*

MAY 4

It has been said by many Christians, sung in many beautiful songs, and heard through wonderful testimonies, "The safest place in all the world, is in the will of God!" To be in God's will, is to be in God's care. And one of the best places to see God's will on earth, is in the house of the Lord! Sure, there are imperfections there, strife, SIN, all manner of sickness, and even misconduct, but also, there is God's will! King David echoed this sentiment when he wrote: "I was glad when they said unto me, let us go into the house of the Lord!" (Psalms 122:1). David said, "Because of the house of the Lord our God, I will seek thy good!" (vs.9). With all that can go on in the church, it's still the best meeting place for God and those looking for HIM!! God sees everything that goes on in the church, but He also knows them who are His! (II Timothy 2:19). His grace is sufficient, and His gift of Salvation is sovereign! They say, "Don't judge a book by its cover." But God is saying: "Don't judge my house, and what's in it, if you don't know my plans for it!" (Jeremiah 29:11). Have a Blessed day, and thanks for allowing me to share the word from *a Pastor's Perspective*...

MAY 5

When Jesus said...."Blessed are the PEACEMAKERS, for they shall be called the children of God" (Matthew 5:9), He was revealing the true nature of those who want more than anything to be at PEACE. It is within all men to want to be heard, to be respected, and to be right! However, if being all these things doesn't yield PEACE, the situation is still not blessed! And it probably isn't the work of a child of God! You must understand that being a child of God starts with being a child of PEACE. Peaceful people are always trying to find ways to promote "God's Presence." Their desire is not just in being RIGHT, but also being RIGHTEOUS! Scripture reveals..."There is no PEACE for the wicked!" (Isaiah 48:22). And in case you don't know, wickedness is essentially yielding your will to the ways of this world! So again, we must remember, that being a child of God, starts with being a child of PEACE! Jesus said..."Peace I leave with you, MY peace I give unto you, and not as the world giveth!" (John 14:27). If you consider yourself a child of Peace, you must keep your heart from the ways of the world! Have a Blessed day, and thanks for allowing me to share the word from *a Pastor's Perspective*...

MAY 6

There is much comfort, strength, and courage to be gleaned from the following: "Trust in Him at ALL times, ye people, pour out your hearts before Him, God is a refuge for US!" Selah (Psalms 62:8). To have God as a place of complete safety, and a sure and strong shelter, is truly something you can rest in. Our hearts can either help our FAITH or perpetuate our FALL! But with God, He never FAILS, and He promises to never FORGET our dependence on His promises. Yes, "He's the same yesterday, today, and forever." (Hebrews 13:8). But He's also; "A strong tower, and the RIGHTEOUS run into it, and are SAFE!" (Proverbs 18:10). To be righteous, is to be in right STANDING with God! And to be STANDING with God, is to be completely protected from falling! The Prophet Jeremiah said, "Our heart is deceitful above ALL things, and desperately wicked, who can know it?" (Jeremiah 17:9). But the Spirit of God reminds us, "And ye shall dwell in the land that I gave to your fathers, and ye shall be MY PEOPLE, and I will be YOUR GOD!" (Ezekiel 36:28). Remember, it's better to have God, and not need Him...than to need God, and not have Him! Have a Blessed day, and thanks for allowing me to share the word from *a Pastor's Perspective*....

Whenever Jesus healed someone, it was because they BELIEVED He could! Our BELIEF in Jesus, grants us our RELIEF in His ability! When the two blind men cried: "Thou Son of David, have mercy on us!" They cried out, because they BELIEVED he could deliver them! And scripture tells us that Jesus asked them, "Believe ye that I am able to do this?" And they replied, "Yes, Lord." (Matthew 9:27-28). Nothing In life hinders God's power like, DOUBT! In the Spiritual sense, DOUBT is choosing Unbelief over Trust! However, you must understand and remember what scripture says about doubt and unbelief; "He that comes to God, must first BELIEVE He is." (Hebrews 11:6), and, "If any man asks of God anything, let him ask in FAITH, nothing wavering! Because, if he doubts, let not that man think that he shall receive ANYTHING of the Lord!" (James 1:5-7). The truth of God's POWER, is revealed in the trials of our FAITH! Sometimes, you must BELIEVE the ridiculous, to receive the miraculous! Have a Blessed day, and thanks for allowing me to share another word from *a Pastor's Perspective…*

MAY 8

The hymn states; "It is well, it is well, with my soul." The songwriter is declaring that; all that concerns me, everything that affects me, and all that may bother me…none of it can touch my soul! Why? Because my soul is anchored in Jesus' care! The prophet Solomon said, "Though a sinner does evil a hundred times, and his days are prolonged, yet surely I KNOW that it shall be WELL with them that fear God, who fear before him!" (Ecclesiastes 8:12). In other words, if the unrighteous can seem to have long life while sinning, it should be WELL with the soul of the saint that fears God! Our lives ought to reflect the substance of that which we hope for in Christ Jesus! When you finally make up in your mind, that you are going to let God's LOVE, be YOUR guide, that's when everything concerning YOU, becomes WELL with your soul. When that which is in heaven has your soul, all that can potentially hurt you, no longer has anything to work with! Why? Because all is WELL, with your soul! You can only declare…it is WELL with my soul, when you can see for yourself, that God has done all things WELL (Mark 7:37). All is WELL, because Jesus hath made you whole! Have a Blessed day and thanks for allowing me to share the word from *a Pastor's Perspective*…

MAY 9

The most important thing in any church, is God's PEOPLE! The spirit of God inspired the Apostle Paul to tell the elders of Ephesus, "Take heed, therefore, unto YOURSELVES, and to ALL the flock, over which the Holy Spirit hath made YOU overseers, to feed the church of God, which HE hath purchased with HIS own blood!" (Acts 20:28). When pastors and elders lose focus on what really matters in the church, the church suffers! However, we as a body of believers also have an important role in the upkeep of our fellowship. As a people, we are, "Fitly joined together and compact by that which EVERY joint supplieth, according to the effectual working in the measure of EVERY part, maketh increase of the body unto the edifying of itself in LOVE!" (Ephesians 4:16). And so, the Spirit of God is telling us…"I will give you pastors and shepherds according to MINE heart, who shall feed you with knowledge and understanding." (Jeremiah 3:15). If God has called you to LEAD His people, it's a big DEAL! Always remember, God's PEOPLE are his PASSION! Have a Blessed day, and thanks for allowing me to share the word from *a Pastor's Perspective*…

MAY 10

When God chose Mary to be the mother of Jesus, and the carrier of His Son, it didn't make her special, as much as it made His choice specific! She was BLESSED among women, and BLESSED was the fruit of her womb, but she herself, was specifically what God was looking for in a woman! (Luke 1:26-30, 39-42). Sometimes we fail to realize that God is a God of specific details. God chose Mary for her virginity and her humility! And God has also chosen you and I with specific goals in mind! (John 15:16). God doesn't have favorites, God's not partial, and He certainly isn't given to making mistakes! No, when God chose you for His glory, He was very specific in what He was looking for in YOU! Is that not the best word of encouragement? To think, everything that I am or am not is exactly what God is looking for, for His glory! Wow! Thank you, God, for your intentions concerning ME! You don't have to be SPECIAL in the eyes of others, but God wants you to know that you are SPECIFICALLY what He was looking for. Have a Blessed day, and thanks for allowing me to share the word from *a Pastor's Perspective*...

MAY 11

When I think of Isaac Watts, writer of hymns, I am awed by his faith in God's forgiveness! He wrote...

At the cross, at the cross, where I first saw the light, and the burdens of my heart rolled away...it was there by faith, I received my sight, and now I am happy all the day!

What blessed assurance! We must NEVER lose sight of the fact that God's FORGIVENESS is greater than our worst moment of WEAKNESS! While true, "For all have sinned, and fallen short of the glory of God." (Romans 3:23). It is also true, that all those who fall *IN* God, fall *TO* God! (Ephesians 1:4-7). If you will start your relationship with God with repentance, he will end your heart's heaviness with forgiveness. He wants to lift the burden of your sin, with the wonderful work of forgiveness! The psalmist wrote, "If thou, Lord, shouldest mark iniquities, who shall stand? But there is FORGIVENESS with thee, that thou mayest be feared." (Psalms 130: 1-4). There is no fall God can't FORGIVE!
Have a Blessed day, and thanks for allowing me to share the word from *a Pastor's Perspective*...

MAY 12

"This is the day which the Lord hath made, we will REJOICE and be GLAD in it!" (Psalms 118:24). We are to REJOICE and be GLAD because, *this day* was given, and *this day* has purpose! Everything may not be perfect, everything may not be as we like, BUT, God gave me another day to be loved by Him! The purpose of this day, is to see the goodness of OUR God! Sunshine, wealth, possessions, and material things are nice to have, BUT God wants you to REJOICE and be GLAD because you have HIM!! (Luke 12:15). To rejoice BECAUSE of God, is the greatest reason to be glad *IN* Him. This day has so much purpose because it's connected to so many promises! (II Corinthians 1:20). God wants you to sit down and think of all He's promised those who love Him (I Corinthians 2:9), and then by faith believe, "No good thing will He withhold from them that walk uprightly!" (Psalms 84:11). If you allow this to sink into your spirit, you will understand why the Apostle Paul instructs us to: "Rejoice in the Lord always, and again I say, REJOICE!" (Philippians 4:4). Have a Blessed day, and thanks for allowing me to share the word from *a Pastor's Perspective...*

The spirit of God told the Prophet Isaiah that He would comfort Jerusalem like a mother comforts her child (Isaiah 66:13). Because a Mother's love is second to none, God understands man's longing for it. There are those who long to see their mother again, (and you will in heaven), there are those who see their mother often, (Praise God), and there are those who've never known their mother at all, (but God has been faithful). God knows your heart, and he knows your circumstance. But praise be to God for being all that we long for in any situation. Not every situation is entangled in tragedy, hardship, and severe circumstances. For some, it was just the will of God, in our lives. However, God inspired the prophet David to encourage us with these words..."When my Father and Mother forsake me, then the Lord will take me up!" (Psalms 27:10). As we honor and celebrate Mother's Day, let us also honor and celebrate God for giving us life through our Mother. Have a Blessed day, and thanks for allowing me to share the word from *a Pastor's Perspective.*

MAY 14

Have you ever wondered why Jesus would heal someone, give them back their sight, or even make the lame walk, then tell them: "Go your way, and tell no one what I did?" (Matthew 8:4). Because of MOTIVES! Jesus wanted to keep His ministry a mystery until people saw His majesty!

There is no way God can touch your life, and you not want to tell somebody! However, Jesus knew that there would always be those who continue to REJECT what has been given to REJOICE about! So, He would make whole the person, but withhold, the minister! I believe He wanted to keep hidden what He did, until we fully understood who He was! But now that we know Him for ourselves, we understand how He inspired the Psalmist to write..."Come and hear, all that fear God, and I will declare what He hath done for my soul." (Psalms 66:16). When Jesus brought grace and truth (John 1:17), God was offering the opportunity to be made whole, and giving you the decree to, "Go ye into all the WORLD, and preach the gospel to every creature." (Mark 16:15). If we're willing to tell it from the mountain, the Messiah will reveal and empower it through the ministry! Have a Blessed day, and thanks for allowing me to share the word from *a Pastor's Perspective*...

MAY 15

When we fail to recognize our nature, we miss the following message: "Come unto me." (Matthew 11:28). We claim to be so broken by the world and others' actions, and therefore struggle to live the life we've been given! We often fail to acknowledge those we have offended but can't wait to report how we've been offended by others! Jesus says, come unto me! For you are *ALL* naughty by nature! Life in the flesh, will always reveal your true identity! You can put a mask on anything, but what's under the mask eventually meets the Messiah and the MESS is exposed! The Apostle Paul wrote: "But I see another law in my members, warring against the law of my mind, and bringing me into captivity to the law of sin, which is in my members." (Romans 7:23).

The Apostle Paul knew the only way to defeat the flesh, was to acknowledge it! "We were by NATURE the children of wrath, even as others." (Ephesians 2:3), "BUT GOD! Who is rich in His mercy, for His great love with which He loved us, even when we were dead in sins, hath made us alive together with Christ!" (Ephesians 2:4) Don't let your nature, hinder your calling! COME!! Have a Blessed day, and thanks for allowing me to share the word from a *Pastor's Perspective...*

MAY 16

When Jesus said to Philip, "He that hath seen ME, hath seen the FATHER." (John 14:9). Phillip said Lord, show us the Father, and it sufficeth us (vs.8). However, there are still those, just like Phillip, who say, "Show us the Father!" Jesus is still responding with, "I and the Father are ONE!" (John 10:30). When we look at all that is, we can see God everywhere! But when we read all that Jesus did, we can clearly see JESUS is GOD! This has always been hard for pessimists and agnostics to grasp! This has been virtually impossible for atheists to grasp! However, just because they struggle with this truth, does not stop it from being TRUTH! Without controversy great is the mystery of godliness. After all, *"God was* manifest in the flesh, JUSTIFIED in the spirit, SEEN of angels, PREACHED unto the nations, BELIEVED on in the world, and RECIEVED up into glory!"* (I Timothy 3:16). Now, I understand why Jesus said, "Let not your heart be troubled (that is, divided), ye believe in GOD, believe also in ME." (John 14:1). Why? Because I and my FATHER are ONE! Have a Blessed day, and thanks for allowing me to share the word from a *Pastor's Perspective...*

MAY 17

One of the greatest ways to move forward in the Lord, is to let FORGIVENESS move in your heart! There are so many people who don't realize that in the same way that God hath dealt to every man a *measure* of faith (Romans 12:3), we must also remember the following: "Having *PREDESTINED* us unto the adoption of sons by Jesus Christ to himself, according to the good pleasure of His will, to the praise of the glory of His GRACE, through which He hath MADE us accepted in the beloved. In whom we have redemption through His blood, the FORGIVENESS of sins, according to the riches of His grace." (Ephesians 1:5-7). So, when you look deep into the word, you can see God's grace, the origin of forgiveness. And so, if it was predestined grace that allows for forgiveness, we have a very PRESENT HELP within, that enables us to FORGIVE! (Psalms 46:1). Now we can fully understand why Jesus said, "But if ye forgive NOT men their trespasses, neither will your Father forgive your trespasses." (Matthew 6:15). If Forgiveness is predestined, then your heart has already been primed, for forward progress! Have a Blessed day, and thanks for allowing me to share the word from a *Pastor's Perspective*...

MAY 18

When the Spirit of God inspired Peter to
write, "And besides this, giving all diligence,
ADD to your FAITH virtue, and to virtue;
knowledge, and to knowledge, self-control;
and to self-control, patience; and to patience,
godliness; and to godliness, brotherly
kindness; and to brotherly kindness, love, for
if these things be in you, and abound, they
make you that ye shall be neither barren nor
unfruitful in the knowledge of our Lord Jesus
Christ." (II Peter 1:5-8). In this lesson Peter
instructs us that the practical approach to
exercising our faith is first in knowing that we
must *ADD* certain things to be fruitful in
some situations! Life and all it entails can be
so diversely challenging and overwhelming at
times, and it can cause you to become
unfruitful! Although we have FAITH, Peter
makes it clear, you still must *ADD* other
things to overcome this world! To be
unfruitful in the Faith, has become common
among the saints, because the world has
SUBTRACTED those things that DRAW
men to God, and replaced them with the
things that DROWN men in Sin! What might
you add to your faith today? Have a Blessed
day, and thanks for allowing me to share the
word from a *Pastor's Perspective*...

It took me some time to really understand the purpose of WEAKNESS. And yes, weakness has purpose. We oftentimes look at weakness as a defect, but in the spiritual sense, WEAKNESS is the cocoon from which our strength is made perfect! When the Apostle Paul wanted relief from his thorn in the flesh, look how God responded to his request: "And he said unto me, my grace is sufficient, for my STRENGTH is made PERFECT in WEAKNESS." (II Corinthians 12:9). Because His Grace is SUFFICIENT, God needed Paul to see his weakness as a means to PERFECTION! Hence, the Apostle Paul concludes, well then...."Most gladly therefore will I rather glory in my infirmities, that the power of Christ may rest upon me!" (II Corinthians 12:9). When you exhibit strength during weakness, others can truly see how sufficient God's grace really is! All things truly do work together for them who are called and love God...even in WEAKNESS! Only weakness WITHOUT God, leads to SORROW. But weakness GIVEN to God, leads to PERFECTION. Have a Blessed day, and thanks for allowing me to share the word from a *Pastor's Perspective*...

MAY 20

If we find ourselves in Divided Places, Dry Places, and Dark Places; we must ask OURSELVES, "How did I get here?" Because according to the Apostle John, God is light. "This then is the message which we have heard of him, and declare unto you, that GOD IS LIGHT, and in Him is no darkness AT ALL!" (I John 1:5).

Now, it is important to understand that constant fellowship with Christ, brings continued LIGHT into the world. "That which we have seen and heard declare we unto you, that ye also may have fellowship with us: And truly our fellowship is with the Father, and with His son Jesus Christ." (I John 1:3). There are times when God has moved on and wants us to follow, patiently beckoning us, but we remain stuck where we are. God may be calling you to higher ground. He knows the plans HE HAS for your future, have a greater reward (Jeremiah 29:11). The only time believers really encounter DIVIDED, DRY, DARK places is when God's plan, is totally different from theirs. Have a Blessed day, and thanks for allowing me to share the word from a *Pastor's Perspective*...

There are so many people who speak with CONFIDENCE, but walk in CONFUSION. It is truly one of the saddest things to witness. The Apostle Paul wrote..."God is not the author of CONFUSION!" (I Corinthians 14:33). When God gives someone discernment, he equips them with the knowledge to see past what's been said! Sure, we want to see the depth in others' conversations, we want to connect with their inner-most feelings, but we can cause more confusion when we turn a blind eye to the BONDAGE that has camouflaged itself as BOLDNESS! The prophet, King Solomon said..."For the Lord shall be thy CONFIDENCE and shall keep thy foot from being TAKEN!" (Proverbs 3:26). Spiritual clutter is the cause of spiritual confusion. Spiritual clutter TAKES up the space that the spirit needs to nurture our understanding. So then, when the Prophet Solomon said..."Keep your heart with all diligence" (Proverbs 4:23), it was the preface, so to speak, for..."The thief cometh but to steal, kill, and destroy!" (John 10:10). We can only heal spiritual confusion when we let others know, spiritual wars TAKE place in our HEADS, but are WON in our HEARTS! Have a Blessed day, and thanks for allowing me to share the word from a *Pastor's Perspective...*

MAY 22

Encouragement comes in a variety of ways. A lot of the time we prefer to hear kindness over counseling. However, look at how Jesus encourages Peter, concerning a plot against his life..."And the Lord said, Simon, Simon, behold, Satan hath desired to have you, that he may sift you as wheat! But I have prayed for thee, that thy FAITH faileth not! And when thou art CONVERTED, strengthen the brethren." (Luke 22:31-32). Jesus told Peter of Satan's plot, but He could not DELIVER the part of Peter that had not yet been DEVELOPED for his glory! So, He simply told him: I'm praying for you brother. We must keep in mind, encouragement is most effective when properly understood, after CONVERSION, not before! And so, Jesus said, "After this happens, you'll have what it takes to strengthen others!"

God wants us to be encouraged, not just feel better, and He knows it is then that we will be equipped to help others!

ENCOURAGEMENT is the good that comes from your testimony, not the wallowing in your test. Sometimes to be ENCOURAGED is to be EMPOWERED, and not consoled! (I Thessalonians 5:14). Have a Blessed day, and thanks for allowing me to share the word from a *Pastor's Perspective*...

MAY 23

The most gratifying thing in all the world, is knowing that...GOD LOVES ME. People may misunderstand you, people may shun you, they may even abandon you altogether, but just remind yourself...GOD LOVES ME. The bible declares that, "God so Loved the world, that He gave *HIS* Son!" (John 3:16). Jesus's mission to save us, was motivated by the Father's LOVE, not the misery of men. His desire to...Always do those things that please God, seemed to cause people to hate him even more! Yet He testified...I'm not alone (John 8:29). When you know GOD LOVES YOU, though doing His will causes friction in your family, with friends, and even in the household of faith, you can understand what Jesus meant when He said..."Greater LOVE hath no man than this, that a man lay down his life for his friends." (John 15:13). It is never God's desire to HURT that which He is trying to HELP through us. However, sometimes God's LOVE doesn't just require us to lay it all on the line for our friends, it requires our friends to stop drawing lines, that limit God's LOVE! If you claim you know GOD LOVES YOU, then humble yourself and let Him love you! Have a Blessed day, and thanks for allowing me to share the word from a *Pastor's Perspective*...

The opportunity to care for others is always there. Anytime you, "Let nothing be done through strife or vainglory, but in lowliness of mind let each esteem OTHERS as BETTER than themselves"(Philippians 2:3), you are taking advantage of the opportunity to care for others. When we do this, we exhibit the true nature of God, and His love for His creation. However, as much as God loves us, He wants us to know the difference between *Caring* FOR us, and *Catering* TO us! God doesn't cater to any of us, but He cares for all of us! He inspired the Apostle Peter to write, "Humble yourselves, therefore, under the mighty hand of God, that He may exalt you in due time, casting all your CARE upon Him, for He CARES for you." (I Peter 5:6-7). There is NEVER a time God doesn't CARE about you, but there will be times when *the way* He Cares for you, will seem like He doesn't care at all! In those moments, God is attending to your needs, and not your notions. (See Psalms 142:1-7). This is when God proves He CARES for you, by CARRYING you safely to the shores of *HIS* love. Have a Blessed day, and thanks for allowing me to share the word from a *Pastor's Perspective*...

If you were to sit and think about the *PROCESS* of building faith, you'd generally find it consists of a series of fault-finding moments. Moments that reveal your HEART to your HELP! And because it is generally our inner challenges that propel our greatest achievements, God tells us, "But you, beloved, building yourselves up on your most holy faith, praying in the Holy Spirit, keep yourselves in the LOVE of God, looking for the mercy of our Lord Jesus Christ unto eternal life!" (Jude 1:20-21). In other words, no matter how difficult destiny may appear to be, *trust the process*. Faith building is not about having all the right tools, it's about having the absolute truth! We oftentimes forsake the reality that, "Faith is the SUBSTANCE of things hoped for, but the EVIDENCE of the UNSEEN!" (Hebrews 11:1). You see, Faith is not just a byproduct of TRUTH, it is a derivative of DIVINITY! And so, to truly add to your faith daily, you must trust the PROCESS, until God manifests the PROGRESS! Most things that turned out GREAT, started from a lump of GRIEF! Just trust the process, and watch your faith grow! Have a Blessed day, and thanks for allowing me to share the word from a *Pastor's Perspective*...

MAY 26

Did you know that the Sermon on the Mount, also known as The Beatitudes, is a message Jesus preached, which spans across Matthew 5:1 through Matthew 7:27? Jesus had a lot to say, because there was so much the multitude needed to hear! However, He started His sermon with the word, *BLESSED*. (Matthew 5:1)

Blessed are....

The poor in spirit

They that mourn

The meek

Those who hunger and thirst after righteousness

The merciful

The pure in heart

The peacemakers

Those that are persecuted for the kingdom's sake

But He concludes his sermon with the WISE.. "Therefore whosoever heareth these sayings of mine, and doeth them, I will liken him unto a WISE man, which built his house upon a Rock." (Matthew 7:24).

Jesus wants us to understand that sometimes the prescription for being *BLESSED*, goes hand in hand with the work of being *BROKEN!* Have a Blessed day, and thanks for allowing me to share the word from a *Pastor's Perspective...*

Jesus asked: "For which of you, intending to build a tower, does not sit down and COUNT THE COST, whether he has enough to finish it?" (Luke 14:28). He asked this question to provoke a deeper understanding of what it really means to be a disciple. It's been said that our destiny travels the corridors of difficulties, and with this truth, it must be understood that the cost of discipleship hinges on the doorpost of our decision making! Jesus said, "Follow me!" (Matthew 4:19). He implores us to do this because He knows where He wants to lead us: to our Heavenly Father! He needs you to accept His leadership, so He can navigate your discipleship! When we follow Jesus, we realize that our JOURNEY is just as important as our DESTINATION. Jesus wants us to count the cost, not because of the potential for loss, but for the perfecting of the promise! "No one, having put his hand to the plow, and LOOKING BACK, is fit for the kingdom of God!" (Luke 9:62). To count the cost is to declare: I have decided to follow Jesus, no turning back, no turning back! Have a Blessed day, and thanks for allowing me to share the word from a *Pastor's Perspective...*

MAY 28

The battles some have died in to save others, are sacrifices that must be acknowledged and never forgotten! Our liberties, just like our salvation, came at a high price! The woman with the alabaster box filled with oil used it in a manner some considered wasteful, whereas Jesus considered it a *good work* (Mark 14:6). Those who criticized her ethics were looking at the VALUE of the oil, but the woman was preparing Jesus for His battle and VICTORY over Sin! Jesus addressed their concern for money over ministry like this: "For you have the poor with you always, and whenever you wish, you may do them GOOD! But Me, you do not have always! She has done what she could. She has come beforehand to anoint my body for burial. Assuredly, I say to you, wherever this gospel is preached in the whole world, what this woman has done will also be remembered as a MEMORIAL to her!" (Mark 14:7-9).

When we memorialize the sacrifices that others have given for our liberty, let's also be sure to memorialize the greater sacrifice that Jesus gave for our souls! Let us salute EVERY soldier, but also give PRAISE to our one and ONLY savior! Have a Blessed day, and thanks for allowing me to share the word from a *Pastor's Perspective...*

MAY 29

If God has prepared a way for you to escape the pollution of this world, you first need to develop an attitude of gratitude, and then be ever mindful not to be entangled by the world again! (II Peter 2:20-21). There are serious consequences for recidivism, worldliness, and reckless living! When the apostle, King David, thought about all of God's mercy towards him, his heart became heavy with purpose, not persecution! He knew God loved him, but he also knew it was time for him to show God, he loved him back. And so, his spirit was ready to surrender to God's sovereignty. God wants to know if you're ready to quit losing in life and start living in it! When David was ready to finally live, he testified, "For I am ready to halt, and my sorrow is continually before me!" (Psalms 38:17). The Holy Spirit reminds us about the wicked works of man, "There is no peace, says the Lord, for the wicked!" (Isaiah 48:22). When we lose the desire for SINNING, we become candidates for WINNING in Christ! Those who abandon sin to truly live, inherit a truth that can never die! SPIRITUAL TENACITY is telling TEMPTATION, "Not today, not tomorrow, not ever!!" Get thee behind me Satan! Have a Blessed day, and thanks for allowing me to share the word from a *Pastor's Perspective*...

MAY 30

The word *FAITHFUL* is most often associated with the relationship between a man and a woman. It seems to validate the core of their commitment to one another! But the true core of being faithful to one another is having FAITH in God first! Jesus asked this question: "When the Son of man cometh, shall He find FAITH on the earth?" (Luke 18:8). The core of this text is often overlooked, because the text is connected to a person's PERSISTENCE and not to the PURPOSE of the persistence! God wants you to look at how many relationships you have put more FAITH in, apart from your having faith in Him. When He returns, He wants to find you FAITHFUL to your FAITH! Just think for a minute; If God dealt to every man a measure of faith (Romans 12:3), then why isn't your FAITH measuring UP?
People of God, if your Faith is all it's supposed to be, when the Son of man returns, He should find all that He's looking for! Therefore, ask yourself today: Is the FAITH that God is looking for on earth still at work in my heart? Those who can't receive WHO God is, can't receive WHAT God has for them! Have a Blessed day, and thanks for allowing me to share the word from a *Pastor's Perspective...*

MAY 31

As we grow in Grace, it becomes our earnest desire to see souls saved, strongholds broken, and the feeble become overcomers in the faith! However, we need to encourage one another daily in this manner: "What you're going through today, does not define your tomorrow!" Those who continue to BELIEVE *God is Able* during a trial (Romans 4:18-25), will have all they need to stand firm in the word, no matter how tempestuous the winds get. "Nay, in all things WE are MORE than conquerors through Him that loved US"! (Romans 8:37). Sometimes we forget that God is just as much our DELIVERER as He is our DESTINY! Today, let your spirit revive in the truth of God's power in your life. God saved you, to serve Him! He wants you and I to understand our deliverance could be someone else's first step in walking with Him. There is no greater feeling than knowing; that which God has delivered me from by faith, I now have dominion over! If we SHARE this truth with others, we can help SHAPE the trust of many...Have a Blessed day, and thanks for allowing me to share the word from a *Pastor's Perspective...*

JUNE 1

If we were determined to speak life into our situations, we would see more clearly *What a FRIEND we have in Jesus.* In the biblical account of Jesus' healing of the Centurion's servant (Matthew 8:5-10), he certainly knew his earthly dominion, he could not fix a situation that needed heaven's authority! The Centurion commenced to tell Jesus how he was not *WORTHY* to have Jesus under his roof, but rather asked Jesus to, "Speak the WORD only, and my servant shall live!" He knew his life wasn't praiseworthy, but he also knew the power of the WORD was worthy to be praised! Today, if you're going through something, and life, bad decisions, or even the naysayers in your midst, have made you feel unworthy of God's help...Speak the WORD into your situation! "Let not your heart be troubled, you believe in God, believe also in me" (John 14:1). Hence, if you can believe in the same way as the Centurion, you will receive. "And Jesus said unto the Centurion, "Go thy way, and as thou hath BELIEVED, so be it done unto thee." (Matthew 8:13). Jesus is willing and waiting to respond to the Saint that lives within our hearts! Have a Blessed day, and thanks for allowing me to share the word from a *Pastor's Perspective*...

It has been said, "Emotions without Devotion, create more, Commotion!" When we choose to exercise unbridled Emotions over Spiritual Excellence, we loosen the works of RECKLESSNESS and bind the works of RIGHTEOUSNESS! However, Jesus said... "For I say unto you, that except your righteousness shall exceed the righteousness of the Scribes and Pharisees, ye shall in no case enter into the kingdom of heaven!" (Matthew 5:20). In addition, the bible tells us that apart from God, our righteousness is as filthy rags (Isaiah 64:6). This is why we can't afford to allow our Emotions to dictate the flow of our Devotion! We must serve God as children of the Most-High. Remember, God is expecting us to live as majestically mature children nonetheless! The Apostle Paul said..."When I was a child, I spoke as a child, I understood as a child, I thought as a child, but when I became a man, I put away childish things!" (I Corinthians 13:11). God is telling us not to allow reckless, child-like Emotions to hinder our Devotion and stunt our spiritual growth! An immature Christian is Spiritual potential lacking Spiritual direction!
Have a Blessed day, and thanks for allowing me to share the word from a *Pastor's Perspective*...

JUNE 3

One of the greatest mistakes Christians make today is stamping a PERMANENT label on TEMPORARY circumstances! Throughout the word of God, the phrase..."AND IT CAME TO PASS," is the written decree letting you know that whatever you're going through, you're going to make it through! And God is going to see to it! When the Prophet Elijah predicted the drought was coming to the land (I Kings 17:1-7), it was still God's job to provide all that the man of God would need to sustain the call on his life! (vs.6). Sometimes God allows situations to occur, that come in the form of opposition, but prove to be one of HIS greatest opportunities at work in your life! The dilemma is this: HE commanded ravens to bring him meat, and the brook at Cherith to provide him water, but the bible also says..."AND IT CAME TO PASS after a while, HE allowed the brook, to dry up!" We must realize that at any given time God can alter our plans, which could challenge our FAITH about tomorrow! Oftentimes, when things COME TO PASS in our lives, it's simply preparation for what's coming! Nothing God says or does EVER returns void! There is no deficiency in God's Sovereignty! Have a Blessed day, and thanks for allowing me to share the word from a *Pastor's Perspective...*

JUNE 4

Those who are serious about ministry have learned to ignore the opinions and sidebar remarks of those who oppose them. The Apostle Paul, while living under scrutiny, asked the following question when he was called to ministry: "For do I now seek the favor of men, or of God? Or do I seek to please men? (Galatians 1:10). Paul understood that he couldn't please men if he truly wanted to serve God! His calling was not only to CONVINCE the gentile that they could receive Christ, but also to CONVICT the Jews regarding their misunderstanding of

GOD IS WORKING

who Christ is! Sometimes conflicts in ministry are NOT the work of the word, but rather related to the person God is working the word through! Each of us has a past and some refuse to let us forget it. And so, the Apostle Paul asks; "For what if some did not believe? Shall their unbelief make the faithfulness of God, of no effect?" Absolutely NOT! The best way to overcome what men may say, is to keep telling others what GOD has said, no matter what!! Have a Blessed day, and thanks for allowing me to share the word from a *Pastor's Perspective...*

JUNE 5

I have discovered that, nothing soothes pain like "PRAISE!" The pastor/singer/songwriter William Murphy wrote,

"PRAISE is what I do, even when I'm going through, I've learned to worship you. Though my circumstance, doesn't even stand a chance, my PRAISE, outweighs, the bad. I vow to PRAISE you, through the good, and the bad...I'll PRAISE you, whether happy or sad. I'll PRAISE you, in all that I go through...because PRAISE is what I do."

King David said, "I will bless the Lord at all times, His PRAISE shall continually be in my mouth!" (Psalms 34:1). David had learned, that in the same way local authorities are first responders to fires, accidents, and tragedies; PRAISE must be a first response to everything. We too should learn to let Praise be our first response to problems. A heart filled with praise, is never really burdened with problems! Remember, what the songwriter said; "PRAISE outweighs the bad!" But even more than these beautiful and encouraging lyrics let's tell God daily that, "Our PRAISE waiteth for thee, O God, in Zion! And unto thee shall the vow be performed!" (Psalms 65:1) Today, give the enemy notice: PRAISE is what I do, even when I'm going through. Have a Blessed day, and thanks for allowing me to share the word from a *Pastor's Perspective...*

JUNE 6

"For the word of God is QUICK, and POWERFUL, and SHARPER than any two-edged sword! Piercing even to the dividing asunder of SOUL and SPIRIT, and of the joints and marrow, and is a DISCERNER of the THOUGHTS and INTENTS of the HEART!" (Hebrews 4:12). There is nothing your heart can hold, your mind can conceive, or your mouth can utter that God's word can't decipher. The word of God is not just a discerner of destiny, it's also a designated developer of our decisions. When believers make decisions, good or bad, our HEART becomes the focal point of our decisions, however our MOTIVES are what go through the WORD's litmus test! It is the word that eliminates a bad thought! And it is the word that gives continuity to good thoughts! We should be oh so grateful that God's word is QUICK, POWERFUL, and SHARP, especially when we are SUBDUED, WEAKENED, and DULLED by Sin! Aren't you glad that God knows more about your life, than you thought you knew about living! We should glorify God for His word because, it not only shows us who HE is, it also showed us what we could be, in HIM! Have a Blessed day, and thanks for allowing me to share the word from a *Pastor's Perspective*...

171

JUNE 7

The Apostle Paul told his young protégé
Timothy that he was going to encounter some
people along his journey that love themselves
more than they love God or the gospel. He
said, these people, "Having a FORM of
godliness, but denying the power thereof!
From such turn away!" (II Timothy 3:1-5).
Paul was warning young Timothy because he
knew that youthful ambition, that lacks proper
perspective, can destroy a ministry! When it
comes to ministry, you can't serve God and
yourself! We can't have a FORM of godliness!
Either we are who God has called us to be or
NOT! One thing the word of God wants us
to be aware of, "A double-minded man is
unstable in ALL his ways!" (James 1:8). The
emphatic truth is this: they're unstable because
the FORM of godliness he or she has, refuses
to CONFORM to what the word of God
says! The Psalmist declared...."Thy word is a
lamp unto my feet, and a light unto my path."
(Psalms 119:105). Therefore, when we refuse
to allow the word of God to shape our hearts,
according to Jeremiah 17:9, life can become a
desperately wicked trap that takes on many
FORMS!......Have a Blessed day, and thanks
for allowing me to share the word from a
Pastor's Perspective...

JUNE 8

"But before FAITH came, we were kept under the law, shut up unto the faith which should afterwards be revealed. Wherefore, the LAW was our schoolmaster to bring us unto Christ, that we might be JUSTIFIED by Him!" (Galatians 3:23-24). The old testament letter or Law was, and is, still applicable to our faith today. The Law (old testament), though relevant, cannot save a soul! What it does do however, is reveal our emphatic need for a Savior! It was given to us by God to teach our hearts how lawless our deeds are! God was gracious and Sovereign to give us the Law, but we were extremely ungrateful and too rebellious to accept it! But because God so loved the world, He made a WAY for TRUTH to give LIFE, so SALVATION could be accepted by FAITH through GRACE! What a plan, What a Love, What a God! Today, take a moment and just thank God for making SALVATION the SOLUTION for the stifling SITUATION of SIN!! If you're saved and glad about it, let the redeemed of the Lord say so! Have a Blessed day, and thanks for allowing me to share the word from a *Pastor's Perspective*...

JUNE 9

We must be mindful of the many different gifts in ministry. God has so many ways, people, and talents with which to express his wonder to this world. And yet, envy, jealousy, and schisms amongst the called remain! So much so, that we deceive ourselves by thinking, "As long as I'm this good at what I do, I don't really need anyone else!" This mindset couldn't be farther from the truth, and it is a disservice to destiny itself! Just think about it, if we all (believer's that is) make up the church and the church is the bride and the groom is God, and the bride and groom are ONE, and the BODY of this union is JESUS, who is ONE with GOD....then the words of the Apostle Paul ring true: "For as the body is one, and hath many members, and all members of that body, being many, are ONE body, so also is Christ! And the eye cannot say to the hand, I have no need of thee! Nor again the head to the feet, I have no need of you! There should be no schisms in the body! But that the members should have the same care one for another!" (I Corinthians 12:12, 21, 25). Though the body of Christ may be a *Members Only* church, that doesn't mean God only wants to use certain Members! Have a Blessed day, and thanks for allowing me to share the word from a *Pastor's Perspective...*

174

JUNE 10

For some of us, we exercise our FAITH in the same way we exercise our bodies. When there is an important engagement or event coming up, we exercise and diet to fit into certain attire to look our best for that MOMENT! But after that event is over, we abort the mission of exercising. We also make exceptions when we don't want to exercise the upkeep of FAITH! Hence, to say we are saved by Grace through FAITH (Ephesians 2:8), and then use the knowledge of salvation to execute mannerisms that allow exceptions over excellence, is unacceptable! Faith is not like the laws of physics...what goes up, must come down! The law of Faith is...progression, not exceptions! (Romans 3:21-28). Your Faith should be adding to your belief, not enabling your fears! Today check your Faith, by lining it up with your choices. If the choices you make, only satisfy the moment you're in, you're headed for spiritual incarceration! Because you continue to break the Law of Faith, the works of your Faith, will die! (James 2:20). "So then, faith cometh by hearing and hearing by the word of God." (Romans 10:17). Exercise your faith each day by reading God's word. Have a Blessed day, and thanks for allowing me to share the word from a *Pastor's Perspective...*

175

JUNE 11

When King Saul took the boy David from his home, he had no idea that his throne, was David's destiny! David did everything King Saul asked of him, but because the spirit of God was with David, the evil spirit of jealousy grew in King Saul (I Samuel 18:1-16). The bible records that King Saul, "Watched David ENVIOUSLY from that day on!" We must remind ourselves that the presence of God in our lives is reason enough for the enemy to be wickedly jealous! We are a MARKED people, because we are a CALLED people! Therefore, we must view spiritual scrutiny as part of the journey! It's been said, that the way of Destiny, comes through the corridors of difficulty! Hence, no matter what King Saul thought about David, or tried to do to David, and even said about David, the bible tells us, "And David behaved himself in ALL his ways, and the Lord was with him!" Consequently, "Wherefore, when Saul saw that he behaved himself very wisely, he was AFRAID of him!" (vs.14-15). The best way to handle people who are jealous of you, is to keep showing them the righteousness of God in you! If you behave yourself wisely, you'll confuse your enemies constantly! Have a Blessed day, and thanks for allowing me to share the word from a *Pastor's Perspective*…

JUNE 12

After David sat and thought about how King Saul felt about him, he told Jonathan, King Saul's son, "There is but one step between me and death!" (I Samuel 20:3). Sometimes we fail to realize how much the devil HATES us! And to walk around uncovered, haphazardly, defenseless, and vulnerable, we lose sight that we too, are but one step from the enemy's reach, and possible death! We need Jesus to cover us every day of the year, every minute of the day, and every second of every minute! There is never a moment we don't NEED

THE NAME OF
THE LORD IS
A STRONG
TOWER

Jesus! Because there is never a moment the devil isn't trying to DESTROY us! The prophet Solomon said, "The name of the Lord is a strong tower, and the righteous run to it, and are safe!" (Proverbs 18:10). Those who aren't SAVED, aren't SAFE! Please reflect on this! Any day without Jesus, whether you believe in Him or not, is another day you're running for your life! Therefore, make your next step, your best step! Come to Jesus and be safe...Have a Blessed day, and thanks for allowing me to share the word from a *Pastor's Perspective*...

JUNE 13

The Love of God is PERFECT! It never fails.
It always seeks to restore. It's full of mercy
and compassion. It's strong, it's revealing, and
it's correcting. It's life changing, it's true, and
it is AVAILABLE to all! There is not one soul
on earth that is not worth saving! No, not
one! No matter what you've done, how long
you've been doing it, or what you might be
planning to do next, God's PERFECT love
can turn your trials into triumphs! His
PERFECT love speaks to our hearts, so it can
comfort our hurt! "Herein is OUR Love made
PERFECT, that we may have boldness in the
day of judgment, because as He is, so are we
in this world! There is no fear in LOVE, but
PERFECT love casts out fear, because fear
hath torment." (I John 4: 17-18). There are
times when we can't accept the PERFECT
love of God, because we live in the stifling
reminder of our own imperfections! Don't let
your fears torment you any longer! Remind
yourself that Jesus went to the cross while we
were yet sinners, so His Love is PERFECT
while I yet live. His PERFECT love, is
connected to his PERFECT promises. "So
that where I am, you may be there also."
(John 14:3) Have a Blessed day, and thanks
for allowing me to share the word from a
Pastor's Perspective...

JUNE 14

King David scribed beautiful and inspiring words, "Teach me to do thy will, for thou art my God. Thy Spirit is good, lead me into the land of righteousness. Revive me, O Lord, for thy name's sake, and for thy righteousness sake bring my soul out of trouble!" (Psalms 143:10-11). Our troubles are often the direct result of our choices and a product of cause and effect. King David did some pretty bad things, yet God still had a pretty awesome plan for his life and used him mightily to write some of the most beautiful and encouraging scriptures of all time The Apostle Paul had a notorious history of persecuting the church, and yet God called him to write two-thirds of the New Testament. Whoever you are, you need not let your PAST block your PATH. If you repented for your past, then presented yourself to God, it's time to continue along your path. Mistakes in life should not define us, they should refine us! Today, speak revival into your soul and remind yourself, "Him who knew NO sin, became sin that I might be MADE the righteousness of GOD in Him!" (II Corinthians 5:21). And then begin to thank God that your STATUS today, isn't measured by the STANDARD of your yesterday! Have a Blessed day, and thanks for allowing me to share the word from a *Pastor's Perspective*…

The bible says..."Choose you this day, whom you will serve!" (Joshua 24:15). There is so much liberalism and self-expression going on in our world today that it's an arduous task trying to decipher the Saints from the Sinners! Yes, all have sinned and fall *SHORT* of the glory of God (Romans 3:23), however, when your faith, lacks the knowledge of the Father, and the coming Day of the Lord, you're not just falling SHORT, you're falling AWAY! For this reason, the prophet Joshua told the children of Israel, that while the Spirit of God was bellowing out to all the earth, it was high time to choose who they were going to serve! Straddling the fence of Faith is no longer acceptable! God is telling us that the coming day of His Son is going to be without warning and unescapable!

(I Thessalonians 5:2, Matthew 24:36). Joshua told Israel, "This is serious people! The same God who has been good to you, will turn and do you harm and consume you, if He is NOT your God!" (Joshua 24: 19-20). Heaven is a choice, but so is Hell! Choose you this day, whom you will serve, before it's too late. Have a Blessed day, and thanks for allowing me to share the word from a *Pastor's Perspective*...

It's amazing how born-again Saints are sometimes referred to as high-minded and accused of thinking too much of themselves. It has been said by unbelievers, and those of other doctrines, that Christians think they are BETTER than others. This couldn't be farther from the truth! In fact, the Apostle Paul said, "Let NOTHING be done through strife and vainglory, but in lowliness of mind let each esteem others BETTER than themselves!" (Philippians 2:3). Therefore, it's not that they think they are *Better* than anyone, it's just that, being born-again has given them an opportunity to become *Better* than what their former sins had labeled them as! And because God's loving kindness is BETTER than life (Psalms 63:3), and therefore life for Christians is so much better! To openly express the newness of life, apart from sin, isn't spiritual arrogance, it's spiritual confidence! So, let's not be too quick to judge a person who has been revived through being born again! They now walk with their heads up high, because they've finally realized they've lived with their heads hung low, for far too long! Have a Blessed day, and thanks for allowing me to share the word from a *Pastor's Perspective...*

JUNE 17

I've read many inspiring and encouraging scriptures along my Christian journey and one of my favorites is, "The Lord shall increase you more and more, YOU and your CHILDREN." (Psalms 115:14). Sometimes we sit and ponder heaven, with all its beauty, its wonder, and every bit of worship eternally taking place there. But in Psalms 115, the writer encourages us to allow ourselves to get caught up in the overflow of God's providence NOW!! You and your children!! It's one thing to be blessed, but it's entirely different to be saturated in the sustaining substance of God's overflow, you and your

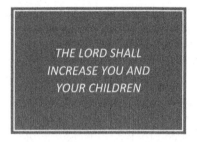

THE LORD SHALL INCREASE YOU AND YOUR CHILDREN

seed! (Psalms 127:3) This morning, give God the praise for increasing your life with an abundance that's going to bless you for generations! Isn't it wonderful to know that God's OUTREACH to you, will continue to REACH OUT to your children, long after you're gone? Have a Blessed day, and thanks for allowing me to share the word from a *Pastor's Perspective...*

JUNE 18

King Solomon said..."Put away from thee a froward or crooked mouth, and perverse lips put far from thee!" (Proverbs 4:24). Our mouths were given to us to Bless God, encourage others, and to do so many other wonderful things for the glory of God. Yet it seems our mouths are used more for destructiveness, than holiness! The Apostle James said..."Out of the same mouth proceeds BLESSINGS and CURSING, my brethren, these things ought not to be so!" (James 3:10) Your mouth can be a wonder of hope, or a whirlwind of hell! We should be diligent to use our mouths to uplift and not tear down, because as believers in Christ...Death and Life are in the power of our tongue!" (Proverbs 18:21). Today purpose to use your mouth to speak life and not death. And always remember; think before you speak, because once the words leave your MOUTH, you may not be able to remove them from someone else's HEART! One of the greatest lies ever told was, "Sticks and stones may break my bones, but WORDS will never hurt me!!!" There are many people who would give anything to be able to take back what they SAID and exchange it for what they should have kept to themselves! Have a Blessed day, and thanks for allowing me to share the word from a *Pastor's Perspective*...

JUNE 19

It is such a blessing just to know God for yourself. He's a lawyer in the courtroom, a doctor when you're on your sick bed, a friend when others turn their back on you, a shelter from the storms of life, and ultimately the savior of your soul. He is COMMITTED to loving you in every way! He inspired the Prophet Solomon to write, "Commit thy works unto the LORD, and thy THOUGHTS shall be established!" (Proverbs 16:3). The Psalmist David wrote, "Thou knowest my down sitting and mine uprising, thou UNDERSTANDEST my THOUGHTS afar off." (Psalms 139:2) Just to know, that one day my thoughts about God will be rewarded with me standing in his presence! Wow! As the song writer declared, "I can only imagine!" (Mercyme). Therefore, let us commit all our thoughts of Him, to Him. The Apostle John declared, "Beloved, now are we the children of God, and it doth not yet appear what we shall be, but we know that, when He shall appear, we shall be like Him; for we shall see Him as He is." (I John 3:2). This morning please know, "God is able to KEEP that which you COMMITT unto Him!!" (I Timothy 1:12). Have a Blessed day, and thanks for allowing me to share the word from a *Pastor's Perspective*...

JUNE 20

The Apostle Paul wrote, "Be not deceived, evil communication corrupts good morals!" (I Corinthians 15:33). In other words, bad company will eventually lead to bad behavior! Jesus said; "You'll know the tree, by the fruit it bears." (Matthew 7:20). God called you out of darkness into his MARVELOUS light (I Peter 2:9), that you might AFFECT those around you, not be INFECTED by everything around you! Therefore, the Apostle Paul says, "Wherefore, come out from among them, and be ye separate saith the Lord, and touch not the unclean thing, and I will receive you!" (II Corinthians 6:17). It doesn't take a rocket scientist to realize that if you lie down with enough dogs, sooner or later you're going to have fleas! If you can tell that your character is changing so much so that YOU don't even recognize YOU anymore, then it's about time you really think about the company you're keeping! If bad company can corrupt your good morals, then good company must have the opposite effect. Those who don't monitor whom they hang around with, often find themselves infected by bad behavior! Remember that for some, the road to Hell was paved with good intentions, but sealed with bad behavior! Have a Blessed day, and thanks for allowing me to share the word from a *Pastor's Perspective...*

JUNE 21

In the words of the song writer, "Oh, how I love Jesus. Oh, how I love Jesus. Oh, how I love Jesus...because He first loved me." I believe this hymn reveals the true emotion of unconditional Love. This truth is substantiated in the scriptures and makes for sound evidence that God's LOVE is our providence!" But God commendeth his LOVE towards us in that, while we were yet sinners, Christ died for us!" (Romans 5:8). Oh, just to know how much God LOVES us,

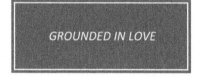
GROUNDED IN LOVE

should be enough to make us LOVE His Son! The Apostle Paul wrote..."For this cause, I bow my knees unto the Father of our Lord Jesus Christ. That Christ may dwell in your hearts by faith, that ye being ROOTED and GROUNDED in LOVE, may be able to comprehend, with all saints, what is the breadth, and width, and length, and depth, and height, and to know the LOVE of Christ. Which passeth knowledge, that ye might be filled with all the fullness of God." (Ephesians 3:14, 17-19). To know Jesus, is to truly know how much God the Father LOVES you. Have a Blessed day, and thanks for allowing me to share the word from a *Pastor's Perspective...*

JUNE 22

If God knows all things and that everything must one day stand before Him in the judgment, why do we deceive ourselves thinking we're safe, within our SECRETS? The Prophet Solomon warned us, "For God shall bring every work into judgment, with every SECRET thing, whether it be good, or whether it be evil!" (Ecclesiastes 12:14). With God there is no such thing as a SECRET! The bible declares, "All things are naked and open unto the eyes of HIM with whom we HAVE to do!" (Hebrews 4:13). Sure, we can pull the wool over each other's eyes, but there is not enough wool in all the earth to block the all-seeing eye of God! To think, God is blind, even in the slightest sense, is SIN! The devil wants us to believe we can have SECRET sins and that God has somehow made allowances for them, in his SECRET love. This is a lie, from the pit of Hell! Jesus says; "I am The Way, The Truth, and The Life!" (John 14:6). Why? Because, "OPEN rebuke, is better than SECRET Love!" (Proverbs 27:5). To truly love God with a pure heart, is to truly let Him into yours. Don't let sin live in your life, by trying to keep SECRETS! God already knows, what you've been trying to hide. Have a Blessed day, and thanks for allowing me to share the word from a *Pastor's Perspective*...

187

By faith, we can look at our BURDENS as a
gateway to our BLESSINGS in life! The
Prophet David said, "Cast thy burden upon
the Lord, and HE shall sustain thee. He shall
never suffer the righteous to be moved!"
(Psalms 53:22). When we cast our cares upon
Him who cares for us (I Peter 5:7), we turn
turmoil into triumph! Situation into solution!
Defeat into dominion! Glory to God! If God
is for you, who or what can stand against you
and prevail? The answer: ABSOLUTELY
NOTHING!!! Our burdens are a blessing if
we give them to God! Placing your burdens in
God's hands, is the greatest disappearing act
you'll ever see! But keeping your burdens to
yourself, is the hardest act you'll ever follow!
When you trust God while *IN* the fire, the
threat of the *furnace* doesn't matter! Just like
the Hebrew boys in the book of Daniel, "Did
not we cast three men BOUND into the
midst of the fire? They answered, true O,
King! But he answered and said, Lo, I see four
men LOOSE, walking in the midst of the fire,
and they have NO hurt, and the fourth is like
the Son of God!!" (Daniel 3:24-25). If you
allow him to, God will use your BURDENS
for wood with which to kindle your
BLESSINGS! Have a Blessed day, and thanks
for allowing me to share the word from a
Pastor's Perspective...

JUNE 24

The scriptures teach, "For the law was given through Moses, but GRACE and TRUTH came through Jesus Christ!" (John 1:17). When Grace and Truth arrived on the scene, so did the hope of our glory. Our hope of salvation rests and abides in our understanding of what GRACE does for the soul, and what TRUTH is to the Spirit! Listen to this incredible exchange of Grace and Truth which took place in the midst of grief and trial: Pilate therefore said to Him, "Are you a King then?" Jesus answered, "You say rightly that I am a King. For this cause, I was born and for this cause, I have come into the world, that I should bear witness *TO* the TRUTH. Everyone who is of the Truth hears my voice." Pilate said to him, "What is TRUTH?" And when he had said this, he went out again to the Jews, and said to them: "I find no fault in Him at all." (John 18:37-38). Because of God's GRACE on Pilate's soul, TRUTH came through Pilate's spirit! He spoke absolute TRUTH, because Jesus is absolute GRACE! Every time Jesus speaks to your heart, Grace and Truth are in your midst. Have a Blessed day, and thanks for allowing me to share the word from a *Pastor's Perspective...*

JUNE 25

The supremacy of God is greater than the audacity of men! In fact, when men try to exalt their finite understanding of ANYTHING, above the omniscience of God, the creator of EVERYTHING, they are doing the works of Lucifer, a fallen angel of PRIDE! (Isaiah 14:11-17). Men who refuse to acknowledge God as supreme, will be suddenly reproved, and taken by surprise, and that without remedy!" (Proverbs 29:1). To think of yourself as higher than *HE* who created you, is just as dangerous as trying to cross a four-lane highway in a wheelchair with a bad wheel! God will never cease to be God, no matter how high you exalt yourself! However, God inspired the Apostle Paul to write...."For I bear them witness that they have a zeal for God, but not according to knowledge. For they, being ignorant of God's righteousness, and going about to establish their own righteousness, have not submitted themselves unto the righteousness of GOD!" (Romans 10:2-3). People of God never forget these words: "God RESISTS the proud but gives Grace to the humble." (James 4:6). "These six things the Lord HATES..." And *PRIDE* is at the very top of the list!!! (Proverbs 6:16-19). Have a Blessed day, and thanks for allowing me to share the word from a *Pastor's Perspective*...

The podium of PROMISE is your belief! Your belief in God through Jesus, allows the promises of God to excel high above every circumstance, every situation, and every potential problem! Jesus said, "And I, if I be lifted UP from the earth, will draw ALL men unto me!" (John 12:32). And because circumstances, situations, and problems can only have purpose through people, places, and things, we need a Savior at all times! One of the most reassuring promises Jesus has ever made to those who believe is: "And lo, I am with you ALWAYS, even unto the end of the age." (Matthew 28:20). With a promise of this magnitude, not only can our ministry within us rest in God's loving care, we are also lovingly compelled to share what God loves within the ministry. God's love for ministry comes through the work of mercy. For it is through mercy that ministry has purpose, but it is through belief that we have the promises of God! And just in case you didn't know, for ALL the promises of God are YES, and AMEN, unto the glory of God by US!!! God is not only true to His word, He has never broken a single solitary promise, EVER! Have a Blessed day, and thanks for allowing me to share the word from a *Pastor's Perspective...*

JUNE 27

The Apostle Paul wrote, "Blessed be God, even the Father of our Lord Jesus Christ, the Father of our mercies, and the God of all COMFORT, who comforteth us in all tribulation, that we may be able to COMFORT them who are in any trouble, by the COMFORT which we ourselves are comforted."(II Corinthians 1:3-4). I believe everyone at some point in their life will miss the mark by confusing that which COMFORTS with that which CONDEMNS! For every time God comforted you in your time of tribulation, He was enabling and equipping you to be a proxy of comfort for someone else. God has shown you what COMFORT is so you could know what a COMFORTER does! While Jesus walked the earth, all those who met Him, were completely comforted. But before He left the earth He said this..."If you love me, keep my commandments. And I will pray the Father, and He shall give you another COMFORTER (that is, the Holy Spirit) that he may abide with you forever. I will not leave you COMFORTLESS."(John 14:15-18). The truest form of comfort in the earth, is showing people the Spirit of Jesus within...Have a Blessed day, and thanks for allowing me to share the word from a *Pastor's Perspective...*

JUNE 28

When God gave Moses the Commandments, He gave man orders! He had already seen what man was capable of without His guidance NOTHING BUT EVIL! (Genesis 6:6-7). God has always made a way for man. He helps man get on his feet, but as soon as he learns to walk, he forgets how to get down on his knees and pray! Moses' calling had its rewards, especially being able to see Israel delivered from Egypt. However, Moses' calling had its grievous moments as well, such as watching some 23,000 Israelites perish in the wilderness, because of their disobedience! (I Corinthians 10:1-12). And when we read this account we ASK ourselves, "Wow! Why did they move away from God during such a miraculous journey?" The Apostle Paul had some questions concerning this matter: "How, then, shall they call on him in whom they HAVE NOT believed? And how shall they believe in him of whom they HAVE NOT heard? And how shall they hear WITHOUT a PREACHER?" (Romans 10:14). When you lose the desire to hear PREACHING, you can best believe it won't be long, before you feel the PRESSURE of disobedience! Have a Blessed day, and thanks for allowing me to share the word from a *Pastor's Perspective...*

JUNE 29

The Apostle Paul said, "For I determined not to know anything among you, except Jesus Christ and Him crucified!" (I Corinthians 2:2). In other words, as far as he was concerned, Paul believed there was nothing else worth talking about, other than the Gospel of Jesus Christ! When Paul had his road to Damascus experience (Acts 9:1-16), he didn't need to focus on anything else! His encounter with Jesus was ALL he needed to follow Him all the days of his life. God asks his creation these three questions; Am I enough God for you? Why do you have to bring so much of the world into our relationship? And, when will **who I am** become **all** I can see **in you**? If we attempt to answer these questions from our nature, our excuses will be hinged to the hardships of life and seemingly validated! However, the Apostle Paul explains that, these questions are connected to purpose, not persecution! "That your faith should not stand in the wisdom of MEN, but in the power of GOD." (I Corinthians 2:5). Today, reflect on these three questions and see for yourself, through yourself! If you can't see JESUS waiting for you at the end of your life, then maybe it's because you're still packing your life, with the things of this world! Have a Blessed day, and thanks for allowing me to share the word from a *Pastor's Perspective*...

Now, more than ever, it's time for all the earth to hearken unto the warning of the Prophet Hosea: "Sow to yourselves in righteousness, reap in mercy, break up your fallow ground! For it is time to seek the Lord, till he come and rain righteousness upon you!" (Hosea 10:12).

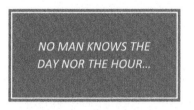

NO MAN KNOWS THE DAY NOR THE HOUR...

With the imminent, inevitable coming of the Lord we should be adamant in these last days about putting our houses in order (Isaiah 38:1). Because the coming of the Lord is inescapable, frivolous living is unacceptable! No man knows the day nor the hour the Son of Man will return (Matthew 24:36), so every man should redeem the time he has and seek the Lord, while he yet can be found! Those who seek him early shall find him." (Proverbs 8:17). "But those who are often reproved and hardeneth his neck, shall be suddenly destroyed, and that without remedy!" (Proverbs 29:1). Get your house in order and wait with joyous anticipation for Christ's return. Have a Blessed day, and thanks for allowing me to share the word from a *Pastor's Perspective...*

JULY 1

The Psalmist declared: "Unless the Lord had been my help, my soul had almost dwelt in silence!" (Psalms 94:17). The writer is not speaking of silence as it relates to complete quiet, no not at all. And this silence cannot have relevance to HELL, because there certainly is NO silence there! I believe this scripture is referring to that place within, where what you THOUGHT meets Him who already KNEW! That place where all your understanding is compelled to bow before the greatness of Him who abides in the hilltops of your help! (Psalms 121:1). Our mountain top experiences are often procured due to the ignorance we exhibit in the valley! Yeah, we would like to think we have it all together, but the truth of the matter is, if it were not for God in all of His sovereignty, we would have perished in the wilderness! Today, remind yourself that you owe God praise!! Just think about it; all your liberty, all your peace, all your strength, and every ounce of your joy come from HIM! Those who abide in the presence of God, always have something to shout about! So, to silence the devil, tell somebody how GOOD God has been to you! God's love is so AMAZING that we just can't keep quiet about it! Have a Blessed day, and thanks for allowing me to share the word from a *Pastor's Perspective*...

JULY 2

The Prophet David wrote..."Create in me a CLEAN heart and renew a RIGHT spirit within me." (Psalms 51:10) I believe it was at this point in his life, that he understood the significance of salvation! He knew he needed a CLEAN heart, to have a clear conscience! I believe it was then that he truly understood, that only through a RIGHT spirit will any man be truly able to see the wrong within himself! In the words of King Solomon, "Every man is RIGHT in his own eyes, but the Lord ponders the HEART." (Proverbs 21:2). We should be constantly asking God for a CLEAN heart, and a RIGHT spirit. Why? Because our soul salvation could be in jeopardy if we don't. Remember, every man CAN LEAN ON HIS OWN UNDERSTANDING, but in the end, the reality of what he THOUGHT, will have to be tried by what truly IS! Hence, ponder these two words today: CLEAN and RIGHT. Be courageous enough to allow everything in you, that is not like Christ, to be washed in the blood of Him, who is pure through and through! And then accept your rightful position as the righteousness of God so that what has been made CLEAN through Christ, can also be made RIGHT with God. Have a Blessed day, and thanks for allowing me to share the word from a *Pastor's Perspective*...

JULY 3

The Prophet Solomon declared: "In all thy ways acknowledge Him, and He shall direct thy paths." (Proverbs 3:6). To have God as the navigator of your will, is to have a blessed assurance that you'll NEVER be lost along your journey. Sure, we all have pivotal moments of misdirection, but somehow, some way, God veers us back onto the right path. After all, He is ordering your steps...right? Now mind you, the scripture says He ORDERS the steps of a good man (Psalms 37:23), and even though He orders the steps, it's still up to you to follow the path! Sometimes the places we end up are of no fault of our adversary. Although it would be easy to blame the devil for all our rough roads in life, that conclusion would not always be true! You would just be giving credit to the author of lies, and he would still be accusing you before God day and night! (Revelation 12:10). Blaming everything around you but refusing to take a good look at yourself and your deeds, is a true sign that you've stopped following God's orders and are in fact lost! Always remember, disobedience never leads to peace! If you let God order your steps now, in the end, you'll walk where Angel's trod. Have a Blessed day, and thanks for allowing me to share the word from a *Pastor's Perspective...*

JULY 4

Sometimes God will place a blessing in your path, not to see what you will do with the blessing, but rather, what you will allow the blessing to do for you! Many really do not understand the principle behind God's providence! When Jesus said, "Behold the fowls of the air, for they sow not, neither do they reap, nor gather into barns, yet YOUR heavenly Father feedeth them. Are YOU not much more than them?" (Matthew 6:26). Sometimes, all we need to understand God's providence, is to remember how God has always made a way, when there seemed to be no way! God has NEVER asked any of us to help him with anything, ever! (Psalms 50:10-15). But rather, He insists on helping us in all things. God is undeniably the epitome of providence! And because of this truth, we should be to Him, the epitome of praise! As you read this devotion, reflect on God's providence and how it has NEVER allowed your trials to raise hands in victory! But rather, He has proven to be a God that doesn't have a problem, with a problem! People of God, we have Champion faith, because God has NEVER lost a battle! Those who let God care for them, don't have a care in this world! (Matthew 6:30-33). Have a Blessed day, and thanks for allowing me to share the word from a *Pastor's Perspective*...

JULY 5

Have you ever read..."A false BALANCE is abomination to the Lord, but a just WEIGHT is his delight." (Proverbs 11:1). This scripture speaks to those who still believe they can somehow balance Sin and Salvation on the same scale! Not only is this completely wrong, God hates any attempt at living this way! Anything that's an abomination to God, is an utter detriment to our walking upright. Please understand, anything abominable, is cursed! King Solomon continues, "But a just weight," that is, a lifestyle conducive to the call of God, and not the call of the world, "Is His delight!" God does not want us to manage Sin on any

LAY ASIDE EVERY WEIGHT...

level, but rather, He wants us to allow the ministry of life to WEIGH so heavy on our hearts, that we refuse to hurt or hinder the happiness He experiences in loving us! God has only one way to love us, through His Son. Yet we find so many ways to hurt Him, through our Sin! The only way to live a balanced life before God, is to lay aside every WEIGHT and SIN that so easily besets us." (Hebrews 12:1). Have a Blessed day, and thanks for allowing me to share the word from a *Pastor's Perspective…*

JULY 6

Our growth in the Faith is essential, because the war with this world is so intense! The Apostle Paul wrote..."For we wrestle not against flesh and blood, but against principalities, against powers, against the rulers of the darkness of this world, against spiritual wickedness in high places!" (Ephesians 6:12). We cannot afford to be out of touch with God, when the war with wickedness is ablaze all around us! While it is true that the real battle field is in our mind, we cannot ignore the fact that the enemy wants nothing more than to turn our worship into worry! If he can accomplish that, he can turn your Faith into Fear, and your heart will inevitably become a gravesite! This is one of the many reasons why the Prophet Solomon said, "Keep thy HEART with all diligence, for OUT of it are the issues of life." (Proverbs 4:23). Let us never deceive ourselves into thinking we can defeat spiritual wickedness with a wayward Faith! Your Faith, must have Spiritual Muscle! And that spiritual muscle, only comes through the exercising of unshakable BELIEF! Always remember, the BIGGER the Faith, the smaller the worry! And the smaller the worry, the BIGGER the Worship! Have a Blessed day, and thanks for allowing me to share the word from a *Pastor's Perspective*...

JULY 7

The Apostle Paul wrote..."For we are saved by hope but hope that is seen is NOT hope! For what a man seeth, why doth he yet hope for it? But if we hope for that which we see not, then do we with PATIENCE wait for it!!" (Romans 8:24-25). If we can be still and know that He is God (Psalms 46:1), we will also run and not be weary, walk and not faint! (Isaiah 40:31). When patience is allowed to have its perfect work (James 1:4), we can rest in the knowledge that the Lord is our shepherd and we don't have to live in WANT! (Psalms 23:1). Our lives are constantly being challenged by circumstances, situations, and all manner of opposition, but if we learn to speak the following words to our adversaries: "Yea, though I walk through the valley of the shadow of death, I will fear no evil! For thou art with me! Thy rod and thy staff they comfort me! Thou preparest a table before me in the presence of mine enemies! Thou anointest mine head with oil and my cup runneth over! Surely GOODNESS and MERCY shall follow me ALL the days of my life! And I will dwell in the house of the Lord FOREVER!!" (Psalms 23: 4-6). If God is for you, it doesn't even matter who is against you! Have a Blessed day, and thanks for allowing me to share the word from a *Pastor's Perspective...*

JULY 8

To live a life of godliness is to live a life filled with heavenly expectation. The Prophet Solomon said: "In the way of righteousness is life, and in the pathway thereof is no death!" (Proverbs 12:28). When we get a good, firm grasp on what Jesus said about our future in Him, our outlook about a life IN Him, becomes incomparably different from those who perish without Him..."I am the Resurrection, and the LIFE! He that believeth in me, though he were dead, yet shall he LIVE!" (John 11:25). The Apostle Peter said, "Blessed be the God and Father of our Lord Jesus Christ, which according to his abundant mercy hath begotten us AGAIN unto a LIVELY hope by the resurrection of Jesus Christ from the dead! To an inheritance INCORRUPTIBLE, and UNDEFILED, and that fadeth not away, RESERVED in heaven for YOU!" (I Peter 1: 3-4). So then, people of God, be encouraged by the words of the Apostle Paul, "For to me to LIVE is Christ, and to die is gain." (Philippians 1:21). Those who die IN Christ, are already IN heaven! Have a Blessed day, and thanks for allowing me to share the word from a *Pastor's Perspective*...

JULY 9

If the scripture promises, "But my God shall
SUPPLY all your needs according to his
riches in glory by Christ Jesus" (Philippians
4:19), then why do we spend so much time
telling God about our needs, when we should
be telling our needs about our God?
Sometimes we forget that a NEED in the
hand of God, is a miracle where man is
concerned! If God is your shepherd and you
shall not WANT, then you must believe that
your NEED is supplied according to the
riches in His Son, and not the severity of your
circumstances! Never second guess God's
ability to SUPPLY what we need, but instead,
make sure our need is NOT because of
something we neglected to nurture in God's
care! "There is nothing God will hold back
from them that walk upright before Him."
(Psalms 84:11). Therefore, our need is
supplied according to His riches, and not
according to our righteousness! Sure, it's
wonderful to live right before God and reap
where you have not sown, however, please
remember, while you were yet a sinner, God
never stopped SUPPLYING what you
NEEDED! Have a Blessed day, and thanks
for allowing me to share the word from a
Pastor's Perspective…

JULY 10

Genuine GIVERS are always eager to serve! They're the first to church on Sunday and the last to leave. They're always in the forefront of someone else's joy! And they never get tired of blessing the Lord with all that He's given them! The bible calls these people..."Cheerful Givers," and the bible tells us that God loves them (II Corinthians 9:7). It is often minimized that, "God so loved the world, that He GAVE His only begotten son. (John 3:16). God demonstrated His love, through His giving! And He expects the same from us. Sometimes people look at givers as overzealous, a bit much, and even weak! But that's not the case with those who genuinely have the heart of God. They desire to GIVE, because they desire to SEE God (Matthew 5:8). So then, if you're a GIVER and people can't seem to understand that, know that your giving is not the issue, it's more about them refusing to do the same! Continue to do all that God has called you to do, and as they continue to see the heart of God in your giving, they'll forever witness why God loves them so much! Givers don't give because they're gullible, they give because God gets the glory!.......Have a Blessed day, and thanks for allowing me to share the word from a *Pastor's Perspective...*

JULY 11

I'm sure you've heard people say: *"Life is what you make it."* I've come to realize this saying is not biblically sound. If Life was something I could shape to my liking, then why do we still have so many battles with the works of our flesh? Not only is this a cliché, it also sits at the center of confusion for so many of God's people. The bible says, "The EARTH is the Lord's and the FULLNESS thereof, the WORLD and THEY who dwell therein." (Psalms 24:1). Know ye not that the Lord, HE is GOD! It is HE who hath made US, and NOT we ourselves! We are HIS people and the sheep of HIS pasture." (Psalms 100:3). And then, to top it off, Jesus makes it crystal clear, "I am the way, the truth, and the LIFE!" (John 14:6). Let me ask you a question; When was the last time you took a good look at what man has done with LIFE? Not only is it totally different from God's plan, but he's slipping further into sin! Man will never be able to make life what it is supposed to be if he continually refuses to live for God! The only thing natural man has made out of LIFE, is a mockery of God's LOVE! So, starting today, go and live life to the fullest within God's plan for you. Have a Blessed day, and thanks for allowing me to share the word from a *Pastor's Perspective…*

King David said, "Search me, O God, and
know my heart! Try me and know my
thoughts! And see if there be any wicked way
in me and LEAD me in the way Everlasting."
(Psalms 139:23-24). Through the language
alone, we can hear David's plea to have all
that he desires, to be saturated in the presence
of God! He was asking God to seek out the
deeds of his flesh, because his objective in life
was to live in the strength of his faith! When
we refuse to look deeper into our own hearts,
we mistakenly ignore the depths of our inner
struggles. Some of our inner pain and
persecutions are the result of our reluctance to
separate our imaginations from reality! When
David's desire for righteousness superseded
the complacency of reckless thinking, he
asked the Lord...*YOU* search me! And see if I
missed anything that should not be in my
heart! When pleasing God becomes your sole
desire, maintaining a clean heart is all that
matters! Today, take inventory of what's in
your heart, and see if what's there can abide in
the presence of God! If it can't, there is only
one solution: it must GO! From the manger
to the cross, Jesus' heart remained PURE in
the presence of God, and ours should also!
Have a Blessed day, and thanks for allowing
me to share the word from a *Pastor's
Perspective*...

JULY 13

Life continues to teach us many lessons. Some
help us understand people. Some lessons help
us understand ourselves. Some help us learn
how to be better listeners. Some are for the
sole purpose of correction and reproof. And
then, there are those lessons that cost you so
much that you'll NEVER need to make that
mistake again! It is teachable moments like
these where we discover that the lesson
LEARNED leads to spiritual GROWTH! The
Apostle Peter wrote, "Wherefore, laying aside
all malice, and all guile, and hypocrisies, and
envies, and all evil speaking, as newborn
babes, desire the pure milk of the word! Why?
That you may GROW by it! (I Peter 2:1-2).
The word of God is given so we can GROW
in grace, not drown in sin! If you continue to
live in this world, you should be constantly
Learning from it! For better or worse! In
addition, the rejection and rebellion against
God's word is clear and evident all around us.
Just because you've LEARNED something,
doesn't mean you're going to LISTEN! So
then, please understand this, if we don't lay
aside the things that stagnate our growth, we
will continue to plant grief in the garden of
our lives! Those who refuse to accept and
GROW in grace, will DIE without it! Have a
Blessed day, and thanks for allowing me to
share the word from a *Pastor's Perspective*...

JULY 14

The bible says that Jesus was led into the wilderness by the Spirit to be tempted of the devil, and in that moment the devil demanded that Jesus turn *stones* into *bread*! (Matthew 4:3). His demand had nothing to do with Jesus' ability, it had everything to do with Jesus' authority! If Jesus would have entertained the devil's demand, the devil would be able to question Jesus' deity! But glory to God..."Greater is he that was Him, than he that was in that moment!" (I John 4:4). And so, in that moment Jesus said..."IT IS WRITTEN, Man shall not live by bread alone, but by every word that proceedeth out of the mouth of God!" (Matthew 4:4). The devil is always challenging our deficiencies! Jesus fasted forty days and forty nights. In his humanity, He was hungry and above all of this, his wilderness had a voice! So it is with us as well! Our wilderness may have a voice, but our Spirit has God's word! When your wilderness starts making demands on your worship, it's not challenging your ability, it's trying to weaken your authority! To stop the devil from speaking to you in the wilderness, you must firmly remind him: IT IS WRITTEN! Have a Blessed day, and thanks for allowing me to share the word from a *Pastor's Perspective...*

JULY 15

The Prophet Solomon wrote..."If thou faint in the day of adversity, thy strength is small." (Proverbs 24:10). This scripture speaks to the seasons in our lives. The seasons that come from nowhere, that pull you in every direction! However, Solomon is telling us all not to let the seasons in your life sap out the strength in your fight! In other words, don't get weary in well doing, for you will reap in due season, if you don't FAINT! (Galatians 6:9). While it is true that seasons bring change, challenges, and choices, seasons also develop champions! If you are adequately prepared for the season, the circumstances surrounding it can never diminish your strength! You

DO NOT GROW WEARY IN WELL DOING

can't fight, the good fight of faith, if you faint during the fight! For your fight to be considered good, you must purpose in your heart, that you'll NEVER give up! People of God, seasons can be symptoms of your problems, or the stairway to your promises! It is a disservice to God to claim His strength yet be in bondage to a season! Have a Blessed day, and thanks for allowing me to share the word from a *Pastor's Perspective*...

JULY 16

One of the most meaningful things you have in this life is TIME! Time is a great companion for the wise, but for the wicked, TIME is a consuming fire of pending consequences! The Prophet David asked, "Lord, make me to know mine end, and the measure of my days, what it is, that I may know how FRAIL I am!" (Psalms 39:4). David no longer wanted to waste his TIME wrestling with temptation and weakness! He was beginning to see how precious TIME was to the development of his worship! It's been said, TIME waits for no man, that's just not true! TIME does wait on men! It took TIME for *YOU* the baby, to become *YOU* the adult! And then it took TIME to develop your relationship with Christ! It took TIME to learn how to walk by faith, and not by sight! It took TIME to learn how to move with the spirit! And while all these things were taking place in your heart, mind, and soul, time *WAITED* patiently as you grew! What some fail to realize is that ETERNAL work is still work! Those who don't use TIME wisely, are always left wishing they had more! Have a Blessed day, and thanks for allowing me to share the word from a *Pastor's Perspective...*

JULY 17

I am often left in complete awe of the elasticity of God's LOVE! While God's love "Covers a multitude of sin" (I Peter 4:8), it also stretches across our widest river of grief. Because He truly is the God of all comfort (II Corinthians 1:3). Amazingly, God's Love is one size fits all! God's Love will be as tight as you need it to be, and it can give you as much room as you need to have. God's Love can accommodate our every need! Sometimes we struggle with OUR strength, but God's LOVE keeps us in OUR weakness! God will use many things, people, and circumstances to cover you. When he inspired the Prophet Jeremiah to write, "I have LOVED you with an Everlasting LOVE, therefore with lovingkindness have I drawn thee." (Jeremiah 31:3). He was saying, my Love, stretches to you, not stresses, with you! My brothers and sisters, God is telling us that he has seen your pain and has witnessed your struggles, and that he is so proud of your faith! As I stretch my hands to you, continue to usher your heart to me. Because those who have tasted and seen that I AM good, know deep down inside, my LOVE, is greater than your grief. Have a Blessed day, and thanks for allowing me to share the word from a *Pastor's Perspective*...

JULY 18

The Apostle Paul wrote: "IF it be possible, as much as lieth in YOU, live peaceably with all men!" (Romans 12:18). Sometimes we go to great lengths to keep the peace with others. We try several methods; keeping silent, keeping our distance, and even try the method of putting image over ignorance! However, we must understand that the bible also says, "There is no PEACE for the wicked!" (Isaiah 48:22). Sometimes it's just NOT possible to live peaceably with those who won't live peaceably before Christ! The Apostle Paul asks the question: "For what fellowship hath righteousness with unrighteousness? And what communion hath light with darkness?" (II Corinthians 6:14). Sometimes we forget..."All things are POSSIBLE with God!!" (Matthew 19:26). And then there are other things that remain IMPOSSIBLE because of the evil of man! IF it be possible live peaceably with men, but IF not, live prayerfully on their behalf! Why should you come in PEACE, but leave in PIECES? Have a Blessed day, and thanks for allowing me to share the word from a *Pastor's Perspective*...

JULY 19

The best way to really get a grip on *WHO* the Lord is, *WHAT* the Lord came to do, and *WHY* he chose you to do it...is by allowing the Lord to *FREE* your mind from the grip of this world! The Prophet Solomon said, "Trust in the Lord with *ALL* thine heart, and lean not unto thine own understanding. In *ALL* thy ways acknowledge him, and he shall direct thy paths."(Proverbs 3:5-6). Sometimes it's hard to trust God, after you've been through a trial you feel God could have prevented. You need to remember that God works *ALL* things together for our good (Romans 8:28). And God does *ALL* things well (Mark 7:37). The prophet Solomon later wrote..."The Lord is a strong tower, the righteous run to it, and are safe!" (Proverbs 18:10). Now ask yourself..."What do I want at the end of my life?" Heaven? A reunion with loved ones? Everlasting worship? Freedom from sickness and suffering? Well, *ALL* these things will come to pass, if you can come to grips with God's process. Either He's God of *ALL*, or He's not God at *ALL*!" Have a Blessed day, and thanks for allowing me to share the word from a *Pastor's Perspective*...

JULY 20

More often than not we give God our OPINION before we give him our OPENNESS! We want God to exalt what we're feeling over what He knows! Not only is this a disservice to His authority and leadership, but it is also a hindrance to our help and inheritance! However, God who is rich in mercy even still (Ephesians 2:4), is pleading with our hearts today saying: "Come now, and let us reason TOGETHER, saith the Lord. Though your sins be as scarlet, they shall be as white as snow, though they be red as crimson, they shall be as wool. If ye be WILLING and OBEDIENT, ye shall eat the GOOD of the land. But if ye REFUSE and REBEL, ye shall be devoured with the sword! The word of the Lord hath spoken it." (Isaiah 1:18-20). We must remember that in spite of all the times our worship was wayward, God never gave up on His love for us! He remained faithful to us, even in our weakness! God already knows you may not have it all together, He just doesn't want you to forget that TOGETHER with Him, you have it all!! Have a Blessed day, and thanks for allowing me to share the word from a *Pastor's Perspective...*

JULY 21

One of the greatest things about being blessed with another day is waking up in peace and quiet! There are those who don't rise and shine, instead they rise with ruckus! They don't realize that, "He that blesseth his friend with a LOUD voice, rising early in the morning, it shall be counted a CURSE to him!" (Proverbs 27:14). God gives us new days with new mercies to rejoice and be glad in them! Not noisy and quarrelsome! (Psalms 118:14, Lamentations 3:23). The start of every day, should involve the solace of devotion. For it is in your quiet place that the Father speaks the clearest. Those who rise to love and commune with God, will be blessed to continue to collect their thoughts in His presence (Proverbs 8:17). It is God's desire that you start your day in acknowledgement of Him. While it is true, many things can happen in a day, there is nothing that happens without God's permission! Those who start the day in quiet devotion, understand clearly that every day is subject to God's decisions. Have a Blessed day, and thanks for allowing me to share the word from a *Pastor's Perspective*...

JULY 22

Some believers forget that as children of
Zion, we are the inheritors of all that heaven
has! (Joel 2:23). We forget that Jesus went
to..."Prepare a place for us there!" (John 14:2).
But in addition to that inheritance in heaven,
he wants us to live in the overflow of his Love
on this side of glory as well. God is our
Jehovah-Jira (our provider)! He longs to love
us! That's why Jesus came to save us! God will
never turn his back on any of us! His love
won't allow it! Our adversary tries to plague us
with shame for trusting God, when we've had
some not so pleasant moments in our lives.
But we must remind ourselves that, "We are
children of Zion, inheritors of all that heaven
has!" And being the beneficiaries of heaven,
we don't have *bad* days, we have *different* days.
Today ponder these words..."BLESSED be
the God and Father of our Lord Jesus Christ,
which according to his abundant mercy hath
begotten us again unto a lively hope by the
Resurrection of Jesus Christ from the dead.
To an INHERITANCE incorruptible, and
undefiled, and that fadeth not away, reserved
for YOU in HEAVEN!" (I Peter 1:3-4). Have
a Blessed day, and thanks for allowing me to
share the word from a *Pastor's Perspective*...

When you purpose in your heart to give God all you've got, you walk with tenacity because you know for yourself that, "Blessed are they who dwell in thy house, they will still be PRAISING thee!" (Psalms 84:4). Keep in mind that maybe God wants to take a moment to teach someone else some spiritual math through your life! Maybe he wants to show them; Unshakable FAITH + unspeakable JOY= continuous PRAISE! Sometimes we must remind ourselves..."Nay, in all things WE are more than conquerors through Him who loved US. And NOTHING shall be able to separate us from the LOVE of God, which is in Christ Jesus, OUR Lord!" (Romans 8:37-39). When you learn to put continuous praise on EVERYTHING, it's hard for ANYTHING to work against you! So then, if you're going through something today, or just feel like something is trying to press in on you...apply the direct pressure of constant PRAISE until your situation changes! Cover it with Faith, then let God's Love for you, maintain His peace in you! Have a Blessed day, and thanks for allowing me to share the word from a *Pastor's Perspective...*

JULY 24

Jesus said..."Either make the tree good, and its fruit good, or else make the tree corrupt, and its fruit corrupt, for the tree is known by its fruit!" (Matthew 12:33). Is the fruit of your life tainted with the rottenness of this world? Or is your fruit considered spiritually edifying to others? Some trees look strong, sturdy, and durable. Though they have thick firm branches, and though the root may be intact, it's the FRUIT that is sought after. The fruit in your life, is the blessedness of God's Spirit in your heart and in your ministry. In fact, it is by the FRUIT that a tree is deemed good or bad! And Jesus makes it crystal clear..."A GOOD tree cannot bring forth bad fruit! Neither can a CORRUPT tree bring forth good fruit!" (Matthew 7:17-18). Today, take a good look at your fruitfulness, then ponder the question of the Apostle Paul: "What fruit did you bear before you gave your life to Christ, that you are almost ashamed to acknowledge today?" (Romans 6:21). Now, because you know God has blessed your life, begin to thank God for nurturing your tree, so you are able to yield GOOD fruit! Have a Blessed day, and thanks for allowing me to share the word from a *Pastor's Perspective*...

JULY 25

The Prophet Solomon said..."Happy is the man that findeth WISDOM and the man that getteth UNDERSTANDING!" (Proverbs 3:13). These two entities are vital components of our character and our sense of direction! Solomon said, WISDOM is the PRINCIPLE thing, therefore get WISDOM! But with all thy getting, get UNDERSTANDING!" (Proverbs 4:7). We must exercise the WISDOM of God in our hearts to be able to walk with God, and then we must allow UNDERSTANDING to give God's purpose the preeminence it needs to push us forward. When a soul is devoid of WISDOM and UNDERSTANDING, the journey of life is joyless. But when you find WISDOM and UNDERSTANDING you find complete joy in knowing: "For the Lord taketh pleasure in His people, He will beautify the meek with salvation!" (Psalms 149:4). Oh, just to know that the wisest thing I've ever done *WITH* my life, was getting a firm understanding that I need God *IN* my life! A wise man will accept God's love, but only a man of understanding will live in it! Have a Blessed day, and thanks for allowing me to share the word from a *Pastor's Perspective...*

JULY 26

Jesus wants us to LIVE by faith, LOVE by faith, and WALK by faith! According to scripture..."Whatever is not of FAITH is sin!" (Romans 14:23). Do you know that the opposite side of faith, is fear? "God hath NOT given us the SPIRIT of FEAR! But of LOVE, POWER, and a SOUND mind!" (II Timothy 1:7). In addition to this truth, God wants us to know, "There is NO FEAR in Love! And *PERFECT* LOVE casts out Fear! Because FEAR torments you! (I John 4:18). The scriptures tell us that Love keeps no record of wrongs or thinks of evil (I Corinthians 13:5). God is never FEARFUL to give His love to us because of what we're capable of, have done, or are yet going to do! His love is as perfect as the blood that covers us! Either you walk in HIS PERFECT LOVE, or you'll live in the torment of FEAR! Hence, "Herein is our Love made perfect...when we live in the PERFECT LOVE of God right now!" (I John 4:17). We must stop acting as if Love is something we can TAKE or LEAVE! Because truth be told, life would be nothing without it! (I Corinthians 13:1-3) Have a Blessed day, and thanks for allowing me to share the word from a *Pastor's Perspective...*

JULY 27

Until we surrender *ALL* to Jesus, we can't
truly receive the fullness of his ONENESS!
"There is ONE body, and ONE Spirit, even
as ye are called in ONE hope of your calling!
ONE Lord, ONE faith, ONE baptism, ONE
God, and Father of ALL! Who is above ALL,
and through ALL, and in you ALL!"
(Ephesians 4:4-6). Until we surrender to the
GREATER in us, the struggle *in* us will
always seem stronger *than* us! But glory to
God when sweet surrender gives way, to
sweet relief! There is nothing like the
experience of having your burdens lifted, and
your soul revived through surrender. Spiritual
surrender is your heart telling your hurt, look
who's coming down the hill, ALL of my
HELP! (Psalms 121:1). "There is ONE God,
and ONE mediator between God and men,
the man, Christ Jesus!" (I Timothy 2:5).
Today, let ALL you do, ALL you say, and
ALL you are, start with an audience of ONE!
Have a Blessed day, and thanks for allowing
me to share the word from a *Pastor's
Perspective...*

Do you realize how uniquely special you are to God? When he created you, He had only *YOU* on His mind! All your uniqueness, all your gifts, all your intuitiveness, He made special your every likeness to Him. And when He was done, the bible says..."He BLESSED you!" (Genesis 1:28). God looks at you every day with a complete and incredible Love! God's love for you is so amazingly awesome that after he blessed you, He said...."Be fruitful and multiply!" (Genesis 1:28). He told us to do this, because in doing so, Jesus said..."In this is my Father glorified, that ye bear much fruit, and so shall ye be my disciples. As the Father hath loved me, so have I loved you, continue in my LOVE!" (John 15:8-9). When we keep the continuity of God's love alive on the earth, HIS joy remains in us, and OUR joy remains full! (John 15:11). We are FEARFULLY and WONDERFULLY made (Psalms 139:14), because God was specific about how special we are to Him...Have a Blessed day, and thanks for allowing me to share the word from a *Pastor's Perspective*...

JULY 29

As we press toward the MARK for the prize of the high calling of God in Christ Jesus (Philippians 3:14), we become a target that the enemy constantly tries to hit! And with every attack, no matter how it comes, we must encourage ourselves in knowing..."Though an host should encamp against me, my heart shall not fear! Though war should rise against me, in this will I be confident...For in the time of trouble He shall hide me in His pavilion! In the secret of His tabernacle shall He hide me! He shall set me up upon a rock! (Psalms 27:3, 5). When you know with blessed

assurance, that you're secure in God's care, you can thrive in God's presence without stress! Being a target for the high calling of God is something to press toward! I'd rather be pressing towards God, than getting points for trying to impress people! Those who are marked for Jesus, are bound for glory! (Ezekiel 9:1-6) Have a Blessed day, and thanks for allowing me to share the word from a *Pastor's Perspective...*

JULY 30

There is a significant spiritual reason God wants us to abandon the works of this world! He knows that all our carousing, worldly activities, and the like are our connections to the world, and that they cause confusion in our conscience! Remember, "You cannot serve two masters!" (Matthew 6:24). We continue to say we're SAVED, until the next worldly invitation! God has a strong reminder for us all..."Wherefore, remember that ye, being in times past Gentiles in the flesh, who are called uncircumcision by that which is called the Circumcision in the flesh made by hands! That at that time ye were WITHOUT CHRIST, being aliens from the commonwealth of Israel, and strangers from the covenants of promise, having NO HOPE, and WITHOUT GOD in the world!!" (Ephesians 2:11-12). Every time we answer the world's call...we hang up on God! God understands the connection to our loved ones and to people who are in the world, but he has called you to be a light OUT OF DARKNESS, not a blind travel guide in it! Have a Blessed day, and thanks for allowing me to share the word from a *Pastor's Perspective*...

The Apostle Paul wrote, "But in a great house there are not only vessels of gold and of silver, but also of wood and of earth, and some to honor, and some to dishonor." (II Timothy 2:20). In other words, God knows exactly who you are, no matter where you are! Sometimes God allows TESTING, not to cause you to STUMBLE, but to convince you to STOP! We don't like the *do's* and *don'ts* of God, but we continue to suffer from the *will* and *wants* of self! Unbelievable! However, this is what the word of God says about it all...."Every man's work shall be made manifest, for the day shall declare it! Because it shall be revealed by FIRE, and the FIRE shall TEST every man's WORK for what it is!" If any man's WORK abides which he hath built upon, he shall receive a REWARD! If any man's work be BURNED, he shall suffer LOSS, but he himself shall be SAVED, yet as by fire!"(I Corinthians 3:13-15). Any test God allows to come your way, is sent to point you in the right direction! God is not trying to shame you, it just hurts God so much to watch you fail an open-book test! Have a Blessed day, and thanks for allowing me to share the word from a *Pastor's Perspective*...

"The Lord is merciful and gracious, slow to anger, and plenteous in mercy!" (Psalms 103:8). We must break free from self-condemnation, because, "Whom the Son has set free, is free indeed!" (John 8:36). When you repented, and meant it, God heard it and received it! When He saved you, He forgave you! He made all things NEW, because He already knew, it would take you some time, to live in the NEW you! But NOW that you're a NEW creature in Christ, there is therefore no more condemnation in your life! (Romans 8:1). Your soul has been redeemed, and you  can now look towards the hills, from hence God sends your help causing you to triumph in everything you may be going through! So today, as you reflect on your redemption, repeat the words of the Prophet David…"Bless the Lord, O my soul, and forget not all His benefits!" (Psalms 103:2). Have a Blessed day, and thanks for allowing me to share the word from a *Pastor's Perspective*...

AUGUST 2

We can truly be encouraged that even after King David experienced life-threatening persecution he declared: "I will LOVE thee, O Lord, my STRENGTH! The Lord is my ROCK, and my FORTRESS, and my DELIVERER! my GOD, my STRENGTH, in whom I will trust! my BUCKLER, and the horn of my SALVATION! and my HIGH TOWER!" (Psalms 18:1-2). God wants us to hold fast, to the HOPE, that holds us close to His love.

THE LORD IS MY ROCK AND MY STRENGTH

(Romans 5:5). When He promised to NEVER leave us, nor forsake us, he wasn't just encouraging us, he was sending a warning all who oppose those that love Him! Our Kinsman redeemer warns our adversary to back up or be broke up! So then, today, know that you are secure, loved, and above all, you are GOD'S PROPERTY, and all trespassers will be dealt with! (I Chronicles 16:18-21, Psalms 105:15). Have a Blessed day, and thanks for allowing me to share the word from a *Pastor's Perspective*...

228

When the Apostle Paul wrote..."There is one BODY, and one SPIRIT, even as you are called in one HOPE of your calling! one LORD, one FAITH, one BAPTISM, one GOD, and FATHER of all! Who is ABOVE all, and THROUGH all, and IN you all!" (Ephesians 4:4-6). The importance of this text is its Perspective! Many religious ideologies and doctrines seem to undermine the Omnipotence and Oneness of God's greatness! When the Spirit of God said: "I am the LORD, that is my name, and my GLORY will I NOT give to another!" (Isaiah 42:8). Things are easily taken out of context, when things are not put in proper Perspective! The PREEMINENCE of God stands alone! And all those who believe in His Son, stand with Him! God is second to none! He can't be compared to anything! And He will NEVER be in competition, with what HE created! Today, put His preeminence in proper Perspective! He IS God and we are NOT! Have a Blessed day, and thanks for allowing me to share the word from a *Pastor's Perspective...*

AUGUST 4

The Prophet Solomon wrote..."A man hath JOY by the answer of his mouth! And a word spoken in due season, how good it is!" (Proverbs 15:23). There is nothing more comforting and consoling than hearing a perfect word, at the perfect time. And it is just as gratifying to hear someone say..."Thank you so much, I needed to hear that." When words are MINISTERED with precision, hearts are moved with compassion! When God allows us to speak a word that is more than just a response, we'll always receive more than a good feeling, and the hearer is always blessed beyond measure! The Prophet Isaiah said..."The Lord God has given me the tongue of the learned, that I should know how to speak a word in season to him that is weary." (Isaiah 50:4). When God puts a PERFECT word in your heart, wait for the PERFECT moment to sow it into someone else's. Those who learn to speak a word in due season, receive unspeakable JOY! Have a Blessed day, and thanks for allowing me to share the word from a *Pastor's Perspective*...

What a blessing it is just to know the Lord! To know how much He Loves us (John 3:16), how He's always interceding for us (Romans 8:26), and has purposed to NEVER leave us, nor forsake us (Hebrews 13:5)! This kind of knowledge tills the fallow ground of our hearts, so that good seed can be planted, and a good harvest can be expected! When you know Jesus, you don't have to look for justice, you're living in it! But, even with this knowledge we must never forget how finite and unfortunately unfinished our flesh can be (I Corinthians 13:9-11). We can shout

hallelujah anyhow, for what we KNOW about Jesus! Because scripture tells us: "Beloved, NOW are we the sons of God, and it doth not yet appear what we shall be. But we KNOW that, when He shall appear, we shall be LIKE Him! For we shall SEE Him as He is!!" (I John 3:2). Have a Blessed day, and thanks for allowing me to share the word from a *Pastor's Perspective...*

AUGUST 6

It doesn't matter if you're a minister of music, on the deacon board, an usher, or even the pastor, your position should promote potential, not inject poison! Because whoso shall offend one of these little ones which believe in me, it were better for him, that a millstone were hanged about his neck, and that he were drowned in the sea!" (Matthew 18:6). Too often, babes in Christ witness ongoing compromise from professing, seasoned Christians! Additionally, they deal with persecution from unbelievers! Discouraged, they decide to live and die apart from Jesus! The word of God tells EVERY believer..."Be ye HOLY, for I am HOLY!" (I Peter 1:16). And Jesus told the disciples: "Let them both grow together until the harvest, and in the time of harvest I will say to the reapers, gather ye together FIRST the tares, and bind them in bundles to BURN them! But gather the wheat into my barn." (Matthew 13:30). Remember, everyone will give an account, in the end! Have a Blessed day, and thanks for allowing me to share the word from a *Pastor's Perspective*...

The Psalmist said..."Through God we shall do valiantly, for it is He who shall tread down our enemies!" (Psalms 108:13). God wants to encourage every soul today with a blessed assurance that He is right by your side. The enemy, the obstacles, and the negativity around you is no match for your JEHOVAH! And because you belong to and trust Him, He has promised..."No weapon formed against you shall prosper!" (Isaiah 54:17). The enemy may come at you one way, but scripture tells us He will flee SEVEN ways! (Deuteronomy 28:7). God is NOT going to stand by and watch you bullied by benevolence! But rather, He said in His word…"When the enemy comes in like a flood, the Lord shall raise a standard against him!" (Isaiah 59:19). Therefore, God wants you to rest in this: "As I was with Moses, so I will be with thee! I will not fail thee! Nor forsake thee! Be strong and of good courage!" (Joshua 1:5-6). If God is for us, who or what can stand against us! (Romans 8:31). Have a Blessed day, and thanks for allowing me to share the word from a *Pastor's Perspective*...

AUGUST 8

"God raised Jesus up, and loosed the pains of death, because it was NOT possible that He should be held by it!" (Acts 2:24). One of the greatest strategies the devil uses to make us GIVE IN, is by applying enough pressure to make us feel like we can't GET OUT of a situation! He tries to make suffering seem like defeat! But let me encourage you today: "Weeping may endure for a night, but joy is coming in the morning!" (Psalms 30:5). It is through our suffering that we learn to stand our ground! It is through our suffering that we overcome this world! And it is through our suffering that we learn how big of a liar the devil really is! After all, "All those that will live godly shall SUFFER persecution!" (II Timothy 3:12). We are NOT trapped by suffering, we are triumphant OVER it, IN Jesus! (II Corinthians 2:14). Our Lord and Savior reigns supreme!! Today, don't allow suffering to be the focus of your faith! Know that your DEVOTION is stronger than any demonic strategy! Have a Blessed day, and thanks for allowing me to share the word from a *Pastor's Perspective...*

As we live, move, and have our being (Acts 17:28), we can clearly see why we must be OBEDIENT and let God have his way! Our understanding of God's order, is oftentimes impeded by our moments of spiritual disorder! "The way of a fool is right in his own eyes, but he that hearkeneth unto counsel is wise!" (Proverbs 12:15). The Prophet Solomon warns us that bad strategy can lead to grave tragedy..."There is a way that SEEMS right unto a man, but the end thereof are the ways of DEATH!" (Proverbs 14:12). It is good practice to PRAY before you SAY, what you will and will not do! And please don't depend SOLELY on your heart either, because sometimes the heart can lead you to places God NEVER intended for you to go! (Jeremiah 17:9). We must get in the habit of following Jesus, no matter how good our own plans may SEEM! Why? "A man's heart deviseth his way, BUT THE LORD DIRECTS HIS STEPS!"(Proverbs 16:9). So today, let Jesus lead the way! Have a Blessed day, and thanks for allowing me to share the word from a *Pastor's Perspective*...

AUGUST 10

Sometimes in your walk with Christ, you will be faced with the decision to TOLERATE or TERMINATE! As I think of this dilemma my mind goes back to something Jesus said: "YE are the salt of the earth. But if the salt has lost its savor, wherewith shall it be salted? It is no longer thenceforth good for NOTHING, but to be cast out, and to be trodden under the foot of men!" (Matthew 5:13). When your ability to savor a situation ceases, you must be careful not to become the doormat of ignorance. "Be not weary in well doing!" (Galatians 6:9). You may be doing well by them, but your heart is a witness, they are NOT doing well by you! It is at this junction that you need to recognize the threat a situation has become to your PEACE. And so, here are your options; TOLERATE or TERMINATE! Never allow circumstances to dictate your level of devotion. You have every right, once you've done all you could to stand, to take a stand in your decision! I've had enough! (Ephesians 6:13-14) Have a Blessed day, and thanks for allowing me to share the word from a *Pastor's Perspective*...

AUGUST 11

When Jesus was teaching the multitude and the disciples how to pray, He said something that helps me understand the Father's willingness to care for me, and all those that believe in the Father. He said, "When you pray do it after this manner; Pray ye, Our Father which art in heaven, hallowed be thy name. Thy kingdom come, thy will be done on earth, as it is in heaven. GIVE US THIS DAY OUR DAILY BREAD... (Matthew 6:11). To ask for daily bread is to trust the provider! Now daily bread could be physical food, but I believe it was far more than that! I believe it was fellowship in His presence! "In His presence, is fullness of joy!" (Psalms 16:11). Now, make no mistake, we do feel great after a good meal! Right? But, when you have God's provision and His presence, you get a totally different feeling of joy!! The bible calls it UNSPEAKABLE!! (I Peter 1:8). Always remember my brothers and sisters, OUR DAILY BREAD, comes from OUR DAILY FELLOWSHIP! Have a Blessed day, and thanks for allowing me to share the word from a *Pastor's Perspective...*

AUGUST 12

Most of our understanding about being made WHOLE, relates to being healed from something or someone harmful. We tend to put being HEALED in the same category as being made WHOLE! Although, they are close in connotation, they are different in manifestation! The Apostle Peter proved to us that we can have deliverance and still not be made whole! (Luke 22:32). When Jesus saw the man at the pool of five porches, he saw a man with the faith to believe in the process, but no means to make the progress! (John 5:1-7). Being Healed is to be delivered from the circumstance, whereas being made whole is to walk in the completed authority of Jesus! Many of us have faith, but no fight and therefore can't seem to move forward! Sure, we believe in the process, but lack the means for the progress! Faith lacking authority, is a

soul that has not been made Whole! Have a Blessed day, and thanks for allowing me to share the word from a *Pastor's Perspective...*

"Behold, how good and how pleasant it is for brethren to dwell together in UNITY!" (Psalms 133:1). UNITY is the opposite of division, vanity, and enmity! In fact, unity in the body of Christ is the ultimate goal of fellowship! "The God of all the universe gave

DWELL TOGETHER IN UNITY

Apostles, Prophets, Evangelists, Pastors, and Teachers for the perfecting of the saints, for the work of the ministry, for the edifying of the body of Christ, till we all come into the UNITY of faith!" (Ephesians 4:11-13). Today, as you reflect on God's work of grace in your life, ponder how Grace came through ONE, namely Jesus Christ, but the greatness of fellowship in the Spirit comes through us all, in UNITY! We've heard this quote: "A family that prays together, stays together." However, it should also be said...UNITY holds together what the world is trying separate: US! Have a Blessed day, and thanks for allowing me to share the word from a *Pastor's Perspective*...

When God told Hezekiah to..."Set thine house in order, for thou shalt die, and not live," (Isaiah 38:1) the bible tells us: He "Turned his face toward the wall and prayed to the Lord." (vs.2). Do we really need to have near death experiences, a bad doctor's report, a severe situation, or a threatening trial before we set our house in order? We should not only want to SET our house in order, we should also want to KEEP it that way! Why? Because where the Spirit of the Lord is, there is liberty to do so! (II Corinthians 3:17). "But if any man provide not for his own and especially for those of his own house, he hath denied the FAITH, and is less than an infidel!" (I Timothy 5:8). Therefore, keep your house in order both in the natural and the spiritual realm! "Take heed, WATCH and PRAY! for ye know not when the time is!"(Mark 13:32-33). Those who fail to keep order in the house, will be unprepared tenants! Have a Blessed day, and thanks for allowing me to share the word from a *Pastor's Perspective...*

It is amazing how many people seem to gravitate towards Hate and set out to destroy Love! King David said..."For my LOVE they are my adversaries, but I give myself unto PRAYER! And they have rewarded me evil for good, and hatred for my LOVE! (Psalms 109:4-5). When people attack, put down, ridicule, and altogether try to discredit your walk with Christ, they're not offended by YOU, they're offended by God's LOVE for you! They may know things that happened in your life, but they know nothing about what happened in your heart! But God does! And through PRAYER and REPENTANCE, God has declared your heart and His LOVE, a perfect match! Jesus said, "Let not your heart be troubled, you believe in God, believe also in me." (John 14:1). Remind yourself today, if Christ died for you while yet a sinner (Roman's 5:8), there's nothing that can separate you from His LOVE now that you're saved! (Romans 8:38-39) It's not your fault, others can't handle God's LOVE! Have a Blessed day, and thanks for allowing me to share the word from a *Pastor's Perspective*...

AUGUST 16

When going through hard times, tears indicate the release of pain, frustration, and in some cases, even love. Know that, "Weeping may endure for a night, but joy cometh in the morning!" (Psalms 30:5). And as encouraging as that scripture is, when we're going through it, it is no less painful! Sometimes, when trying to comfort others, we try to rush the grieving PROCESS by using a fair amount of spiritual rhetoric. But that sometimes makes things worse and doesn't always speed up deliverance! The Psalmist said..."They that sow in tears shall reap in joy! He that GOETH FORTH AND WEEPETH, bearing precious seed, shall doubtless come again with rejoicing, bringing his sheaves with him!" (Psalms 126:5-6). God will restore you

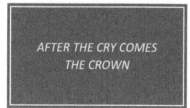

AFTER THE CRY COMES THE CROWN

following every wilderness experience. We tend to forget that after the CRY, comes the CROWN! Have a Blessed day, and thanks for allowing me to share the word from a *Pastor's Perspective...*

When the Son of Man returns it will truly be
something to behold! "And before Him shall
be gathered all nations, and He shall separate
them one from another, as a shepherd divides
his sheep from the goats!" (Matthew 25:32).
The thought of eternal separation is nothing
to take lightly! The separation process alone
should get your attention...."And He shall set
the sheep on his right hand, but the goats on
the left. Then shall the King say unto them on
His right hand, Come, ye blessed of my
Father, inherit the kingdom prepared for you
from the foundation of the world." (vs.33-34).
As for the goats, they will have a totally
different assignment...."Then shall He say also
unto them on the left hand, depart from me,
ye cursed, into everlasting fire, prepared for
the devils and his angels!"(vs.41). Your eternal
DESTINY, will be determined by your
DECISIONS! If you don't choose the eternal
life OF the FATHER, you will suffer the
eternal death IN the FIRE. Have a Blessed
day, and thanks for allowing me to share the
word from a *Pastor's Perspective...*

AUGUST 18

Some people talk BIBLE, though their lives are a BURDEN! The Apostle Paul warns us that they are deceitful workers, transforming themselves into the apostles of Christ (I Corinthians 11: 3-15). But more importantly, he goes on to say..."Satan himself is transformed into an angel of light." (vs.14). Warnings of this magnitude, are specifically for the multitude! Sometimes we get caught up in a person's WORDS and fail to realize we're entering their WORLD! The Psalmist said...BLESSED is the man who walketh NOT in the counsel of the UNGODLY! (Psalms 1:1). Everyone you LISTEN to, may NOT be a BLESSING to you! They may appear as light but are actually lost souls with a corrosive understanding! "Beloved, believe NOT every spirit, but test the spirits whether they are of God! Because many false prophets are gone out into the world!" (I John 4:1). Remember, don't get caught up in how people SPEAK, pay attention to how they LIVE! Have a Blessed day, and thanks for allowing me to share the word from a *Pastor's Perspective...*

WORSHIP must have a place in our lives! "Lord, remember David, and all his afflictions! How he swore unto the Lord, and vowed unto the mighty God of Jacob: surely I will NOT come into the tabernacle of my house, NOR go up into my bed, I will NOT give sleep to mine eyes, NOR slumber to mine eyelids, UNTIL I FIND OUT A PLACE FOR THE LORD! an habitation for the Mighty God of Jacob!" (Psalms 132:1-5). Our place of WORSHIP should be just as important as our place of rest! Many professing believers don't settle on a home church, because of the accountability factor. Nevertheless, David had this to say about his place of WORSHIP: "One thing have I desired of the Lord, that will I seek after, that I MAY DWELL IN THE HOUSE OF THE LORD ALL THE DAYS OF MY LIFE! To behold the beauty of the Lord, and to inquire in His temple!" (Psalms 27:4). When you neglect to find a place to WORSHIP, you neglect to give God a place to DWELL! Have a Blessed day, and thanks for allowing me to share the word from a *Pastor's Perspective...*

Jesus said..."Notwithstanding, in this rejoice NOT, that the spirits are subject unto you, but rather rejoice, because your names are written in heaven!" (Luke 10:20). Sometimes we get excited about fleeting situations. We make the mistake of stamping PERMANENT on that which is TEMPORARY! Our assessment of things is often obscured. Our rejoicing should always be propelled by our relationship with Christ! It is our relationship with Christ, that gives

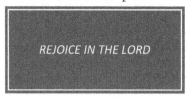

REJOICE IN THE LORD

our righteousness relativity and causes our hearts to

rejoice in the Lord! The Apostle Paul said: "Rejoice in the Lord! And again, I say, Rejoice!!" (Philippians 4:4). He was inspired to write this because he understood that the peace of God is not only a promise, it is PERMANENT! Today, the Spirit of God is saying, don't REJOICE about the things God has rejected, but rather REJOICE for the one thing God has accepted, namely, YOU...Have a Blessed day, and thanks for allowing me to share the word from a *Pastor's Perspective*...

AUGUST 21

To celebrate LIFE, is to acknowledge JESUS! When we lift up the name of Jesus, we crush the works of the enemy! Jesus said..."If I be lifted up, I will draw ALL me unto me!" (John 12:32). He went on to say..."I am come a light into the world, that whosoever believeth on me should not abide in darkness!" (vs.46). Our celebration today is about having the light of our Savior and dispelling the darkness of our adversary!

When God the Father declared, "Let there be light," (Genesis 1:3) Jesus, the Son started writing out invitations for our salvation celebration! The Lord is saying..."Come, for all things are now ready!" (Luke 14:17). He's telling us that all are invited to this celebration, and that He's expecting a FULL house (vs.23), so please come! This joyous occasion will be like no other! And the after-party will be completely, OUT OF THIS WORLD!!! I TRULY HOPE TO SEE YOU THERE! Have a Blessed day, and thanks for allowing me to share the word from a *Pastor's Perspective...*

"He who heeds the word wisely will find GOOD, and whoever trusts in the Lord, HAPPY is he!" (Proverbs 16:20). True HAPPINESS is only found in the truth of Jesus! As believers, our happiness is sustained by our trust in the Savior's care. The Lord is our shepherd therefore, we don't have to want for anything! (Psalms 23:1). "The Lord supplies all our needs according to His riches in glory!" (Philippians 4:19). And when we

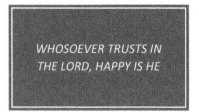

WHOSOEVER TRUSTS IN THE LORD, HAPPY IS HE

make our prayers and requests known to God, He gives us a peace that carries our thoughts beyond our concerns! (Philippians 4:6-7). So then, those who say they're happy WITHOUT Jesus, they're not only living a LIE, they've convinced themselves to believe it also! If your HAPPINESS isn't connected to heaven, your HAPPINESS is fleeting! Have a Blessed day, and thanks for allowing me to share the word from a *Pastor's Perspective*...

As believers, we do our best to WALK in the Lord, LIVE in the Lord, and ABIDE in the Lord. But how often do you allow your heart to LAUGH in the Lord? The Prophet Solomon declared that, "There is a time to LAUGH!" (Ecclesiastes 3:4). The Psalmist said when Israel thought about how God had turned their captivity around, it was like living a wonderful dream! So much so, that their mouths were filled with LAUGHTER! Why? "The Lord hath done great things for them, and they were glad!" (Psalms 126:1-3).

Today, God wants you to release some good godly LAUGHTER in your soul! And if it's hard to find something good and godly to LAUGH about, let me help you. For all the times the devil brings up your past, burst into LAUGHTER and remind him of his future! There's always room for Good, Godly LAUGHTER in balancing the truth between being BLESSED and being BLAMED. Have a Blessed day, and thanks for allowing me to share the word from a *Pastor's Perspective*...

AUGUST 24

When Jesus said, "He that hath ears to HEAR, let him HEAR!" He was explaining that there is a difference between HEARING what I say and listening to what you HEARD! In the parable of the sower and the soils (Matthew 13:1-9), Jesus spoke to the multitude to help them understand that the expected harvest from HIS seed, is substantiated by the condition of YOUR soil! He said, "Some seed fell by the WAYSIDE (unattended and not cared for), some fell upon STONEY ground (there were more stones than soil) and some fell among the THORNS and THISTLES (as soon as the seed sprouted, the thorns and thistles strangled the life out of it). Are you tending to your soil daily? Are you careful to remove the stones, that is, the hardness of your heart? And are you making sure that thorns and thistles (people, places, and things) aren't choking the life out of your works? He that hath ears to HEAR, let him HEAR! Have a Blessed day, and thanks for allowing me to share the word from a *Pastor's Perspective*...

The Apostle Paul said..."In everything GIVE THANKS, for this is the will of God in Christ Jesus concerning you." (I Thessalonians 5:18). When we give thanks to God, we're saying, "Lord, I appreciate you!" And in return, the Psalmist reminds us...."For the Lord takes pleasure in his people." (Psalms 149:4). Giving Thanks to God is about reverence, not penitence. When we give thanks unto God it should be from an adoration that is perpetuated from all HIS sovereignty, all HIS goodness, all HIS Grace, and all HIS mercy! Because the Apostle Paul said, all of this was HIS will in Christ Jesus concerning YOU. Sure, we could all find something to complain about, but if you were to be critically honest about things, you too would testify that your GOOD days far exceed your BAD ones! And for that alone, it's worth letting God know, "Lord, I GIVE THANKS for all you've done, all you're doing, and all you're going to do, in my life!" Have a Blessed day, and thanks for allowing me to share the word from a *Pastor's Perspective...*

Our JOY in the Lord, is maintained by our relationship with Him! "The JOY of the Lord is our STRENGTH!" (Nehemiah 8:10). Abiding in His presence is fullness of JOY! (Psalms 16:11). When we've made mistakes and poor decisions, it is the Lord who restores our JOY! (Psalms 51:12). And because our relationship with Him is something we desire and even treasure,

THE JOY OF THE LORD IS OUR STRENGTH

Jesus said, "His JOY would remain in us! So our JOY might be full!" (John 15:11). Today, God wants you to purpose in your heart not to let anything or anyone steal your JOY! Because, that JOY you have...the world didn't give it to you! And the world can't take it away! When you have Jesus in your heart, there's JOY in your life! And because of that, you are BLESSED!! Have a Blessed day, and thanks for allowing me to share the word from a *Pastor's Perspective*...

AUGUST 27

The Psalmist said..."Blessed is that man who maketh the Lord his trust, and respecteth not the proud, nor such as turn aside to LIES!" (Psalms 40:4). The greatest LIAR of all time is the devil (John 8:44). And his greatest lies have been spent on the rebellious minds of unbelievers! When he sees, hears, and witnesses your rebellion, he immediately offers you his version of happiness! But by the time it's clearly understood what has happened, the soul in question has already been corrupted and the mind is in complete disarray. Jesus told us that the devil wants to steal, kill, and destroy all your potential! (John 10:10). Today, God wants you to abandon worldly influence and ALL its wickedness! The devil desires to sift you like wheat, but you need to worship God like never before! The LIES of the enemy won't stop while you accept the ways of the world as truth! Those who are complacent with LIES, will live in the company of HELL! Have a Blessed day, and thanks for allowing me to share the word from a *Pastor's Perspective*...

The world tells us that the best things in life are free! Not only, is this NOT TRUE, it is designed to minimize the finished work of JESUS at the cross! Which explains why the Apostle John recorded..."Jesus came unto his own, but His own received him NOT!" (John 1:11). If the world can turn the hearts of men away from worshipping Christ, it leaves room for temptation to antagonize our flesh with dissatisfaction! But glory be to God for the Apostle James putting the blame of dissatisfaction, where it belongs: "Let no man say when he is TEMPTED, I am TEMPTED of God! For God CANNOT be tempted with evil, neither tempt he any man! But every man is tempted when he is drawn away by HIS own LUST and ENTICED!" (James 1:13-14). Those who are not SATISFIED with the

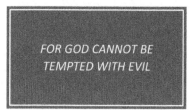

FOR GOD CANNOT BE TEMPTED WITH EVIL

Son's finished work at the cross, won't be satisfied with the blood He shed at Calvary either! Have a Blessed day, and thanks for allowing me to share the word from a *Pastor's Perspective*...

The six words Jesus wants us to remind the DEVIL when he tries to attack our faith are as follows: IT IS WRITTEN (Matthew 4:4), and IT IS FINISHED (John 19:30)! When "It is Written" is used in spiritual warfare, what is heard becomes what is TRUE! When you speak what is TRUE to a lie, God allows YOU to cross-examine the double-crosser! The devil will soon realize he can't victimize you with his lies, overthrow you with his deception, and hoodwink you with his hellish ways, because God has given you the authority to say: "It is Finished!" Scripture tells us, "For the accuser of our brethren is cast down, who accused them before our God day and night!" (Revelation 12:10). He was cast down from the presence of God, because the case he brought against blood bought, blood covered saints lacked evidence! He didn't know every saint had been ACQUITTED at the cross!! Therefore, the case was thrown out and the devil was cast out of God's presence, while YOU remain rapture ready! Have a Blessed day, and thanks for allowing me to share the word from a *Pastor's Perspective*...

AUGUST 30

King David prayed..."Keep back thy servant also from presumptuous sins, let them not have dominion over me! Then shall I be upright, and I shall be innocent from the transgression." (Psalms 19:13). After David came to grips with his God, he no longer desired to be a slave to grief! He wanted to live in the liberty of which the Apostle Paul speaks of in II Corinthians 3:17. When we came to Christ, repented, received forgiveness, and were born again, we entered a covenant that covered it! Whatever IT was, IT is now GONE! And so, when David prayed to be kept from presumptuous sins, he wanted God to know he was finally ready to stop taking grace for granted and was truly ready to start taking his worship seriously! (Psalms 38:17). Likewise, you are greater than your grief! And even your worst transgression is no match for His grace! Accepting God's GRACE for your GRIEF is the greatest transaction, you'll ever make! Have a Blessed day, and thanks for allowing me to share the word from a *Pastor's Perspective...*

AUGUST 31

Each day we should set out to UNDERSTAND more and more about the will of God for our lives. And because our lives are a puzzle of purpose, our

SERVE GOD WITH YOUR
WHOLE HEART

UNDERSTANDING is constantly being pieced together! The Psalmist wrote..."Give me UNDERSTANDING, and I shall keep thy law, yea, I shall observe it with my WHOLE heart." (Psalms 119:34). However, you must UNDERSTAND that to serve God with your WHOLE heart, you must give Him EVERY piece of it! This way we will cease to get caught in the WHEELS of this world! King Solomon wrote: "And with all thy getting, get UNDERSTANDING!" (Proverbs 4:7). The only reason someone is reluctant to come to Jesus and receive all that He is, is because they don't UNDERSTAND...JESUS IS the WILL of God, concerning them. (I Thessalonians 5:12-24) Have a Blessed day, and thanks for allowing me to share the word from a *Pastor's Perspective*...

SEPTEMBER 1

When Jesus is the center of your joy, you don't have time to be in the middle of someone else's mess! Amen! You are so consumed with trying to follow God's order for your life, you just can't run the risk of being ruined because of the foolishness of others! You must allow God to reveal to them that you don't think you're better than others, you've just come to the knowledge that you're better than that! Jesus said: "That which cometh out of the man is what defiles the man. For from within, out of the HEART OF MEN, proceed evil thoughts, adulteries, fornications, murders, thefts, covetousness, wickedness, deceit, lasciviousness, an evil eye, blasphemy, pride, and FOOLISHNESS! All these EVIL things come from within and defile the man." (Mark 7:20-23). In the center of every man is the heart, and God wants his Son at the center of every heart! If Jesus is not the center of who you are, you run the risk of one day being asked: "WHO ARE YOU?" Have a Blessed day, and thanks for allowing me to share the word from a *Pastor's Perspective*…

SEPTEMBER 2

"When a man's ways please the Lord, he maketh even his enemy to be at peace with him!" (Proverbs 16:7). If you were to sit down and really think back over your life and all the times God protected you in situations YOU got yourself into, you would have good reason to give him an unhindered praise! Amen! But now that you're saved, sanctified, and delivered...Oh hallelujah somebody! We find out that when our ways please our God, our enemies can't do anything but be at peace with us! You may be thinking: "I receive it, but I still don't understand it!" Allow me to help...When our sole desire is to please God, and we yearn to be one with Him, the things that were once in pieces around us are now made whole in us! Get this in your spirit today: only the TRUTH of God, can make a TRUCE with the enemy! It's time to stop thinking PEACE while living a life that's in PIECES! If you want peace commit your works to the Lord (Proverbs 16:3). Have a Blessed day, and thanks for allowing me to share the word from a *Pastor's Perspective*...

SEPTEMBER 3

King David wrote these words to encourage and comfort us: "The Lord is NEAR unto those who are of a broken heart, and SAVETH such as be of a contrite spirit. Many are the afflictions of the RIGHTEOUS, but the Lord DELIVERETH him out of them ALL!" (Psalms 34:18-19). While it is true that Life is constantly happening all around us, it is also true, that God is there right by our side! No wonder, no weapon formed against me can prosper, because, there's no weapon stronger than my God! When we truly repent from the depths of our soul for ALL our disobedience, rebellion, and blatant sin, God takes our broken heart and our contrite spirit and lifts the ENTIRE burden! "It is GOOD for me that I have been afflicted, that I might learn thy statutes!" (Psalms 119:71). When God uses affliction to point you in the right direction, His purpose is Devotion! Why? Because Devotion always leads to Deliverance! Have a Blessed day, and thanks for allowing me to encourage you from a *Pastor's Perspective...*

SEPTEMBER 4

A lot of what we DO is impulsive. A lot of what we SAY is emotion. And a lot of what we THINK is passion. But no matter what we DO, SAY, or THINK it should all be driven by the spirit of God, and have its PURPOSE, in God! "For what shall it profit a man, if he shall gain the WHOLE world, and lose his own soul? Or what shall a man give in EXCHANGE for his soul?" (Mark 8:36-37). To build on a foundation other than the one Jesus has purposefully laid out is to exercise natural thought through spiritual ignorance! We Should Always SEEK to Please God because it is written, "Let this MIND be in you, which was also in Christ Jesus." (Philippians 2:5). Jesus raises the bar even further with this parable: "For which of you, intending to build a tower, sitteth not down FIRST, and counts the cost, to see whether he has what he needs, to finish what he has purposed!" (Luke 14:28). Today, as you venture out, let all you Do, Say, and Think have PURPOSE! Have a Blessed day, and thanks for allowing me to share the word from a *Pastor's Perspective...*

SEPTEMBER 5

Have you had moments when your life feels off course because your circumstances appear greater than your confidence! What about those days when your heart seems full of uncertainty and your faith feels like it's failing! And let's not forget the days when your past mistakes seem to cut down all your growth, and your heart is bombarded with grief! When these things begin to happen, it's because the truth of your DESTINY is wiping out the record of your past! Satan does not want you to rest in the following: "For I will be merciful to their unrighteousness, and their sins, and their iniquities will I remember NO MORE!" (Hebrews 8:12). If that truth gets in your heart, the devil now must contend with you and the fact that you are, "Being RENEWED in the spirit of your MIND!" (Ephesians 4:23). "For as a man thinketh in his HEART, so is he!" (Proverbs 23:7) To receive ALL God HAS for you, you must have the mind of Christ and be on the same page with His goals for you! Rejoice in your renewal! Have a Blessed day, and thanks for allowing me to share the word from a *Pastor's Perspective*...

SEPTEMBER 6

Waiting on the Lord is not always easy, but it is always necessary! There are many scriptures that express God's understanding about what we go through in this life. Scriptures like: "Let not your heart be troubled, you believe in God, believe also in me!" (John 14:1). "Be not weary in well doing; for in due season we shall reap, if we faint not!" (Galatians 6:9). And one of my favorites: "The race is not to the swift, nor the battle to the strong, neither yet bread to the wise, nor yet riches to men of understanding, nor yet favor to men of skill; but TIME and CHANCE happen to us ALL!" (Ecclesiastes 9:11). However, none of these soul-stirring words of encouragement will have any impact, if we run out of perseverance! We must be so steadfast and unmovable, that our hearts will only yield to the God we know, and not to the things we feel! "Wait on the Lord; be of good courage, and he shall strengthen thine Heart. WAIT, I SAY, ON THE LORD!" (Psalms 27:14). Have a Blessed day, and thanks for allowing me to share the word from a *Pastor's Perspective*...

SEPTEMBER 7

Did you know that prayer to God that moves mountains is the same fervent prayer that makes all things possible? It's been said that PRAYER is the key, but that FAITH unlocks the door! Listen to this..."So Jesus said to them, because of your UNBELIEF; for assuredly, I say to you, if you have FAITH as a mustard seed, you will say to this mountain, MOVE from here to there, and it will MOVE; and nothing will be IMPOSSIBLE for you!" (Matthew 17:20). A man brought his epileptic son forward for healing, but the disciples could not deliver him. They were so focused on the mountain (the epilepsy), that they were negligent of the ministry (the power of their prayer). God allows your faith to move mountains, so your prayers can establish authority! God wants us complete in our devotion, so we can defeat all of life's demons! Remember, mustard seed faith can move the biggest of mountains! You don't need a lot, to accomplish a lot! Have a Blessed day, and thanks for allowing me to share the word from a *Pastor's Perspective*...

SEPTEMBER 8

It is truly wonderful to see the SUN shining
and all of nature responding to God's creation
in complete surrender. But how much more
amazing is it when His SON shines within us!
When God sent His Son as a ransom for us
all, Jesus announced His purpose by telling us:
"For the Son of Man has come to SEEK and
to SAVE that which was lost!" (Luke 19:10).
Though there is an adversary in your midst,
whose motive is to seek and devour, Jesus has
come to seek and deliver! Between the
onslaught of the enemy, the trials of life, and
the battle in your flesh, it has become a reflex
to run from God, and lean on your own
understanding! However, when we lean on
our own understanding, we don't stand for
very long! Today, surrender to the spirit of
God by simply declaring...I know you've been
searching for me, here I am Lord! Therefore,
he that hath ears to hear, let this be the day,
you come out with your hands up! Because
remember, God can only COVER what you
SURRENDER! Have a Blessed day, and
thanks for allowing me to share the word
from a *Pastor's Perspective*...

Do you know that VICTORY in Jesus means not allowing yourself to be tainted by the cares of this world! A victorious mindset refuses to live beneath the privilege of being an OVERCOMER! Let's break it down further; if greater is HE that is in ME, than he that is in the world (I John 4:4), and if I can do all things through Him who is greater, namely, Jesus (Philippians 4:13), and if no weapon formed against me has a chance of prospering (Isaiah 54:17), then I must give God praise and remind myself that VICTORY IS MINE! Thanks be to God, who gives us this VICTORY through our Lord Jesus Christ! (I Corinthians 15:57). Don't allow circumstances, situations, romance, family, or financial issues, not even death to taint the VICTORY you have in Jesus! Starting today, put your problems in their place, by putting your life in proper perspective! You'll never live beneath your privilege when VICTORY is ALL you'll accept! Have a Blessed day, and thanks for allowing me to share the word from a *Pastor's Perspective*...

Jesus said..."If you continue in my word, then are you my disciples indeed. And ye shall know the TRUTH, and the TRUTH shall make you free!" (John 8:31-32). When we purpose in our hearts to operate in truth, we're expressing a desire to live as free people. It is an absolute burden to talk freedom in Jesus yet live in bondage according to the flesh! We need to continue in His word if we want to live free in this world! There are so many ways to get caught up in bondage, but there is only one way to be made free...the TRUTH of Jesus! Jesus said, "I am the WAY, the TRUTH, and the LIFE!" In other words, our knowledge of Him keeps us on the right path, FREE to live in liberty, and soul secure with the authority of ETERNITY! Today, purpose to be FREE in your heart by letting TRUTH disciple you. Let all your yesterday's get lost in the TRUTH of today's wonderful possibilities! Because the TRUTH of the matter is what makes all the difference! Have a Blessed day, and thanks for allowing me to share the word from a *Pastor's Perspective*...

SEPTEMBER 11

Jesus prayed, "And now come I to Thee; and these things I speak in the world, that they might have my joy FULFILLED in themselves." (John 17:13). He was praying to the Father on behalf of US, His children, about the joy of being one with Them! This prayer helps us understand that the JOURNEY is just as important as the DESTINATION! God the Father is filled with indescribable joy because of our acceptance of His Son Jesus. However, His joy is truly fulfilled when we have a steadfast mind to stay the course and fulfill our purpose while on our way to see Him! Jesus is truly expecting to see us all in that place that He went to prepare for us! I want you to head out for work, school or the kitchen, filled with the knowledge that God the Father and Jesus the Son are awaiting your arrival with unspeakable joy! And one day, it's going to be just as the song says: "When we all get to heaven...what a day of rejoicing that will be...when we all see Jesus, we'll sing and shout the victory!" Have a Blessed day, and thanks for allowing me to share the word from a *Pastor's Perspective*...

SEPTEMBER 12

On this Christian journey we will face difficulties, experience all manner of disappointment, question God's plans, and sometimes even feel like we're all alone. But Jesus said: "All authority is given unto ME in heaven and in earth and lo, I am with you always, even unto the end of the age!" (Matthew 28:18,20). And because He truly knows how it feels to experience tribulation, He tells us: "These things I have spoken unto you. That in ME ye might have peace. In the world ye shall have tribulation but be of good cheer; I have OVERCOME the world!" (John 16:33). Jesus wants us to find comfort in the victory He has won! Though He experienced the world in all points like a man, our Savior is a champion of change, a champion of chance, and a champion of challenge. But more than all this we should be of good cheer because He's THE champion of His children! When Jesus has your back, just keep moving forward! Have a Blessed day, and thanks for allowing me to share the word from a *Pastor's Perspective...*

Preparing for promise requires PATIENCE. "Knowing this, that the testing of your faith worketh patience!" (James 1:3) Even though scripture explains the gist of the work does nothing for the reality of the test! Depending on the expected outcome and lessons needed, God determines the severity of the test and what it will take to accomplish the goal! God will not allow the promise, His purpose, nor His passion to be poisoned by...impatience! When God has something specific in mind, we must be patient! What God has for you, is tailor made and will fit YOUR faith perfectly! His plan and purpose may require tremendous patience, nevertheless, at the end of the test, look at the promise..."Because thou hast kept the WORD with PATIENCE, I also will keep thee from the hour of temptation, which shall come upon all the world, to try them that dwell upon the earth."(Revelation 3:10). Which is why Jesus said..."In your PATIENCE possess ye your souls!" (Luke 21:19). Have a Blessed day, and thanks for allowing me to share the word from a *Pastor's Perspective...*

When you PRESENT your body a living sacrifice (Romans 12:1), God becomes the very PRESENT help that makes what you bring to the alter, Holy. With consecration, establishing what you are presenting, your reasonable service becomes perfect and acceptable unto God! The greatest sacrifice any man can give God is his Life! When you give of yourself for the service of preserving life, you show forth and prove what is that Good and perfect sacrifice within! To present your body a LIVING sacrifice for Christ, is to accept being crucified with Christ! Nevertheless, it must be understood that sacrifice is not always about dying for someone. Sometimes sacrifice is also about being alive because of someone! So today, take a quiet moment of solitude and present to God, what Jesus presented for you...His BODY! There is no sacrifice too great when it leads to salvation! Have a Blessed day, and thanks for allowing me to share the word from a *Pastor's Perspective...*

SEPTEMBER 15

Jesus asked His disciples this question..."And why call ye me, Lord, Lord and do not the things which I say?" (Luke 6:46). To be a true follower of the Lord, you must be a committed listener of Him! We must remember what the Lord is looking for in the man He has called out from among the worldly! He already knows..."We are shaped in iniquity, and in sin did our mothers give birth!" (Psalms 51:5). And..."NO good thing dwelleth in our flesh!" (Romans 7:18). However, because He is the same yesterday, today, and forever (Hebrews 13:8), He is asking us...But if you've truly been BORN-AGAIN, why is it so hard to do the things I ask of you? Jesus wants ALL of US to understand: "Verily, verily, I say unto thee, except a man be BORN AGAIN, he cannot see the kingdom of God!"(John 3:3). Remember that the Holy Spirit will guide you and give you the strength to do what He asks. Only when you listen TO the Lord, do you truly have a right, to call him LORD! Have a Blessed day, and thanks for allowing me to share the word from a *Pastor's Perspective...*

SEPTEMBER 16

When your spiritual growth is hindered, stagnant, or seemingly on hold, it could be a sign that defiance is causing deficiency. Remember, "WE wrestle not against flesh and blood, but against principalities, against powers, against the rulers of darkness of THIS WORLD, against spiritual wickedness in high places." (Ephesians 6:12). However, when we "Set our affections on things above" (Colossians 3:2), our spiritual growth rises above what God has purposed to abide beneath us! Never forget we have a fight, headed our way! Just think about it...if there is spiritual wickedness in HIGH PLACES and we are trying to go HIGHER, it's inevitable, we're going to cross paths with the enemy! And when we do, we must not become deficient through defiance...that is, don't try to avoid the confrontation. To avoid spiritual deficiency, you must have spiritual determination! And having done all to stand, you just STAND! (Ephesians 6:13-14). Have a Blessed day, and thanks for allowing me to share the word from a *Pastor's Perspective*...

SEPTEMBER 17

The story of the woman at the well is the account of a woman whose inner struggle finally met the living word! (John 4: 5-25) She was on her way to Jacob's Well, probably where she went every day to get water. But on this day, Jesus met her at the edge of her conscience! First, as a Samaritan she probably felt ostracized. Secondly, having had five different husbands, and currently with a man who was not her husband, she probably felt unworthy. And lastly, she was confronted by a Jewish rabbi, someone who is not supposed to have any dealings with Samaritans. She had never met this man, yet he knew all about her! She must have felt shame! Jesus knew that her HEART was in desperate need of worship! The well could only give water, but Jesus met her there with what gives worship: the living word! The well is symbolic of the place of worship, but the living water is you and I, alive in Jesus springing up into everlasting life! Don't miss your opportunity to worship at the well! Have a Blessed day, and thanks for allowing me to share the word from a *Pastor's Perspective*...

SEPTEMBER 18

Sometimes we spend far too much time entertaining people and things that have nothing to do with the call and purpose for our lives! We listen to frivolous chatter, accommodate compromise, and debate with carnality, only to be frustrated in our spirituality! We even suffer hardships because we fail to realize, anything opposed to Godliness will never be real friendship! "Therefore, to him that knoweth to do GOOD, and doth it not, to HIM it is sin." (James 4:17). "For to be CARNALLY minded is DEATH, but to be SPIRITUALLY minded is Life and Peace." (Romans 8:6). "But the natural man receiveth not the things of the Spirit of God; for they are foolishness unto him, neither can he know them, because they are spiritually discerned." (I Corinthians 2:14). There may come a time in your walk when you'll just have to say; "And lead me not into temptation but deliver me from evil." (Matthew6:13). Even though you can't reach everyone in this world, you yourself must keep reaching for Jesus! Have a Blessed day, and thanks for allowing me to share the word from a *Pastor's Perspective...*

The Psalmist asked the Lord to: "Order my steps in thy word and let not any iniquity have dominion over me!" (Psalms 119:133). When was the last time you examined your walk for INIQUITY? Which is essentially an immoral pattern of behavior. Oftentimes, when we hear the word immoral, we immediately think sensual and although sensuous sins are immoral, immorality is connected to all sin and every unethical behavior. When we allow iniquity to become familiar, we allow our lower desires to have greater dominion! Can you imagine what our existence would be like if Jesus when Jesus was in the wilderness he would have responded to temptation in the FLESH, instead of by FAITH? (Matthew 4:1-11). Satan doesn't have dominion because Jesus' steps were ordered in what was written! God's written word is all you need to lead the

ORDER MY STEPS LORD...

way, but it takes a made-up mind to stay off the path of iniquity! Have a Blessed day, and thanks for allowing me to share the word from a *Pastor's Perspective...*

Every shift in the kingdom purpose, starts with a kingdom thought! Jesus prayed..."Our Father who art in heaven, hallowed be thy name. Thy KINGDOM come, thy will be done, on earth as it is in heaven!" (Matthew 6: 9-10). This prayer not only gives reverence to Kingdom authority it also reveals Kingdom agenda! When we become caught up in our own agenda, we hinder the work of God's will in our lives and experience the disappointing reality that *His Kingdom hasn't come*! The prayer in Matthew Chapter 6 is God's way of letting each of us know that, for the kingdom to come, we must HALLOW (that is, honor as Holy) what's ordained in His name! God did not sacrifice Jesus because it made Him happy, He sacrificed Jesus because it made US holy! So today, if you want God's kingdom to come into your life, you must be willing to let what's done in heaven, be done in you! If heaven can't be expressed through you, you'll find it hard to understand the purpose of the kingdom working in others! Have a Blessed day, and thanks for allowing me to share the word from a *Pastor's Perspective*...

Believers go through three stages of understanding: LESSONS, LEARNING, and then LEANING...I look at it like this: "The grass WITHERETH, the flower FADETH, but the WORD of God shall STAND forever!" (Isaiah 40:8). God's purpose for His WORD, is so you can STAND right where you are! God, His Son, and His Spirit, are always in total agreement concerning YOU! "To have life and have it more abundantly!" (John 10:10). God allows LESSONS to come into our lives that help us LEARN to LEAN on His WORD! When God uses your hardships and pain as teachable moments, he's never trying to increase your agony, but rather, he's desiring to draw you closer to his Sovereignty, that you might be able to LEAN on His Everlasting Arms! Whatever God is trying to show you... LOOK! Whatever God is trying to teach you... LISTEN! And whatever direction God wants to take you...LEAN! I guarantee if you listen to God's WORD, you'll learn God's WILL! Have a Blessed day, and thanks for allowing me to share the word from a *Pastor's Perspective*...

SEPTEMBER 22

The Apostle Peter is most noted for denying Jesus three times…But regardless of his weaknesses, Jesus knew that one day Peter would be all he was called to be… "Simon, Simon, Satan has asked to sift you as wheat. But I have prayed for you, Simon, that your faith may not fail. And when you have turned back, strengthen your brothers!" (Luke 22:31-32). When difficult times in ministry arrive, and they will come, remember that your calling doesn't always travel down the street called straight. But glory to God, the Father has promised that when your heart is pure, your motives are ministry, and your gift brings him glory; every valley shall be EXALTED, and every mountain and hill shall be made LOW, and the crooked shall be made STRAIGHT, and the rough places PLAIN! And the glory of the Lord shall be revealed, and ALL flesh shall SEE it TOGETHER! for the mouth of the Lord hath spoken it! (Isaiah 40:4-5 KJV). Never allow your Fears to hinder your Faith! Have a Blessed day, and thanks for allowing me to share the word from a *Pastor's Perspective*…

We are made in the likeness of God! (Genesis 1:26). The Prophet David said: "I will PRAISE thee: for I am fearfully and wonderfully made!" (Psalms 139:14). You are created with an incredible purpose! We are the center of God's creativity and the pleasure in His will! When God made two great lights, day and night, He saw, it was GOOD! Even when God made the beasts of the field after its kind, God saw, it was GOOD! But when God said let us make man in our own IMAGE, this time God saw HIMSELF! Saints of the Most-High, after all was completed, the bible tells us..."God saw everything that he had made, and behold, it was VERY GOOD!" (Genesis 1:31). So, the next time you question your identity and second guess your purpose, remember what God saw when he made you! And remember what God calls you, every time he looks at you! VERY GOOD! It's not important WHAT people call you, it's WHO you answer to that matters. Have a Blessed day, and thanks for allowing me to share the word from a *Pastor's Perspective*...

SEPTEMBER 24

Sometimes the greatest challenges in life, are those that test our patience. Patience is so important that Jesus said, "In your PATIENCE possess ye your souls."(Luke 21:19). Jesus shared the parable in (Luke 8:4-8,10-15), because He wanted the disciples to understand there is WAYWARD ground, ROCKY ground, THORNY ground, and then there is GOOD ground. The Good ground describes those who hear the word, hold the word, and through PATIENCE, harvest the word, and bring forth fruit! The best way to keep YOUR heart in Good ground, is to sow it in Good word! Your patience becomes perfect, when your purpose becomes fruitful! There will be times when you won't have to water, you won't need to prune, you won't even need to give the plant light. All you'll need is a dose of PATIENCE, then watch God give the increase! He's saying: "Just be patient, your destination is just ahead!" Have a Blessed day, and thanks for allowing me to share the word from a *Pastor's Perspective…*

SEPTEMBER 25

The Apostle Paul was inspired to remind us that..."For the Kingdom of God is not food and drink, but RIGHTEOUSNESS, and PEACE, and JOY in the Holy Spirit!" (Romans 14:17). Over time we've misconstrued what the Kingdom of God is and forgotten who can get in! We shun and ostracize those with tattoos, certain shades of make-up, hairstyles, hair color, blue jeans, pants as opposed to a dress or skirt, etc. While God does REQUIRE holiness without compromise, he also makes it clear in this text that you cannot both CRUCIFY and EDIFY then call it Kingdom work! "For he that in these things serveth Christ is ACCEPTABLE to God and men. Let us, therefore, follow after the things which make for PEACE and EDIFY one another." (Romans 14:18-19). When your judgment doesn't leave room for the Grace of God, you can be sure your assessment is not from God! Never judge what you don't understand! Let the Kingdom come! Have a Blessed day, and thanks for allowing me to share the word from a *Pastor's Perspective...*

There is a huge difference between reading the Bible and KNOWING the Author! Today, there are many different opinions, theories, and leaders claiming to know God. But they teach, live, and do things that are totally contrary to the will and word OF God! Jesus said: "Ye hypocrites, well did Isaiah prophesy of you, saying, "This people draw near unto me with their mouth, and honor me with their lips, but their heart is FAR from me!" (Matthew 15:8). The earth is in bad shape! Violence everywhere and events are coming to pass as prophesied. Don't allow yourselves to believe that Men can solve the problems of this world, because they can't! We often forget these words can be applied now and that day..."I never KNEW you, depart from me, ye that work iniquity!" (Matthew 7:23). If you say you KNOW Him, then you should do your best to make a difference because of Him! It's virtually impossible to meet the Lord, and not want to change the world, in which we live...Have a Blessed day, and thanks for allowing me to share the word from a *Pastor's Perspective*...

SEPTEMBER 27

I often say..."God's mercy, is for man's misery!" If I had to explain God's mercy to someone who doesn't understand it, I would say this: "MERCY is the part of God, that won't let our flesh have the last word! Mercy is so divine, it separates our salvation from our current situation! Mercy is a divine

GOD'S GOODNESS
TRUMPS OUR SIN

assignment, but it is also a reminder of how God's goodness trumps our sins and

transgressions!" (Psalms 23:6 & 25:7). Award-winning singer Calvin Hunt sings:
"The justice of God, saw what I had done....
but MERCY saw me, through the Son....
Not what I was, but what I could be......
That's how MERCY, saw me..."
Today, give thanks unto God for seeing His Son in you through the eyes of Mercy. Those who have a heart filled with MERCY can also see exactly what God sees in YOU...Have a Blessed day, and thanks for allowing me to share the word from a *Pastor's Perspective*...

As we prepare for seasonal change, it is imperative that we adjust accordingly. Jesus said...."It is written, Man shall not live by bread alone, but by every word that proceedeth out of the mouth of God." (Matthew 4:4). We need ALL of God's word, to survive ALL the different seasons in our life! During the sunny season things couldn't be better. We don't mind the rainy season cause we can still find our way, but when the forecast includes, "Severe Storm Warning headed your way with Destructive Winds! In the same way that we can't LIVE on bread alone, we can't survive the storm alone! People who perish IN the storm, are those who fail to prepare FOR the storm! Today, make Jesus your storm shelter! Jesus, the living Word rebuked the winds and said to the sea..."Peace Be Still!" (Mark 4:39). And that same authority is still available today! If you trust Jesus before the Storm arrives, you can "Be Still", during the storm...Have a Blessed day, and thanks for allowing me to share the word of from a *Pastor's Perspective*...

SEPTEMBER 29

God is not only omnipotent, omniscient, and omnipresent, He is masterful in all His deity! "There hath no temptation taken you, but such as is COMMON to man: but God is faithful, who will not suffer you to be TEMPTED above that ye are able; but will with the temptation also make a way to ESCAPE, that ye may be able to bear it." (I Corinthians 10:12). First, suffering is COMMON to man. Secondly, the suffering that comes from being TEMPTED is the standard that God uses, to show He is able! And finally, with that very temptation, God uses the commonality of being tempted to limit the effects of bondage, and through his Sovereignty turns burdens into blessings, that you may ESCAPE! If God can be faithful in YOUR mess, imagine His faithfulness in your ministry! Your life, is your ministry! Don't ever lose sight of that! You can't foolproof your ministry if you continue to allow your flesh to make a fool out of you! Use the provided ESCAPE! Have a Blessed day, and thanks for allowing me to share the word from a *Pastor's Perspective*...

"But whosoever looketh into the perfect LAW OF LIBERTY, and continues in it, he being not a forgetful hearer, but a DOER of the WORK, this man shall be BLESSED in his deed!" (James 1:25). We miss a lot of blessings, because of missed assignments! And please realize that missed assignments ARE subject to future judgement! When God calls you to do something, He wants you to look at yourself through the PERFECT LAW OF LIBERTY, not through the smudged lens of the past! It is the perfected law of liberty, that gives your work, its wonder! Jesus said...they will know you by the fruit you bear." (Matthew 7:15). Not by how many people accept the fruit! If you keep operating in the perfect law of liberty, those who are looking for good fruit shall appear, and not only will they be pleased by the fruit, but they will be amazed at how BLESSED the tree is! Don't ever forget, PERFECT Love casts out fear." (I John 4:18). It's up to you, to walk in the BLESSINGS! Have a Blessed day, and thanks for allowing me to share the word from a *Pastor's Perspective...*

OCTOBER 1

Though God has every intention of delivering you from them, one of the most humbling things God does in every believer's life is to allow trials. He declared that He will never leave you, nor forsake you (Hebrews 13:5). The Psalmist wrote: "God is our refuge and strength, a VERY PRESENT HELP in trouble!" (Psalms 46:1). The Prophet Solomon said: "The name of the Lord is a strong tower, the righteous run into it, and are SAFE!" (Proverbs 18:10). So then, why does God allow affliction to linger, when his plan is to deliver? First, that the Son of God might be glorified by it (John 11:4), and secondly, that your faith should not stand in the wisdom of men, but in the POWER of God! (I Corinthians 2:5). God wants you to understand that just because He allows trials, doesn't mean you should lose trust! God uses trials to train your trust! Therefore, if God is using trials to reveal the TRUTH of His love, He wants your faith to be fit enough for the kingdom call! Have a Blessed day, and thanks for allowing me to share the word from a *Pastor's Perspective...*

OCTOBER 2

As the Psalmist reflected on the greatness, majesty, and beauty in all that God had seen him through he concluded: "For this God is our God forever and ever, He will be our guide even unto death!"(Psalms 48:14). To know that God will ALWAYS be our God, is good reason to ALWAYS be His people. Our lives, with all the many things that happen and all the changes, it is nice to know that God is the only thing that will never change! Each of us has probably experienced a number of storms. Storms where the winds blew hard,

PEACE BE STILL

the waters of life raged vehemently, and the rain was so relentless it was blinding. But through it all, not only was God there, He was our shelter! "Great is the Lord, and greatly to be praised." (Psalms 48:1). Today, God wants you to know that whatever storm you're in, He's in it with you and therefore it was just declared, the PERFECT storm! Consequently, you can tell your PEACE, to be still...Have a Blessed day, and thanks for allowing me to share the word from a *Pastor's Perspective...*

289

OCTOBER 3

Have you given much thought to how MUCH God LOVES you? We try to sum it up with.... "For God so Loved the world that He GAVE his only begotten Son!" (John 3:16). We try to evaluate it by..."Greater Love hath no man than this, that a man LAY DOWN his life for his friends." (John 15:13). And, how about: "And why take ye thought for raiment? Consider the lilies of the field, how they grow, they toil not, neither do they spin: And yet Solomon in all his glory was not arrayed like one of these. Wherefore, if God so clothe the grass of the field, which today is, and tomorrow is cast into the oven, shall He not much more clothe you, O ye of little faith!" (Matthew 6:28-30). God wants you to experience His LOVE for you, through His PROVISION for you! God's Love for you is not just for the comfort of today, it's from Everlasting to Everlasting! God LOVES you and there is nothing you can do to change it, but there is something you MUST do to receive it...simply, ACCEPT IT! Have a Blessed day, and thanks for allowing me to share the word from a *Pastor's Perspective...*

OCTOBER 4

It's been said, "What goes up, must come down," however, for the people of God we have but one direction leading to our destiny...UP! When the bible says, "Looking unto" or even "Looking forth," it implies moving forward and progress toward the expected end. In the account of the Apostle Stephen being stoned for his faith, the bible says..."But he, being full of the Holy Spirit, looked UP steadfastly into heaven, and saw the glory of God standing on the right hand of God!" (Acts 5:55). Be sure to maintain faith, knowledge, and an understanding that is constantly moving you in the right direction: UP! Even when Jesus was being tempted by the devil, (Matthew 4:5,8,) When the devil saw he couldn't hinder Jesus in any way the scripture records this: "Then the devil leaveth Him, and, behold, the angels came and ministered unto Him."(vs.11). When the devil sees your focus is fixed on the Father, you'll have all you need to say to every temptation: UP, UP, and AWAY........Have a Blessed day, and thanks for allowing me to share the word from a *Pastor's Perspective...*

OCTOBER 5

When you woke up this morning, it was nothing but the goodness of God that allowed it! Clothed in your right mind, blood still running warm in your veins, roof over your head, food on your table, and health as good as He would have it! The psalmist said: "Enter into His gates with THANKSGIVING, and into His courts with PRAISE! Be thankful unto Him and bless His name!" (Psalms 100:4). Oftentimes we forget, or should I say we lose sight of the fact that, somewhere, someone, is going through the struggle of their life. While it is true, some calamities result from poor decisions, others come out of nowhere and leave unanswered questions and heaviness of heart. If things are seemingly blessed in your life today and God made death behave one more time, so you could live one more day, you need to stop, take a moment, and say, "Lord I THANK YOU!" You ought to find you a spot and give God a PRAISE! Hallelujah, have a Blessed day, and thanks for allowing me to share the word from a *Pastor's Perspective...*

OCTOBER 6

The greatest dynamic duo to EVER exist is not Batman and Robin! It's not Michael Jordan and Scottie Pippen! It's not even Cake and Ice Cream! (smile). It's none other than, Repentance and Forgiveness! Listen to the Apostle Peter's message: "Him hath God exalted with His right hand to be a Prince and a Savior, to give REPENTANCE to Israel, and FORGIVENESS of sins! And we are witnesses of these things, and so is also the Holy Spirit, whom God hath given to them that obey him!" (Acts 5:29-32). When we Repent (turn away from our sin) and ask for Forgiveness (confess and truly tell God we're sorry) the restoration and renewing process immediately ignites revival! God desires our hearts and minds be free from the burden of sin and bondage! Today, start with a one-two punch that knocks your accusers and your past actions completely out! Repent and ask God for Forgiveness and let this day, be your new beginning!! Have a Blessed day, and thanks for allowing me to share the word from a *Pastor's Perspective*...

OCTOBER 7

Did you know that as children of God there are two things, He always wants us to have? His PRESENCE and His PROVISION! The Prophet David had this to say about it: "I have been young, and now am old; yet I have NEVER seen the righteous FORSAKEN nor His SEED begging for bread!" (Psalms 37:25). Even when difficult times arise, God is present and able! Faith is about TRUST not PROOF! The Prophet David encourages us through his knowledge of God by concluding his thoughts of God with this: "He is ever merciful and lendeth, and His Seed is BLESSED!" (Psalms 37:26). As children of the Most-High God we HAVE His PRESENCE and His PROVISION! These two pillars of our faith solidify the security that comes from knowing God for ourselves! The cause of your circumstances is never prepared for God's presence, therefore, be confident in knowing that God has already provided a solution concerning your every situation! Have a Blessed day, and thanks for allowing me to share the word from a *Pastor's Perspective...*

Let me teach you some simple spiritual math: 1 Cross + 3 Nails = Forgiven! This equation is just too easy for some people to receive. Jesus said..."If we confess our sins, He is faithful and just to FORGIVE us our sins, and to cleanse us from ALL unrighteousness!" (I John 1:9). You may be wondering how God can forgive your sin? When Jesus WENT to the cross, he was writing our problems on the board! But when he DIED on the cross, he was erasing the problem, and giving us the answer!! God wants you to know that He specializes in *addition* and *multiplication*...He has no kingdom desire for *subtraction* and *division*! So today is a glorious day for some of you who have struggled with math (smile). God wants you to have your first open book math test, because He truly wants you to get and *A!* 1 Cross + 3 Nails = ____...If you know the answer, tell everyone you know, because this is an each one, teach one test! Lord willing I'll see you all at the Heaven's Academy Graduation! Have a Blessed day, and thanks for allowing me to share the word from a *Pastor's Perspective*...

OCTOBER 9

"It is because of the Lord's Mercies that we are not consumed, because His compassions fail not. They are new every morning, great is thy faithfulness!" (Lamentations 3:22-23). It doesn't matter if yesterday was the BEST day of your life or the WORST day of your life, if God allows you to wake up, it's the NEXT day of your life, full of compassion and brand-new MERCIES! There are moments we want to relive because they were remarkable! Then there are moments we want to forget altogether, because they were just that horrible! Nonetheless, if God woke you up, and the blood is still running warm in your veins, and even if everything is still the same as it was yesterday, Good or Bad, just remember, it's no longer yesterday! This is a New Day, with New Mercies to work with! Anything that falls in God's care, falls into God's hands! His faithfulness is great, but His Love is AMAZING yesterday, today, and forever! Have a Blessed day, and thanks for allowing me to share the word from a *Pastor's Perspective...*

OCTOBER 10

Have you ever said the Lord's prayer then stopped to think about what you just prayed? "Our Father who art in heaven, hallowed be thy name, thy kingdom come, thy will be done, on earth, as it is in heaven. Give us this day our daily bread. And forgive us our debts, as we forgive our debtors. And lead us not into temptation but deliver us from evil. For thine is the kingdom, and the power, and the glory, forever." Amen. (Matthew 6:9-13). What you prayed was this: Father God in heaven, I truly respect your name. I know your kingdom purpose is being fulfilled even as I speak, just as it is being fulfilled in heaven. Please give me all I need to run this race without becoming weary. Strengthen my will, to forgive just like you do, and receive the forgiveness that only you can assure. And Father please let nothing harmful hinder my worship. And because you are the only authority I will listen to, when you return, I promise you will find me doing exactly what you called me to do! Selah! Have a Blessed day, and thanks for allowing me to share the word from a *Pastor's Perspective*...

OCTOBER 11

With all the issues in our world today, it is more obvious than ever that, JESUS is necessary! Our Savior spoke these words over 2,000 years ago...."Without me, you can do nothing!" (John 15:5). Man has become so blinded by technology, the wisdom to gain wealth, knowledge of medicine, and the many success schemes that we have almost abandoned the necessity of Jesus! We have traded being spirit lead for intellect! We are reminded with extremely costly outcomes that intellect is limited, while the Spirit is not only eternal, but willing! The necessity for Jesus is now! From government to the very foundation of family, JESUS is necessary! We are slowly drifting away from the only ONE who can save us from ourselves! Please don't be like many who entered the grave then realized..."It was better to have Jesus and not NEED Him, than to need Jesus and not HAVE Him!" Have a Blessed day, and thanks for allowing me to share the word from a *Pastor's Perspective*...

The believer's life is hidden with Christ in God! (Colossians 3:3). We are not only untouchable, we are undetectable. Our adversary is like a roaring lion seeking whom he may devour (I Peter 5:8). Our secret place is under the shadow of the Almighty! (Psalms 91:1). Sometimes we become vulnerable because of our own agendas, rebellious ways, and deliberate sin, all of which can expose us to an adversary's attack. While at other times, it is God's will that we experience certain things for OUR good! Never lose sight of knowing, God will KEEP, the soul that is COMMITTED to Jesus!" (II Timothy 1:12, John 17:12). Think about it; you weren't left in SIN and instead, you've been redeemed by the blood! Therefore, remind yourself that no matter what you go through, your life is hidden WITH Christ, IN God! And that's all the encouragement you need, to tell your circumstances: "You Can't Touch This!!" Have a Blessed day, and thanks for allowing me to share the word from a *Pastor's Perspective*...

OCTOBER 13

If you were to look back over your life and ponder the moments where God protected and delivered you from the enemy's attack, from your own mistakes, and even from sin, you would truly see that God is a good God! He is so worthy to be praised! While you were yet sinners Christ died for you! (Romans 5:8). "Him who knew no sin, became sin, that we might be made the righteousness of God!" (II Corinthians 5:21). "God is our refuge and strength, a very present help in trouble!" (Psalms 46:1). "His name alone is a strong tower, the righteous run into it, and are SAFE!" (Proverbs 18:10). And "NO weapon formed against you, can prosper!" (Isaiah 54:17). God is reminding us: "He hath not dealt with us after our sins, nor rewarded us according to our iniquities!" (Psalms 103:10). God loves us so much that He gave his only begotten Son as a ransom for us all! No man alive, can out LOVE, the very God that brings LOVE to life! Have a Blessed day, and thanks for allowing me to share the word from a *Pastor's Perspective*...

OCTOBER 14

In 1977 Roberta Flack and Donnie Hathaway released a smash hit entitled: *The Closer I Get to You*. This romantic love song is the epitome of two becoming one. The Apostle James instructs us to..."Draw nigh to God, and He will draw nigh unto you."(James 4:8). The closer we get to God, the more He helps us see; his Love, His purpose, His direction, and ultimately, His Son! It is truly soul stirring to know that the closer I get to God the more heaven is revealed to me! Jesus said..."NO man can come to me, except the Father, who hath sent me, draw him; and I will raise him up at the last day." (John 6:44). Jesus' sole purpose is to have eternal communion with you. He wants you and I to start making our way back to Him NOW. "For your redemption draweth near!" (Luke 21:28). We were separated because of sin, but because of His atoning blood at the cross, He's made a way for all to be redeemed! He ransomed what He loved, because He wants to keep, what He's called! Have a Blessed day, and thanks for allowing me to share the word from a *Pastor's Perspective…*

OCTOBER 15

"Faith without Works is dead." (James 2:17). But did you know that before Faith can really prove itself to you, you must apply yourself to it! "ADD to your Faith virtue, to virtue, knowledge, to knowledge, self-control, to self-control, patience, to patience, godliness, to godliness, brotherly kindness!" (II Peter 1:5-7). Adding these character traits to your faith, reveals that your faith has all it needs to be OF God, and IN God! If you don't exhibit any of these qualities in your works, the bible declares your faith is dead! And God, is the God of the living, not the dead! (Luke 20:38). Because faith is your belief in a God on the move, you have to trust God when He moves! Sometimes His moves are so different from the ones you would have taken, that you question whether it's God at all! But let me remind you, God has countless ways of working His wonder! Don't forget, Faith is about trust, not proof! Today, allow your faith to reveal its character, by trusting God with its contents. Have a Blessed day, and thanks for allowing me to share the word from a *Pastor's Perspective*...

OCTOBER 16

As believer's there are times when we CAN'T see with our eyes, what we CAN see in our spirits. These moments are called VISIONS. I believe these encounters provide our possibilities with purpose! The Prophet Solomon said: "Where there is no vision, the people perish." (Proverbs 29:18). The purpose of a vision is to keep your hope alive! Visions have the Power to transform a trial into a triumph, a burden into a blessing, and rejection into rejoicing! Jesus said..."The lamp of the body is the eye, and if therefore thine eye be healthy, thy whole body shall be full of light."(Matthew 6:22). Hence, because VISIONS give our possibilities purpose, God expects our purpose to expand! Why? Because just like in the Prophet Jeremiah's day; when the Daughter of Zion's men would not seek the Lord..."The prophets also find no visions from the Lord!" (Lamentations 2:9). Don't let what's destined to live in you DIE for lack of vision! With God, all things are POSSIBLE (Matthew 19:26). Have a Blessed day, and thanks for allowing me to share the word from a *Pastor's Perspective*...

The only direction any believer should want to GROW, is UP! Our desire to go farther starts with a determination to be better! Listen to the heart of the Psalmist: "Lord, my heart is not haughty (arrogant), nor mine eyes lofty (high-minded), neither do I exercise myself in great matters, or things too high for me!" (Psalms 131:1). When we become self-proclaimed judges, analysts, and examiners of others, our understanding becomes ingrown in us! Anything ingrown, is growing, in the wrong direction! Today, ask yourself: "Am I so involved in the affairs of others, that I'm actually hindering my own growth? People of God, if your self-proclaimed growth is constantly surrounded by GRIEF and not GRACE, I strongly advise you to stop right where you are and ask God for direction! Ingrown unrighteousness, is just as painful as overgrown grief! Be sure to examine yourself often to make sure that whatever is growing inside of you, is growing in the right direction! Have a Blessed day, and thanks for allowing me to share the word from a *Pastor's Perspective...*

OCTOBER 18

Bad motives can corrupt good ministry! Obviously, Ministry is the work of a Minister. It is easily understood that ministry is spiritual work, with religious affiliation according to one's core beliefs. But the real definition of ministry is: to Serve! When Jesus Pointed out the motive of the prodigal son's brother, He revealed how we can sometimes misconstrue the work of ministry, for that disappointment found only in misery! (Luke 15:29). Misery can disguise itself as a form of ministry! How? Because of its ability to serve with a self-seeking understanding! Anytime YOUR gain, is more important than God's glory, YOUR ministry is nothing more than misery in disguise! The reason why so many believers struggle to see the JOY in serving Jesus is because, they haven't taken a moment to understand the word JOY! You can't minister, with a mind filled with misery...and you can't serve the Lord, when everything is all about YOU! Have a Blessed day, and thanks for allowing me to share the word from a *Pastor's Perspective*...

OCTOBER 19

I was taught early in my Christian walk that emotion without devotion promotes commotion! There is so much going on in church today, that it's hard to decipher *Praise* from *Performance*! But there is One who is never fooled and who knows exactly who's who and what's what! If Jesus is asking you: "And why call ye me, Lord, Lord and do not the things which I say?" (Luke 6:46). It's because He already has deep knowledge of you. "I know thy works, that thou art neither cold nor hot. I would that thou was cold or hot! So then, because thou art lukewarm, and neither cold nor hot, I will spew thee out of my mouth!" (Revelation 3:15-16). Jesus has an expectation of you that will never change! He is ALWAYS looking for a heart of pure DEVOTION! With Jesus, He knows who's in the church, and He knows who the church is NOT in! It's one thing to fool each other, but it's an entirely different thing to *make* a fool of yourself! Because in the end, it won't be a laughing matter! Have a Blessed day, and thanks for allowing me to share the word from a *Pastor's Perspective*...

"For the preaching of the cross is to them that are perishing foolishness, but unto us who are saved, it is the power of God!" (I Corinthians 1:18). So why was the CROSS the chosen symbol of salvation? I believe the duality of the cross is that it represents the two main components connected to our existence...Life and Death! It was ON the cross that Christ died, but it was also AT the cross he brought life! The cross is sacred because it is symbolic of both light and darkness. Either way, it is either our meeting place, or our place of departure! And only you can decide that! This morning, let the preaching of the cross reveal the truth of redemption, so you can receive the glorious truth God promises for all your suffering. (Romans 8:18). It's been said, no CROSS, no CROWN...but let's not forget, there will be no REJOICING, for those who aren't REDEEMED! Let what Jesus did on the cross, reveal what's going on in your life! The first step to glory, starts at the foot of the CROSS! Have a Blessed day, and thanks for allowing me to share the word from a *Pastor's Perspective*...

OCTOBER 21

Have you ever praised God for all He's done through others towards perpetuating your purpose? The providence of God, is His protective spiritual care! The Apostle Paul understood the importance of acknowledging those who labored in our purpose, but he had a deeper understanding of who is to be glorified for the increase of our providence! Listen to how he addresses the Corinthian church concerning this matter: "I have planted, Apollos watered, but God gave the increase." (I Corinthians 3:6). We should never lose sight of the fact that, "In Him we live, move, and have our being." (Acts 17:28). Please understand, God should be the fulfillment of all that brings you contentment! Your purpose and all your aspirations can yield temporary satisfaction, but only God in all His wonder can give you lasting increase! I dare you to give all you have to God, and then trust him to give it all back to you and then some! Have a Blessed day, and thanks for allowing me to share the word from a *Pastor's Perspective...*

If you could trade everything you're going THROUGH, for all that Jesus has prepared for YOU, would you be ready? I mean, are you living your life rapture-ready? Or has everything you've allowed to ENTER your life, taken your focus off the day you will EXIT this life? Jesus taught a parable about ten virgins, five wise and five foolish. (Matthew 25:1-13). One of the lessons here; we spend so much of our time sacrificing for what we WANT, and then the rest of our time begging for what we NEED! But the greater lesson in this parable is this: when Jesus does return, there will be no time to GET ready! You must BE ready! While it is true, life is to be lived, it is also true that this life has an unavoidable expiration date! There is nothing wrong with the pursuit of happiness, but don't allow it to pave the way to Hell! Sometimes we take for granted all that Jesus has prepared for us. But the day is coming when all those who aren't rapture-ready, will be rapture rejected! Have a Blessed day, and thanks for allowing me to share the word from a *Pastor's Perspective*...

OCTOBER 23

It's amazing how the expression of praise, helps remove mental clutter! The Psalmist wrote: "Why art thou cast down, O my soul? And why art thou disquieted within me? Hope in God; for I shall yet PRAISE him, who is the health of my countenance, and my God!" (Psalms 43:5). Sometimes you not only have to encourage yourself, you need to have your own Praise party! And you know what makes Praise so powerful? It can convert pressure into promise! O my brothers and sisters when you allow praise to minister to your soul, your circumstances don't stand a chance! A true praise offered to God is the result of a complete trust in God! Know this however, because PRAISE is a God fueled power, He will not allow HIS power to be housed in the wrong heart! If God is worthy to be praised, we must be willing to be HIS! Please remember saints, Praise is not just what we SAY to our circumstance ...Praise is what we DO in our soul! Nothing is sweeter, than to feed your soul PRAISE! Have a Blessed day, and thanks for allowing me to share the word from a *Pastor's Perspective*...

When the prophet David wrote, "Let the words of my MOUTH and the meditation of my HEART, be acceptable in THY SIGHT, O Lord, my STRENGTH and my redeemer," (Psalms 19:14). I truly believe he was speaking from the depths of a heart filled with spiritual commitment. He wanted all that he and God shared to be totally pure and completely holy! When what we say and what we think, is acceptable to God, our spirits can rest assured of God's attention, and our hearts can find comfort in God's provision. The souls that find solace through holiness, are never really victimized by a spirit of heaviness! Their perspective is so Father filtered, that their faith in Him is untouchable!! When God deems your intentions holy and acceptable, there is no reason to let your heart be troubled, about ANYTHING! When holy meditation promotes holy dedication, your peace can be still, and your thoughts can still be filled with peace. Have a Blessed day, and thanks for allowing me to share the word from a *Pastor's Perspective*...

OCTOBER 25

The Apostle Paul teaches that a professing saint who responds to calamity and circumstances with doubt, fear, and uncertainty has a "FORM of godliness, but they are denying the power thereof!" (II Timothy 3:5). On the other hand, the Apostle James points out that when a professing saint responds to adversity through confident prayer: "The effectual, fervent PRAYER of a righteous man, availeth much!" (James 5:16). As children of the Most-High God, our prayers have Most High God power! When Your PRAYERS Are Purposed through unwavering belief, your results are manifested through unstoppable POWER! When the Apostle Paul wrote: "Be anxious for nothing, but in EVERYTHING, by PRAYER and SUPPLICATION with THANKSGIVING, let your requests be made known unto God" (Philippians 4:6), he was letting us know that when we bring our heart's desire to God, we can thank Him in advance, for what we know He is able to do! Have a Blessed day, and thanks for allowing me to share the word from a *Pastor's Perspective*...

OCTOBER 26

The 23rd Psalm is one that every born-again
believer should commit to memory! Saints of
God, what makes this Psalm such a spiritual
keepsake, is that it reveals the relevancy of
prophecy. "The LORD Is my Shepherd, I
shall not want... Yea, though I walk through
the valley of the shadow of death, I will fear
no evil; for thou art with me; thy rod and thy
staff they comfort me. Thou preparest a table
before me in the presence of mine enemies....
Surely goodness and mercy shall follow me all
the days of my life; and I will dwell in the
house of the Lord forever." The beauty of this
Psalm, is its sustaining comfort! This scripture
doesn't just talk about being cared for by
God, it brings the manifestation of God's
providence to your circumstance! Take a
moment to meditate on the entire Psalm, I
mean really meditate on it. After you've given
it some time to sink in, watch how this flow
of truth adds to your faith and comforts your
heart! There is no need to WANT, what's
already in God's WILL for you! Have a
Blessed day, and thanks for allowing me to
share the word from a *Pastor's Perspective...*

OCTOBER 27

As we grow in grace and yield our hearts to God's ways, our daily prayer is generally along these lines..."Teach me to do thy will; for thou art my God. Thy Spirit is good; lead me into the land of uprightness." (Psalms 143:10). The Spirit of God is never wrong, partial, nor carnal! The person of the Holy Spirit is only one way...HOLY! It is through God's holiness that His leadership helps us walk upright. Because we are prone to waver and wander, God assigned GOODNESS and MERCY to follow the believer all the days of our lives! (Psalms 23:6). The leadership of the Lord always leads us in the path of RIGHTEOUSNESS for His name sake! His desire for you and I is that our will becomes His! Surrender is sweet when the outcome is Salvation. Today, allow the Spirit of God to lead you in the path of righteousness, so you can inhabit the land of uprightness. What better place to settle down, than the place God has prepared for you? Have a Blessed day, and thanks for allowing me to share the word from a *Pastor's Perspective*...

I'm realizing now more than ever before that the more *I* desire to be humble, the more *God* adds to my happiness! God has many ways of bringing about humility. Chastisement, affliction, trials, deficiencies of all sorts, and sometimes even death. But when WE desire to be humble in the sight of the Lord, the scripture says, "He shall lift you up!" (James 4:10). Now you may ask, lift me up how? The answer: in every way! You see, a humble heart is to God what happiness is to us: a reason to smile! But do you know what really happens when our humility touches the heart of God? He giveth *more* GRACE! (James 4:6). And any heart, that has an abundance of GRACE covering it, has good reason to rejoice! So today, "Humble yourself under the mighty hand of God, that He may exalt you in due time." (I Peter 5:6). When God lifts you up because of your humility, Grace doesn't allow even your humanity to steal the happiness that fuels your heart! Have a Blessed day, and thanks for allowing me to share the word from a *Pastor's Perspective...*

OCTOBER 29

Allow me to ask a question: Are the things that matter in your life, making a difference to your life?" Jesus said: "Verily, verily, I say unto you, except a grain of wheat fall to the ground and die, it abideth alone; but if it die, it bringeth forth much fruit." (John 12:24). Essentially, when a kernel of wheat is buried in the soil and dies, it dies alone. But its death will produce a plentiful harvest and many new kernels of wheat. As believer's, everything that matters in our lives, should make a difference in the lives of others! We should always be trying to establish a kingdom purpose that has a kingdom impact! Even in the natural sense, before something can live, something else must die. In addition, although the wheat dies alone, the yielded life is what really matters! Today, dare to let your life make a difference, through your willingness to die as a grain of wheat...alone! Jesus moved the multitude with the word when He preached to them, but He delivered generations by faith, when He died for them...ALONE! Have a Blessed day, and thanks for allowing me to share the word from a *Pastor's Perspective*...

Trusting God requires having the knowledge that He is not only ABLE, but also WILLING! The Prophet Solomon wrote..."Trust in the Lord with all thine heart and lean not unto thine own understanding." (Proverbs 3:9). There are times when you'll have to TRUST God on your own! Why? Because you KNOW him, for yourself! This doesn't mean you're walking alone, rather, though none go with you, your focus remains on following Jesus. Trusting God is knowing that He will be a, "Lamp unto your feet, and a light unto your path."(Psalms 119:105). It's knowing He's ordering your steps and directing your path for his righteousness sake! But it also requires a willingness to follow, with nothing more than YOUR faith! When you TRUST God, you're declaring to those all around you, my Father in heaven and my Faith within, have met! And because my Faith knows my Father, my Heart refuses to fear! (Job 13:15). You can't TRY to TRUST God...you either do or you don't! Have a Blessed day, and thanks for allowing me to share the word from a *Pastor's Perspective*...

Many have made this day about ghouls and goblins, costumes and masks. The truth surrounding this pagan celebration is found in its name: Hallow-een! Jesus told us to pray saying, "Our Father...Hallowed be thy name! (Matthew 6:9). Jesus wanted us to give the Father's name a holy reverence that would be set apart and Hallowed through our worship. Quite different from parading around dressed like witches, warlocks, and other images! The enemy, on the other hand, has always tried to duplicate God's glory by making jest out of being lost! Hallowing anything apart from the Father has no substance. It's void, its empty, and it certainly doesn't glorify God! I know to some it's just fun and laughter, but the futility of its indoctrination is not! Today celebrate because this is the day the Lord has made! And know that God always appreciates a Hallelujah party honoring His name, especially if it involves children, candy, friends, and worship! Have a Blessed day, and thanks for allowing me to share the word from a *Pastor's Perspective...*

This is the day that the Lord has made, let us rejoice and be glad in it! (Psalms 118:24). Let's celebrate and rejoice over the three most amazing words Jesus ever spoke..."IT IS FINISHED!" (John 19: 30). His assignment was complete! Our Sin atonement was made! Our past, present, and future falls, flaws, and failures were fixed! Our hope was restored! And last, but certainly not least, death was defeated by His resurrection! It is no wonder saints all over the world celebrate the completion of His triumphant work! IT IS FINISHED are words that should NEVER leave our conscience! What Jesus did for us, can't be repaid! It is such a glorious honor and privilege to celebrate the life and work Jesus FINISHED! His life here on earth was short, His ministry was shorter, but His WORKS are ETERNAL! What Jesus FINISHED *then,* is *now* FATHER approved! Though the crowd shouted, "Crucify Him," what was accomplished at the cross, could not be reversed by the crowd! Have a Blessed day, and thanks for allowing me to share the word from a *Pastor's Perspective...*

NOVEMBER 2

As I sit and reminisce on some old school gospel songs; *Can't Nobody, do me Like Jesus! This Joy, That I Have! Walk With me LORD, walk with me*, my mind immediately recalls Jesus' promise..."Lo, I am with you always, even until the ends of the world, Amen." (Matthew 28:20). Amen means, "So be it." When Jesus concluded with those words to the disciples, he was indicating: This will never change, because, *I* will never change! Blessed assurance from Jesus, is the greatest comfort you'll ever receive! Knowing that Jesus said, "No matter what happens in your life, I will always be there with you," is not only encouraging, it's blessed assurance! A promise of God's presence, keeps problems in proper perspective! There is no situation too big for our Savior! I implore you to smile at adversity! Why? Because your redeemer lives! (Job 19:25). And you can rest assured...*Jesus Will Fix it, After a While*! Have a Blessed day, and thanks for allowing me to share the word from a *Pastor's Perspective*...

NOVEMBER 3

There are many things that truly amaze me about God! He is such a wonder, that at times I'm speechless concerning the power and authority we have in him! Jesus said..."Verily, verily, I say unto you, he that BELIEVETH on me, the works that I do shall he do also; and GREATER works than these shall he do, because I go unto my Father!" (John 14:12). As believers we are equipped with authority to achieve things that surpass our natural abilities. While it is true that believers and unbelievers alike possess talents, when you're GIFTED, your abilities are spiritually elevated from common wonder to incredible! The God authority in you, is the *GREATER than He*, in you! Just think about this...If I possess the power of the Almighty to do GREATER things through my belief, imagine all the things I've left undone because of my unbelief! We've all had moments when we humbly asked God..."LORD, I believe, but help my unbelief!" (Mark 9:24) Have a Blessed day, and thanks for allowing me to share the word from a *Pastor's Perspective*...

NOVEMBER 4

King David said something to God that is both inspiring and encouraging. "For thy name's sake, O Lord, pardon mine iniquity, for it is great!" (Psalms 25:11). He said this AFTER his many trespasses and sins and because David was after the heart of God, He created a new heart in him! (Psalms 51:10). Listen to what he said, "Oh, keep my soul, and deliver me; let me not be ashamed; for I put my trust in thee. Let INTEGRITY and UPRIGHTNESS preserve me, for I wait on thee." (Psalms 25: 20-21). Your past is something you can't outrun, nor outlive! The only way to avoid the burden of Shame, is to stop listening to the voice of the past! Repent then walk by faith. As you allow INTEGRITY and UPRIGHTNESS to preserve you, strengthen you, and encourage you, you'll begin to shed the layers of shame, like unwanted clothing! The Lord will PERFECT, everything concerning you!" (Psalms 138:8) There's no reason for shame, when sure of God's Love...! Have a Blessed day, and thanks for allowing me to share the word from a *Pastor's Perspective*...

NOVEMBER 5

Jesus said, "Therefore, doth my Father love me, because I lay down my life, that I might take it again. NO MAN TAKETH IT FROM ME! But I lay it down of myself! I have power to lay it down, and I have power to take it again!" (John 10:17-18). Jesus did more than just give up his life for us, he actually saved US from US! We like to blame all our iniquities on the devil. We blame him for everything defiled and destructive! Everything lascivious and lustful! Everything contaminated and condemned! But all these variables mean nothing without US making the choice to give life to SIN! While the devil is a force to be reckoned with, Hell is a choice! Jesus laid down His life, to save yours! Death is unavoidable in the natural, but so is Hell in the spiritual, if you don't accept Jesus! The devil's destiny was set long before you and I committed our first offense. It was not for the devil but for us that Jesus laid down his life, so we could stand redeemed before Him! Hallelujah! Have a Blessed day, and thanks for allowing me to share the word from a *Pastor's Perspective...*

NOVEMBER 6

While we will soon enjoy Thanksgiving festivities with family and friends, somebody somewhere may be going through unthinkable hardship and loss. Perhaps many whom they thought would be there for them, have left them all alone. This reminds me of Jesus' encounter with the disciples (John 6:60-66) when he tried their discipleship by questioning their spiritual understanding (vs.61) and then their spiritual commitment (vs.66). Jesus endured all things for us, because He wants us to rest assured that we can count on him! Nothing that ever took place in His life, took His focus off OURS! And that, all by itself, is something to give thanks for! Today, if you know of someone who could really use your help, don't turn your back on them. Ask Jesus to strengthen their heart, by giving them the LOVE that's in yours. Sometimes all they need is to hear, "I'm here with you, and I'm here for you." The best way to give THANKS, is to give BACK! Have a Blessed day, and thanks for allowing me to share the word from a *Pastor's Perspective…*

The most amazing thing about being born again is that despite everything we must endure until we finally get TO God, we know we are heaven bound! Behold, what manner of Love the Father hath bestowed upon US, that we should be called the children of God! Therefore, the world knoweth us not, because it knew him not. Beloved, NOW!! ARE WE THE CHILDREN OF GOD, and it doth not yet appear what we shall be, but we know that, when He shall appear, WE SHALL BE LIKE HIM! We shall SEE Him as He is. (I John 3:1-2). You'll be like HIM, who called you to BE! And I believe the Apostle John started the text off with "Behold" because the truth of who we really are, is too much for some of us to grasp just yet. With God, the color of your eyes, the length of your hair, the size of your waist, nor your complexion will matter on that day! Because in the twinkle of an eye, you'll be a twin to the trinity! Just, BEHOLD that! Have a Blessed day, and thanks for allowing me to share the word from a *Pastor's Perspective...*

"You are the salt of the earth, but if the salt loses its flavor, how can it be seasoned?" (Matthew 5:13). Christians are not BLAND people who lack the flavor of Favor! We are salt with the capability of seasoning every situation on this earth! And we have been given this flavor, so that the people on earth can "Taste, and see that the Lord is Good!" (Psalms 34:8). Every word you speak, every song you sing, every prayer you pray, every testimony you share, every heart you touch, for the glory of God, you're seasoning the earth! God's expectation of us being the salt of the earth, is that, there will be so much flavor in the earth, that others can literally eat from our hearts! People don't turn down a word that's seasoned with perfection! They turn down words seasoned with corruption! You'll never be able to season a BLESSED soul, with a BLAND word! But you can BLESS a BLAND soul, with a seasoned word! When your Favor has Flavor, our Heavenly Father gets the glory! Have a Blessed day, and thanks for allowing me to share a word from a *Pastor's Perspective...*

NOVEMBER 9

Sometimes we act as if God needs us, more than we need Him! We rebel against His call! We reject His Son! And then we expect His Sovereignty to be our safety net! I believe we all need to be reminded of the Divine Authority and reverence GOD deserves! "For every beast of the forest is mine! and the cattle upon a thousand hills are mine! I KNOW all the fowls of the mountains, and the wild beasts of the field are mine! If I were hungry, I would not tell thee!! For the world is mine!! And ALL the fullness thereof! Offer unto God THANKSGIVING!! And pay thy vows unto the MOST-HIGH!" (Psalms 50:7-14). We need to give thanks that His MERCIES are new every morning, and that his compassion, despite our rebellion, never fails! (Lamentations 3:22-23). Today, be THANKFUL that He who owns it all, is always willing to share it with YOU! Taking our eyes off self and praising the ONE who owns the cattle on a thousand hills does the heart good. Have a Blessed day, and thanks for allowing me to share the word from a *Pastor's Perspective*…

NOVEMBER 10

Do you know that when you were SAVED in JESUS' name, you inherited gifts that would make your name GREAT! Accepting Jesus brought you ETERNAL life and got your name written in HEAVEN! (Luke 10:20). Secondly, you now have a spiritual endowment so powerful that you can LOVE unconditionally (I Corinthians 13:4-8), FORGIVE others from a pure heart (James 3:17), and have the word of RECONCILIATION committed to you, because of your commitment to Christ! (II Corinthians 5:19). And last, but not at all least, you are a living Epistle connected by Faith, to THE name, that is above EVERY name! (Philippians 2:9). Once saved, He promises to lead you in the path of righteousness for HIS name's sake (Psalms 23:3), and in return, all that you do for him, will be remembered by all, as a memorial unto YOU! (Matthew 26:6-13). Serve and accept the name of JESUS now, so yours will be respected and remembered when you leave. Have a Blessed day, and thanks for allowing me to share the word from a *Pastor's Perspective*...

There are times that for Jesus to develop CHAMPION faith IN you, He must allow extreme CHALLENGES to happen TO you! When Jesus said..."And I am glad for your sakes that I was not there, to the intent ye might believe, nevertheless, let us go to him."(John 11:15). The disciple did not understand what Jesus meant by, "Our friend Lazarus sleepeth, BUT I GO, that I may awake him out of sleep"(John 11:11). Though, He makes it very clear what manner of sleep he was speaking of when he said, "Lazarus is dead!" (John 11:14). God will sometimes let death challenge your faith, hurt challenge your heart, struggle challenge your strength, and if that's not enough, take His time answering your prayer! But could you imagine hearing Jesus say to YOU, "I am glad I was not there, but I hope you still believe!" Those pivotal moments when we seem to need Jesus most, are the moments Jesus wants us to BELIEVE even more! Have a Blessed day, and thanks for allowing me to share the word of encouragement from a *Pastor's Perspective*...

NOVEMBER 12

Our lives are a series of ups and downs, but our God is a deliverer through them all! We have a Testimony every time we've come through a test! You can speak those things that be not, as though they were (Romans 14:17). You can speak to the mountain until it moves (Mark 11:23). You can even P.U.S.H. (Pray Until Something Happens) (Matthew 21:22), but none of that becomes Testimony, until you're delivered from the test! And so, with each chapter in life, we build our testimonial resume! The Lord wants you delivered so you can close this chapter of your life and shout OVERCOME! And they OVERCAME him by the BLOOD of the LAMB, and by the WORD of their TESTIMONY!" (Revelation 12:11). The most encouraging words you could give to anyone going through something is...GOD IS ABLE TO DELIVER! Have a Blessed day, and thanks for allowing me to encourage you from a *Pastor's Perspective*...

"Therefore, being justified by Faith, we have peace with God! By whom also we have access by Faith into His GRACE in which we Stand and Rejoice in Hope of the glory of God!" (Romans 5:1-2). The bible tells us, "For as much, then, as the children are partakers of flesh and blood, He also himself likewise took part of the same, that through death he might destroy him that had the power of death, that is, the devil!" And deliver them who, through Fear of death were all their lifetime subject to bondage!"(Hebrews 2:14-15). A life sentence

in the natural, is BAD, but a life sentence in the spiritual is far WORSE! However, as believers by faith, and because of our acceptance of the blood sacrifice and the gift of Grace...the charges against us were dropped and the verdict is NOT GUILTY!! Remember, Jesus can't overturn your life sentence, if you don't turn your life over to Him! Have a Blessed day, and thanks for allowing me to share the word from a *Pastor's Perspective*...

NOVEMBER 14

We've all heard people say, "Only God Can Judge Me!" Obviously, there are a whole lot of people who haven't read, "Do you not know that the saints (God's people) shall judge the world? And if the world shall be JUDGED by YOU, are you not worthy to JUDGE the smallest matters?" (I Corinthians 6:2). What we often refer to as judgement, relates to actions of the flesh! If you saw someone in a store put a candy bar in their pocket without paying for it, would it be JUDGING them to say they are stealing? No! Because your analysis is measured against what is acceptable according to law! Hence, when spiritual matters are in question, they are JUDGED by the standards of Heaven and it is God who governs the standard. It may NOT always be about people judging you, it might be Jesus revealing how low you've allowed your standards to drop! Judge your own behavior by examining God's STANDARDS and you'll remain in right STANDING. Have a Blessed day, and thanks for allowing me to share the word from a *Pastor's Perspective*…

NOVEMBER 15

Grammy award-winning Gospel artist Kirk Franklin and The Family released a platinum single entitled *The Reason Why I Sing*. This song revolutionized worship in its time because, it spoke to every form of oppression. Job experienced physical affliction, personal loss, and relentless outside accusations, yet he declared, "Lo, mine eye hath seen all this, mine ear hath heard and understood it! What you know, the same do I know also! I am not inferior unto you! Surely, I would speak to the Almighty, and I desire to REASON with God!!" (Job 13:1-3). If you maintain a reason to Sing, Rejoice, Hope, and Believe, you'll see that the Lord will speaking directly to you in the midst of your situation so you can, "Be ready always to give to every man that asks you a REASON for the hope that is in you!" (I Peter 3:15). As long as we have Jesus, whatever HAPPENS in life is no match for the HALLELUJAHS in your heart! He's the REASON why we sing. Have a Blessed day, and thanks for allowing me to share the word from a *Pastor's Perspective*...

NOVEMBER 16

This generation seems to be very liberal and tolerant of unrighteousness. It celebrates sinfulness and mocks the ways of God! The word of God expressly says, "Be not deceived, God is not mocked, for whatever a man soweth, that shall he also reap!" (Galatians 6:7). We seem to have forgotten what the scriptures say about God's perspective on unrighteousness: "And God saw that the wickedness of man was great in the earth, and that every imagination of thought of his heart was only evil CONTINUALLY! And it repented the Lord that he had made man on the earth, and it GRIEVED him at his heart! And the Lord said, I will DESTROY man whom I have created, from the face of the earth!" (Genesis 6:5-7). You may have the liberty to live loose in this earth, but it is sure that you won't have the liberty to leave the place of HELL! Give God some thought, while He's still thinking of you...Have a Blessed day, and thanks for allowing me to share the word from a *Pastor's Perspective*...

The Psalmist declared, "As the deer panteth after the water brooks, so panteth my soul after thee, O God!" (Psalms 42:1). Jesus is always willing and able to quench a thirsty soul! His unlimited source is made known through the account of the woman at the well. There, at the place she frequented daily to draw water, she was instead drawn to the soul-stirring sustenance that leads to salvation (John 4:7-15). Many things in life leave us wanting, hungering, and thirsting! And because of their connection TO life, we deem these sensations necessities. As was the case with this woman. She went to the well daily but left unfulfilled every time! Jesus made mention of the water that would take away her thirst and become a "Well of water springing up into everlasting life." (vs.14). Her IMMEDIATE response was: "Sir, give me this water, that I thirst no more, and have to come back here!" (vs.15). God wants you to know, that He can also fill your heart with something that even the deepest well can't hold! Come, drink from the well that never runs dry. Have a Blessed day, and thanks for allowing me to share the word from a *Pastor's Perspective…*

NOVEMBER 18

Have you ever had the disturbing experience of watching while others fall and/or experienced your own decline? No matter the reason for a fall, whether it's refusing to give life over to the Lord or poor management, falling is no laughing matter!! Sure, you can have temporary success, momentary magical moments, and periods, even long periods where you seem to have outrun hardships, but Jesus warned, "If your foundation is not on the ROCK, your falling is inevitable, sooner or later, and GREAT will be that fall!" (Matthew 7:24-27). When Jesus said, "Without me, you can do nothing," (John 15:5), He wasn't speaking of short-term EFFORTS, he was speaking of long term EFFECTS! God wants us to realize that the Temporal should not trump the Permanent. (II Corinthians 4:18). Often, we fall because we are quick to stamp PERMANENT on things that could never be anything other than TEMPORARY! Why fall when you can PERMANENTLY lean on the Lord! Put your faith in Him and avoid a fall. Have a Blessed day, and thanks for allowing me to share the word from a *Pastor's Perspective…*

NOVEMBER 19

There will be times when people you thought you knew, will forget your labor of love! But God will never forget it, nor your love! In fact, scriptures reveal, "For God is not unrighteous to forget your WORK, and LABOR of love, which ye have showed toward his NAME, in that ye have ministered to the saints, and do minister!" (Hebrews 6:10). And because you have purposed in your heart to let Jesus remain the same yesterday, today, and forever in you, God wants you to know; "O Jacob and Israel, for thou art my servant: I have formed thee, thou art my servant: O Israel thou shalt not be forgotten of me!"(Isaiah 44:21). Many fail to realize that the LOVE of God is a kingdom commandment! And that those who serve through love will never be forgotten! Therefore, let all you do for God, be a labor of LOVE, knowing, that your labor is not in vain! (I Corinthians 15:58). Those who remember to LOVE, will always leave something to remember. Have a Blessed day, and thanks for allowing me to share the word from a *Pastor's Perspective...*

NOVEMBER 20

King David was encouraged that in spite of all his sin, his moments of doubt, and all the blood his hands had shed, he knew that when his life on this side of glory was over, he would depart forgiven, restored, and would experience the following truth: "As for me, I will behold thy face in righteousness, I shall be SATISFIED, when I awake, with thy likeness!" (Psalms 17:18). Question is: if today was "that day" and you're standing before Jesus, would he be SATISFIED with how you lived, and would you be SATISFIED with your eternal destiny? Remember, your birth deeply affected those who were expecting your arrival. Your death will affect those who weren't ready for you to leave. But, on the day you meet Jesus face to face, YOUR decisions will only affect YOU! The Psalmist said, "With long life will God SATISFY him who loves him and will show him his salvation!" (Psalms 91:16). God SATISFIES the longing soul (Psalms 107:9). Have a Blessed day, and thanks for allowing me to share the word from a *Pastor's Perspective…*

The Apostle Paul asked: "Know ye not that ye are the temple of God, and that the Holy Spirit dwelleth in you?" (I Corinthians 3:16). Wherever there is a born-again believer, there's a CHURCH! And because there are born again believers EVERYWHERE, there are CHURCHES everywhere. However, it's not enough to just be a CHURCH, God wants you to be a CHURCH of purpose and power! Why? Because the Holy Spirit has made your SOUL, its sanctuary! The Spirit of God wants to preach the message of your ministry from the pulpit of your heart! How many churches have you passed along your journey where there's a sign over the door, but no power in the building! When the Apostle Paul asked, "Know ye not that you are the temple of God?"...He was really saying, if you give the Holy Spirit a dwelling place, wherever YOU are, becomes the perfect place to have CHURCH! Your CHURCH will never lose power, if God is PRESENT! Have a Blessed day, and thanks for allowing me to share the word from a *Pastor's Perspective...*

NOVEMBER 22

The Apostle Paul indicated that circumstantial uncertainties can befall any man, at any time, "Wherefore, let him that thinketh he standeth take heed lest he fall!" (I Corinthians 10:12). In other words, don't be so high minded to believe that LIFE could never happen to you! Because truly, LIFE happens to all of us! Things happen that are often not understood, and certainly never forgotten! And because God is God, he's often blamed for not protecting us from certain things. And yet, LIFE happened to Jesus as well. So much so, that in the flesh he wanted answers: "My God, My God, why hast thou forsaken me?" (Matthew 27:46). God had not forsaken Him, but pain and loss feels the same to us all. (Hebrews 4:15). Therefore, cherish life and listen to the words of the Apostle James…"Whereas ye know not what shall be on the next day. For what is your LIFE? It is even a vapor that appeareth for a little time, and then vanisheth away!" (James 4:14). Troubles won't last…Have a Blessed day, and thanks for allowing me to share the word from a *Pastor's Perspective*…

The joy of not being judged by Jesus on "that day" (Matthew 7:22) provides the motivation to be obedient in this day! Some people pray like heaven is right next door but live as though hell doesn't exist! To secure your soul salvation you must repent and be saved then live as thou you have a savior! There is a peace that accompanies right living. We spend too much time wrestling with agnostic theories, trying to convince those who say they would rather be convicted than converted, and then we try to exalt our efforts by becoming judge and jury over things out of our spiritual jurisdiction! However, there is coming a day when all the wrestling will cease! Those who rejected Jesus will come face to face with the righteous judge! Nevertheless, "Notwithstanding, in this rejoice not, that the spirits are subject unto you! But rather, rejoice because YOUR names are written in the Lamb's book of life! (Luke 10:20). The only way to avoid the judgement on that day, is to accept the joy of salvation offered in this one! Have a Blessed day, and thanks for allowing me to share the word from a *Pastor's Perspective…*

When you know that God is a strong tower and refuge (Proverbs 18:10), all your prayers become praise! And all the broken pieces of your life, become, the spoken promises of your destiny! What are "Spoken Promises?" They are the words God spoke into your situation. For example, when God rejected King Saul, "But now thy kingdom shall not continue! The Lord hath sought him a man after His own heart."(I Samuel 13:14). It didn't matter that BOY David didn't know how to be a man yet! But, because of a spoken promise, the God of this BOY knew that one day He would be the God of this KING!! When God told Samuel to anoint him, He said: "For this is he!" (I Samuel 16:12). Don't let anything keep you from fulfilling a spoken promise. YOU are who God is looking for! God sought out your heart, because He knew, you were after His! There is a kingdom purpose inside of you, and it's the call of a Spoken Promise! Have a Blessed day, and thanks for allowing me to share the word from a *Pastor's Perspective…*

NOVEMBER 25

The Apostle Paul's summation of God's purpose for clergy is important to behold..."And he gave some, Apostles, and some, Prophets, and some Evangelists, and some Pastors, and some Teachers; For the PERFECTING of the saints, for the WORK of the ministry, for the EDIFYING of the body of Christ! Why? Till we all come in the UNITY of the faith and the KNOWLEDGE of the Son of God!" (Ephesians 4:11-13). Isn't it just like God to provide all we need for unity in the faith, and just like man to lean on his own understanding and pervert the purpose of UNITY! The bible speaks expressly of being on one accord: "How can two walk together unless they agree?" (Amos 3:3). God desires the unity of our faith, because our adversary is counting on finding stray sheep, who believe they can stand away from the fold, only to destroy them! God has provided you with great leaders. And, when God has UNITY amongst his people, a new leader is always in the making! Have a Blessed day, and thanks for allowing me to share the word from a *Pastor's Perspective...*

NOVEMBER 26

When we sing, "*What a FRIEND we Have in Jesus...*" the message becomes far more profound than the melody! We are declaring that we not only know Jesus, but He knows us as well! But what makes Jesus a true friend to anyone who really knows Him is His unconditional and uncompromising Love for us! I mean, He does exactly what the scripture says friends do: "A friend loveth at all times."(Proverbs 17:17). And because of this love, his friendship is no ordinary one! The scriptures tell us: "A man that hath friends, MUST first show himself friendly!!" (Proverbs 18:24). Because we abandoned the works of the flesh that led to sin, repented, and accepted Salvation, Jesus is talking about us when he declares: "Henceforth I call you not servants; for servants knoweth not what his Lord doeth: but I have called you FRIENDS!"(John 15:15). Rejoice this morning, and remember that having a FRIEND in Jesus, is to have a FRIEND always. Have a Blessed day, and thanks for allowing me to share the word from a *Pastor's Perspective*...

NOVEMBER 27

Resting in Jesus is not just something to say, it is something good to do! Many people lay down at night to sleep, but don't get any REST! Jesus said: "Come unto ME, all ye that labor, and are heavy laden, and I will give you REST!" (Matthew 11:28). We need to know for ourselves that we have the privilege of being able to take EVERYTHING to God in prayer! Otherwise, our concerns wind up in a place not meant to bear burdens: the MIND! So then, the place reserved for peace has become the place where we hold memorials for our worries! God wants us to know that his endless Mercy extends even to our moments of misery. But His Grace becomes Amazing the minute we allow Him to bear our griefs! God doesn't want you to lay down at night with weary worship, then wake up the next morning with empty Faith! Instead, He wants us to REST in Him! Those who have been rescued by faith, can fully REST in Jesus! Have a Blessed day, and thanks for allowing me to share the word from a *Pastor's Perspective...*

NOVEMBER 28

As we embark upon this new day, with its new challenges and uncertainties, it is very encouraging to know that Jesus is the same... "Yesterday, Today, and Forever!" (Hebrews 13:8). Look how the bible describes Jesus' immutability: "But this man, because he continueth ever, hath an UNCHANGEABLE priesthood! "Wherefore, He is able also to save them to the uttermost that come unto God by Him, seeing He ever LIVETH and maketh INTERCESSION for them!" (Hebrews 7:24-25). Even when we miss the mark, fall short, or even waver in our faith, God is still God! Things are subject to change from day to day...but God is the same EVERY DAY! There has never been a day that God didn't make! JESUS said: "Have faith in God!" (Mark 11:22). Because there will be days where you'll just have to trust me and know that I am still GOD!" (Psalms 46:10). That applies to today and every day! Have a super fantastic day, and thanks for allowing me to share the word from a *Pastor's Perspective*...

NOVEMBER 29

God wants us to become champion CHOICE makers! Choice is not about making random decisions, rather it is about skilled, calculated, and above all, God ordained choices! "Choose you this day, whom you will serve!" (Joshua 24:15). In addition, choice has three components that ultimately make your decisions a detriment or a delight; probability, relativity, and accountability. We need to talk with God daily about our choices! There have been countless times when I didn't consider the consequences of a decision. There were times my decisions were overshadowed by my reckless, irrational thinking. And ultimately, accountability has always proven that CHOICES determine OUTCOME! God has given you another day to decide whom you will serve. The CHOICE to serve God, is a chance to truly be blessed! Choosing to follow Jesus is the CHOICE champions make! Have a Blessed day, and thanks for allowing me to share the word from a *Pastor's Perspective*...

NOVEMBER 30

Before we touch and agree with one another in PRAYER, we need to at least make sure our FAITH is on one accord in JESUS! There is nothing worse than praying for *Victory* with a person who has accepted being a *Victim*! Only righteous people, receive righteous results! (James 5:16). At times, it may APPEAR that unbelievers, the doubtful, and even the wicked achieve success, but that is not the case! Instead it's God giving them a season of sovereignty, but afterwards a season of consequences is sure to follow! Therefore, sincere PRAYER must be yoked up with sincere BELIEVERS! Prayer is the attorney of your Faith! It tells God all that's in your heart, but keep in mind that, like a relentless prosecutor, the enemy is always and forever cross-examining your case before God with accusations! (Revelation 12:10). Therefore remember, who you PRAY with is also who you're fighting with! Hence, you need to be praying with people, who want to WIN, and not WHINE! Winners are not victims and whiners are not victorious! Have a Blessed day, and thanks for allowing me to share the word from a *Pastor's Perspective*...

DECEMBER 1

As we approach the New Year, I hear the Lord's words loud and clear: "Remember not the former things, neither consider the things of old. Behold, I will do a NEW thing, now it shall spring forth, shall ye not know it? I will even make a way in the wilderness and rivers in the desert!" (Isaiah 43:18-19). And keeping things in perspective, this NEW thing is not a replacement of the old thing, but an upgrade from the old way! Sometimes our greatest successes come because we decided to change how we go about reaching our goals! To try the same THING in the same way, using the same subject, you are sure to receive the same result! But if you take that life-long dream, goal, or idea and let God do that NEW thing His way, I'm sure you can have a WORSHIP service in the wilderness! On the eve of this New Year give God all your OLD things and let Him do a NEW thing with them. You don't have to make resolutions, when you live in God's revelation! Have a Blessed day, and thanks for allowing me to share the word from a *Pastor's Perspective...*

DECEMBER 2

It's encouraging to know that for each day you suffer with Christ you'll also reign with Him! (II Timothy 2:12). We ought to serve God with an assurance that represents all the power of his presence, according to His promise! And because God is not a man that he should lie, (Numbers 23:19) we are believers that cannot fail! Some of our service is actually the revealing of our oneness with His suffering. He inspired the Apostle Paul to pen these words of encouragement: "For I reckon that the sufferings of this present time are not worthy to be compared with the glory which shall be revealed in us!"(Romans 8:18). Therefore, let me leave you with this: "Cast not away therefore your CONFIDENCE, which has great recompense of reward. For ye have need of patience, that, after ye have done the will of God, ye might receive the PROMISE." (Hebrews 10:35-36). God has never made a promise that He didn't keep. Have a Blessed day, and thanks for allowing me to share the word from a *Pastor's Perspective...*

DECEMBER 3

"In the beginning God created the HEAVENS and the Earth." (Genesis 1:1). However, according to scripture God called the dry land EARTH (vs.10), but everything in the firmament, that is, the sky or His presence, He called Heaven (vs.8). While Chapter I of Genesis explains the origin of creation, the bigger picture is Heaven's blueprint! The place where Time meets Eternity! Because it was declared, "This is the history of the heavens and the Earth," (Genesis 2:4 NKJV), we need to understand that, wherever the presence of God is, such is the Kingdom of God! Which is why Jesus preached, "Repent, for the Kingdom of God is at hand!" (Matthew 4:17). As born-again, blood washed believers, please know that Heaven is not just an expectation, Heaven is also the presence of God in you! Today, be that foreshadow of Heaven, so that those around you will know that truly the Lord is in this place!! Have a Blessed day, and thanks for allowing me to share the word from a *Pastor's Perspective...*

DECEMBER 4

It has been said, FEAR accepted, is FAITH contaminated! The bible declares that "Every man has been dealt a measure of faith." (Romans 12:3). And from that measure of faith, God is expecting your ministry of BELIEF to grow! And yes, belief is ministry. For without it, you cannot please God! (Hebrews 11:6). If we don't allow BELIEF to be the yeast in our FAITH, our expectations, our trials, and even our circumstances will have dwarfed outcomes! Big Faith, fuel by Big Belief should yield Big Rejoicing! Let's just think about this for a minute...If God is BIGGER than anything you could ever go through and your FAITH is Bigger than all your Fears put together, and your Belief IN God, is Bigger than the burden upon you, then the Ministry within you will survive the Misery that surrounds you! Today and every day, allow the comforting words of Jesus to soothe your circumstances and add to your Faith. Have a Blessed day, and thanks for allowing me to share the word from a *Pastor's Perspective*...

DECEMBER 5

Our Christmas story began with the wise men following a star, but the story continues with us following the light! Now that we have been called out of darkness into His marvelous light (I Peter 2:9), God wants us to walk in that light, because God is light (I John 1:7). Why? Because the Father and the Son are one and there could never be darkness in Him at all!! And last but certainly not least, Jesus is the ONLY light capable of dispelling the darkness of this world! He reminds us..."I AM THE LIGHT OF THE WORLD, HE WHO FOLLOWS ME SHALL NOT WALK IN DARKNESS, BUT HAVE THE LIGHT OF LIFE!! (John 8:12). He wants us to follow the light, so we won't get lost in the dark! If you walk in the light, even in the valley of the shadow of death, God will provide His reassuring presence! It takes light in darkness to create a shadow, and it takes an obedient follower to make it to God! If you follow the light of Jesus, you're guaranteed to make it to the glory of God! Have a Blessed day, and thanks for allowing me to share the word from a *Pastor's Perspective*...

DECEMBER 6

The Apostle Paul reminds us, "Among whom also we ALL had our manner of life in times past in the lust of our FLESH, fulfilling the desires of the FLESH, and the MIND, and were by NATURE the children of wrath, even as others!" (Ephesians 2:3). However, the next verse starts with two words that eliminate confusion, infuse confidence, and crush the works of the flesh with faith: "BUT GOD!" (vs.4). Every testimony that begins with those words is no ordinary testimony! A "BUT GOD" testimony is an EXPERIENCE so spiritually infused with God's presence, that it takes the Holy Ghost in you to tell about it!! Your intellect alone can't testify to a *BUT GOD* experience! Your intelligence speaks according to what's been learned or taught! Nevertheless, Saints of God, every time your PAST tries to block your PATH...let the Holy Spirit speak two words that will ALWAYS make a fool of your fears: "BUT GOD!" You may have to live WITH your past, "BUT GOD," you don't have to live IN your past! Have a Blessed day, and thanks for allowing me to share the word from a *Pastor's Perspective...*

DECEMBER 7

The Christ of Christmas is also the ANOINTING on everything ANOINTED! His birth led not only to our justification from Sin, but He became the power in OUR purpose! In fact, the angel of the Lord said to Mary, "The Holy Spirit will come upon you, and the POWER of the Highest shall overshadow thee, therefore also that Holy thing which shall be born of thee shall be called the Son of God!"(Luke 1:35). The power of our purpose, is in the person of the Son of God! God tells us that as long as MY POWER is what fuels YOUR PURPOSE...All your impossibilities, become Possible! (Luke 1:37). Today, let us be reminded that Christmas is a Holy day, and the impossible became possible because of the POWER of God's PURPOSE for our lives...just think about this...When God declared you a Holy thing, you became His POWER according to HIS Purpose!!Don't ever forget, everything Holy, has Holy Ghost Power and Holy Ghost Purpose! Have a Blessed day, and thanks for allowing me to share the word from a *Pastor's Perspective...*

DECEMBER 8

The Apostle Paul wanted the Corinthian church to know that the source of his authority is God! He encouraged them by letting them know, "For all the Promises of God in Him are YES, and in Him AMEN, to the glory of God through US!!" (II Corinthians 1:20). Wow, what a phenomenal passage for putting the Promises of God in proper perspective! When the Apostle Paul declared, "To the glory of God THROUGH us," he wanted us to understand that a PROMISE from God should reveal His PRESENCE in us! We are the glory of God in the earth! We are the sheep of His pasture! And We are the manifestation of YES and AMEN! Have you ever been told...You'll never be this or that, and then God says, "Oh YES she will!" Have you ever heard "you'll never be the same after this," and then God said, "Oh YES he will!" Glory to God saints! Let God's promises order your steps and I guarantee that your hope in God, won't let you down! Have a Blessed day, and thanks for allowing me to share the word from a *Pastor's Perspective...*

DECEMBER 9

God wants us to open our hearts, our arms, and especially our minds. "Then He (Jesus) opened their understanding that they might understand the scriptures." (Luke 24:45). The Apostle Paul was encouraged to instruct us to open up so that, "Christ may dwell in our hearts through faith, that you, being rooted and grounded in LOVE, may be able to COMPREHEND with all the saints what is the WIDTH, and LENGTH, and DEPTH, and HEIGHT: to know the LOVE of Christ which passes knowledge, that you may be filled with all the fullness of God!!" (Ephesians 3:17-19). Therefore, I challenge you today to take full advantage of this glorious opportunity to be filled

FILLED WITH THE FULLNESS OF GOD

with God and full of faith! Though you may have trouble opening up to people, most certainly opening up to God is the beginning of life lived in all of its fullness. Have a Blessed day, and thanks for allowing me to share the word from a *Pastor's Perspective...*

DECEMBER 10

When you know you're BLESSED, your outlook on life is superior to anything that life throws you! "BLESSED is he whose transgression is forgiven, whose SIN is covered. BLESSED is the man unto whom the Lord imputeth not iniquity and in whose spirit there is no guile." (Psalms 32:1-2). People say: "I'm Blessed," with no real understanding of what they're declaring! When you're Blessed, you're implying that you are above reproach because you're covered by Grace! And that you personally know the Blesser! But saying, "I'm Blessed," without knowing Jesus, is deceiving yourself! (Galatians 6:7-8). Please understand, the crux of being BLESSED is knowing the Lord! To leave this life and not know the Lord, is the opposite of being eternally BLESSED! Therefore, to make good on your declaration of "being BLESSED", make sure you have a real relationship with Him from whom all blessings flow! Have a Blessed day, and thanks for allowing me to share the word from a *Pastor's Perspective*...

DECEMBER 11

"Fear not, for behold I bring good tidings of
great JOY, which shall be to all people! (Luke
2:8-10). And this Great Joy grew up and
became our Savior, our healer, our provider,
and our protector! And although Jesus is
standing at the door of so many hearts
knocking, His knock often goes unanswered!
But those who have answered, did so because
Jesus said: "I am the Good Shepherd and
know my sheep, and am known of
mine."(John 10:14). The sheep needed a
Shepherd then, and His sheep need a
Shepherd now! Unattended sheep always have
something to Fear! But any Sheep with a good
shepherd need not fear at all, because a good
shepherd will protect the sheep's life, even if
it costs him his! God has been watching you
travel the fields of life without a Shepherd,
but He has sent His Son to knock at the door
of your heart. Today; answer and let Jesus in,
then let the Good Shepherd take care of you.
Have a Blessed day, and thanks for allowing
me to share the word from a *Pastor's
Perspective*...

DECEMBER 12

"Weeping may endure for a night, but JOY cometh in the morning."(Psalms 30:5b). I believe David wanted to shed light on the fact that our circumstances don't need to hold us hostage. David's understanding of God's love for him came through loss, betrayal, and his own selfishness. God used all of David's afflictions to establish the power of His majesty! David said..."For His anger endureth but a moment, in His FAVOR is life!"(Psalm 30:5a).

Therefore, TRIALS only come to pass! PAIN will not prevail! CIRCUMSTANCES will not control you! LOSS in this life, does not mean God has left you anywhere! Your WEEPING, will become WORSHIP one day, if you trust him! One day JOY will come again, and you will gain enough strength to get up and pull out of that night experience. Saints of God, life is filled with things that try to bring us down, but we are filled, with the ONE who is able to pick us up! Have a Blessed day, and thanks for allowing me to share the word from a *Pastor's Perspective*...

DECEMBER 13

One of the most trying things every believer must deal with at some time or another is the battle of our WILL versus our WORSHIP! Our WILL can be cleverly demanding at times, which is why we commit our WORKS to the Lord! On the other hand, our WORSHIP is the sustainer of our strength when the desires of the flesh want to have their way! It is your WORSHIP that helps you win this war! It is your WORSHIP that turns temptation into testimony! And it will be your WORSHIP to God that will establish your thoughts in God! Today, if a battle between your WILL and your WORSHIP is going on, let me encourage you first, with the words of Jesus..."God is spirit, and those who WORSHIP him, must WORSHIP in spirit and truth."(John 4:24). And after you have suffered a while the God of ALL grace will Perfect, Establish, Strengthen, and Settle you!"(I Peter 5:10). Remember, the victory is in Jesus, but the war is won through WORSHIP! Have a Blessed day, and thanks for allowing me to share the word from a *Pastor's Perspective...*

DECEMBER 14

The Prophet Solomon said...."A man hath JOY by the answer of his mouth, and a word spoken in due season, how good is it!" (Proverbs 15:23). When scripture tells of "DUE" season, it is referring to a time of refreshing! We all have seasons that don't yield continuous JOY, but the Prophet Solomon said the refreshing begins with how we RESPOND to the season! Sure, we could use a hug from those that love us. And it's always nice to sit and laugh with people. And sometimes just having someone there for you makes all the difference. But true refreshing in a DUE season, must start with you and is best endured, by drawing on the remarkable refreshing power, from within! Today, let the true YOU, speak life into your DUE season! You're going to find that He is greater in you,

 and bigger than anything you're going through! Have a Blessed day, and thanks for allowing me to share the word from a *Pastor's Perspective...*

DECEMBER 15

Now, I realize the holidays can be trying for some for many reasons but sometimes the best way to remain JOYFULL around this time of year, is to separate ourselves from negativity! Which is exactly what God the Father did! Jesus' birth could not be tainted by the negativity of others! Everything Christ came to do, was done with JOY! (Hebrews 12:2). It was by design that Herod was unable to locate the baby Jesus! God would not allow Herod's negative mindset to snuff out our reason to rejoice! The birth of Jesus was God's answer, for the sins of his people! (Matthew 1:21). We may not have all that we want under a tree, but as believers, we have all that we need to rejoice in our hearts! This holiday season, let the JOY of our Savior's birth brighten your day. The wise men followed a star that lead them to Christ, and now the one who was to come is leading us to glory! As we celebrate this holiday season, remember that His birth, is our JOY!... Have a Blessed day, and thanks for allowing me to share the word from a *Pastor's Perspective*...

DECEMBER 16

Sometimes we can't seem to see our way through things, and everything around us seems too much to bear. Or a dark cloud seems to follow us everywhere we go. Let me remind you that in times like these, "Thy word is a LAMP unto my feet, and a LIGHT unto my path!" (Psalms 119:105). Many of us approach dark times groping and feeling our way through obscurity only to experience a fear that literally cancels our faith! Sure, we may attempt to move a little in these night experiences, but the truth of the matter is, you can't truly maneuver in darkness and instead you must displace it with LIGHT!! Today, allow the word of God to be a LAMP for your endeavors and let the LIGHT of his word illuminate your path! Remember this..."God is LIGHT, and in Him, is NO DARKNESS AT ALL!!" (I John 1:5). The best way to see your way through everything, is to let God shine His LIGHT everywhere you go! Have a Blessed day, and thanks for allowing me to share the word from a *Pastor's Perspective*...

DECEMBER 17

Have you ever really sat and pondered Psalms
139 in its entirety? When David asked:
"Where shall I go from thy spirit? Or whither
shall I flee from thy presence?" He is
revealing that he understood that no matter
where he went, God would be there! (vs.7).
We are so surrounded by God's love that
when you accepted Jesus as your Lord and
Savior, you received Heaven's Almighty
Insurance Policy! You have full coverage, no
matter where you are! Nothing happens by
accident! There is no need for collision
insurance, because you are consecrated! And
there will never be a deductible no matter
what the circumstances are because you have
the promise of complete deliverance!
Periodically, review your policy and ask God
to: "Search me, O God, and know my heart,
try me, and know my thoughts. And see if
there be any wicked way in me and lead me in
the way everlasting."(Psalms 139:23-24). To
have God all around you, is full coverage at its
best! Have a Blessed day, and thanks for
allowing me to share the word from a *Pastor's
Perspective*...

DECEMBER 18

The Centurion told Jesus: "Lord, I am not worthy that thou shouldest come under my roof, but speak the word only, and my servant shall be healed!" (Matthew 8:5-8). What an awesome picture of Care, Compassion, and Confidence! The Centurion's servant was dear to him and he didn't see him as a mere slave or worker. When he found the Healer, he had total trust in Him! This is the same truth in our relationship with Christ. Jesus said: "Henceforth, I call you not servants, for the servant knoweth not what his Lord doeth, but I have called you friends!" And guess what? "You have not chosen me, but I have chosen you!" (John 15:15-16). How you see your circumstances and even yourself, is one thing, but how you see yourself and circumstances in Christ, is altogether different! The healing, the deliverance, and even the circumstance changer is just a WORD away! It is good to know that the WORD works, if YOU work it! Have a Blessed day, and thanks for allowing me to share the word from a *Pastor's Perspective*...

DECEMBER 19

We are so blessed to inherit ALL that springs from the heart of God! The living waters of life that flow in us are from Him! (John 4:14). The peace we have in us is from Him! (John 14:27). The comfort we receive in the difficult times comes from Him! (John 14:18). Even the JOY we experience is from Him! (John 15:11). God has WILLED us so much, and today He wants to know if you'll accept all He has for you and abandon all that weakens your WILL? "Love not the world, neither the things that are in the world. If any man loves the world, the love of the father is not in him. For all that is in the world, the lust of the flesh, and the lust of the eyes, and the pride of life is not of the Father but is of the world. And the world passeth away, and the lust of it! But he that doeth the WILL of God abideth forever!"(I John 2:15-17). Our Godly inheritance is our assurance that we belong to God! Examine your spiritual WILL then rejoice in the fact that everything you have, is according to HIS will! Have a Blessed day, and thanks for allowing me to share the word from a *Pastor's Perspective*...

DECEMBER 20

King Solomon declared... "The fear of the Lord prolongeth days, but the years of the wicked shall be shortened!" (Proverbs 10:27). We are living at a time when people take the supremacy of God's majesty for granted! There seems to be a lack of reverence for the creator! Wickedness is widespread! Violence is rising everywhere! Morality has taken a backseat to physical pleasure! However, the Apostle Paul reminds us...."Now the spirit speaketh that, in the latter times, some shall depart from the faith, giving heed to seducing spirits, and doctrines of demons!" (I Timothy 4:1). God is to be reverenced, because of who HE is! He has allowed us to express the many gifts we possess, but that does not mean we are to stop giving HIM all the glory HE deserves! Our world is in the state it's in, because our hearts have been corrupted by SIN! The only way to keep God in perfect and proper perspective, is to put SIN in its place! Have a Blessed day, and thanks for allowing me to share the word from a *Pastor's Perspective...*

King Solomon said, "The blessing of the Lord, it maketh rich, and he addeth no sorrow with it." (Proverbs 10:22). However, he also wrote: "They that trust in their wealth and boast themselves in the multitude of their riches; None of them can by any means redeem his brother, nor give to God a ransom for him." (Psalms 49:6-8). He continues… "For He seeth that wise men die! Likewise, the fool and the stupid person perish! And leave their wealth to others!" (vs.10). Jesus reiterated what they said, when he warned: "Lay not up for yourselves treasures upon earth, where moth and rust doth corrupt, and where thieves break through and steal. But lay up for yourselves treasures in Heaven, where neither moth, nor rust doth corrupt and where thieves do not break through, nor steal!" (Matthew 6:19-20). Never bury your HEART in a place that's not fit for your soul to rest! "For where your treasure is, there will your HEART be also." (Matthew 6:21). Have a Blessed day, and thanks for allowing me to share the word from a *Pastor's Perspective*...

DECEMBER 22

When we were children we dreamed of the future. But now that we're all grown up, God needs us to understand, "When you were a child, you spoke as a child, you thought like a child, but the more you grew, I expected you to put away that childish mindset." (I Corinthians 13:11). Why? Because now God wants you to know that, "A man's heart deviseth his way, but the Lord directs his path!" (Proverbs 16:9). If what you dreamed as a child, doesn't fulfill your destiny as God's elect, not only is your vision subject to change, but your heart gets exposed to heaviness, because your expectations don't match up with what God has predestined. Instead of being frustrated with YOUR plans, ask God what HIS plans are for your life. And give God time to respond to your heart. It is very hard to hear God tell you his plan, if you're constantly listening to YOURSELF talk about yours! Have a Blessed day, and thanks for allowing me to share the word from a *Pastor's Perspective*...

The Psalmist said..."Let the REDEEMED of the Lord say so!" (Psalms 107:2). And you might be saying...Say what? And the spirit of God is saying...Tell somebody how good I am!! There is so much pain, so much death, so much suffering all around us. But through it all, YOU the REDEEMED have GOD all around YOU! We are not exempt from pain, death, and suffering but we are covered by a Grace, that won't allow grief, to grow! God wants your TESTIMONY to give someone else hope, encouragement, and ultimately victory! You don't have to be an ordained preacher to lift up Jesus' name! If you've been REDEEMED, you're fully equipped to speak the goodness of God you've experienced into the trying situation of others! God wants someone, somewhere to witness that He's able! And He wants to hear it said, from those who have been delivered! So, today let every Saved, Sanctified, and Blood Washed believer shout...God is Able! Because the REDEEMED of the Lord say so! Have a Blessed day, and thanks for allowing me to share the word from a *Pastor's Perspective*...

DECEMBER 24

We all desire to enjoy life, peace, and happiness. However, like anything worth having, it takes effort and vision. The Prophet Solomon said..."Where there is no vision, the people perish!" (Proverbs 29:18), and he concludes in that same verse: "But he that keepeth the Law, HAPPY is he." Trying to achieve Happiness IN life, apart from the creator OF life, is like stepping over a dollar to get to a penny and constantly saying: "If I just had a little more, everything would be alright!" No, things will remain the same! When your actions go against God's vision for you, what's inside you, slowly perishes! Instead, co-labor with God in bringing to fruition his vision for you! And then, to make the blessing even more bountiful, you'll get the privilege of watching and witnessing everything you envisioned give birth to HAPPINESS! If you're looking for anything from God, you're sure to find it in Jesus! Have a Blessed day, and thanks for allowing me to share the word from a *Pastor's Perspective*...

DECEMBER 25

Christmas is the time of year we acknowledge the birth of our Savior. It's the season we sing carols and where spirits are high on family, food, and festivities. We even go the extra mile by exchanging gifts with one another. But the significance of Jesus' spiritual birth is what gives your life its eternal worth! When Jesus came to earth, God the Father, was acknowledging US! "For he shall save HIS people from THEIR sins!" (Matthew 2:21). From the very moment of his introduction to the world, God's saving grace has been in effect through His son! Sometimes we get so caught up being blessed that we forget to give God the glory for the blessing! There is one significant point we cannot deny...if God did not send Jesus to redeem our souls, there would be no Justice against the courts of Hell! But because Jesus' birth was a "Holy thing"(Luke 1:35), our life in Him, is an eternal thing! Let me remind you that every bright spot in your life was lit by the light of the world (John 8:12). Have a Blessed day, and thanks for allowing me to share the word from a *Pastor's Perspective*...

DECEMBER 26

As we try to focus on today and all its possibilities and challenges, we still have some things going on that are an extension of yesterday. But praise be to God that "Jesus is the same yesterday, today, and forever!" (Hebrews 13:8). It is comforting to know that even when situations linger, our triumphant Savior is still victorious over all our affairs. There are times we lean on our own understanding, and usually those are the times we get unfavorable results. But if you were to think about all the times you truly trusted God in whatever was going on in your life, the end result was blessed of the Lord! To be able to declare, "it is well with my soul," Jesus must be a well deep in your heart! It's because of Jesus... "We LIVE, MOVE and HAVE our BEING!" (Acts 17:28) And because He lives, we can face tomorrow! Today as you give thanks, allow yesterday's successes to strengthen today's possibilities. Because Jesus stays the same...today will be a good day! Be Blessed, and thanks for allowing me to share the word from *Pastor's Perspective*...

DECEMBER 27

When the Scribes and Pharisees brought a woman caught in adultery to Jesus, they were looking to test Jesus' authority, but instead they encountered the Messiah's meekness! (John 8:1-11). The LORD never needs our help judging sin! He wants us to show compassion. Please understand, this does not mean we stop striving for purity, holiness, and righteousness. Nor does it mean we turn a blind eye to unrighteousness. No, not at all! However, He does want us to do all we can to RESTORE a soul, before we decide to REJECT one! When Jesus said, "He that is without SIN among you, let him cast the first stone at her!"(vs.7). He knew that none of them were SINLESS, but it was still His desire for them to SIN LESS! Therefore, when He told the woman..."Go, and Sin no more," (vs.11) He wasn't telling her to go and be perfect, He was telling her "Go, and be a testimony to this moment!" The best way to stop the destruction of condemnation, is to exercise the gift of compassion. Have a Blessed day, and thanks for allowing me to share the word from a *Pastor's Perspective*...

DECEMBER 28

For every action, there is a reaction. With every Pro there is a Con. What goes up, must come down. These are just a few of the many earthly clichés that have sadly set the course for some believers. Solomon clearly said, "Let us hear the conclusion of the whole matter: Fear God, keep his commandments, for this is the WHOLE duty of man!"(Ecclesiastes 12:13). Clichés are opinions or phrases that are over used and that betray ORIGINAL thought. God's word says: "The grass may wither, the flowers may fade, but the word of God will stand forever!?" (Isaiah 40:8). God's

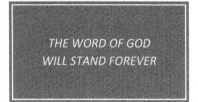

THE WORD OF GOD
WILL STAND FOREVER

original plan for man, will one day be just what he declared it to be from the beginning (Isaiah 11:1-16). We've all heard, "Godliness is next to cleanliness," and "What doesn't kill you, makes you stronger," neither of which is in the bible. We really need to stop passing catchy phrases off as if God said them, in fact, we probably shouldn't use them at all...Have a Blessed day, and thanks for allowing me to share the word from a *Pastor's Perspective*...

DECEMBER 29

When Jesus assembled together with the disciples, He told them not to leave Jerusalem, but to wait for the promise of the Father! "But you shall be baptized with the Holy Spirit not many days from now, SO DON'T LEAVE!" (Acts 1:5). Church attendance is one thing, but an encounter with the Holy Spirit is something completely different! Jesus wanted the disciples to wait on the Holy Spirit because they needed SUPERNATURAL POWER within them that would prevent the world from changing them! If you wait on the Holy Spirit, you'll receive the POWER that gives your EXPERIENCE...PURPOSE! You're not ineffective, you're not any less of a believer than anyone else...God simply wants you to understand that you may have left your EXPERIENCE too soon! He wants you to go back to the place of your EXPERIENCE and wait because the Holy Spirit wants to come upon you, so you can receive POWER from on high. Have a Blessed day, and thanks for allowing me to share the word from a *Pastor's Perspective...*

DECEMBER 30

The shoreline of Salvation is Romans 10:9-10.
"That if thou shall CONFESS with thy
MOUTH the Lord Jesus and shall BELIEVE
in thine HEART that God hath raised him
from the dead, thou shall be SAVED! For
with the heart man BELIEVETH unto
RIGHTEOUSNESS, and with the MOUTH
confession is made unto SALVATION."
When you get to this point, you've actually

swum
through the
unchartered
waters of
uncertainty,
eluded

dangers seen and unseen, endured enormous
winds, waves, and storms, and have finally
reached the shore! God kept the BEST of
you, to save the REST of you! And now, you
can see for yourself that your REDEEMER
lives! (JOB 19:25). God delivered you from
the waters that you might bring forth
WORSHIP unto Him! The survival of your
soul is solidified when you speak of your
belief in Jesus' death, burial, and resurrection.
Hallelujah! Have a Blessed day, and thanks for
allowing me to share the word from a *Pastor's
Perspective...*

DECEMBER 31

One of the greatest spiritual misconceptions is in thinking, that now that you're SANCTIFIED, you ought to always be SATISFIED. While the Apostle Paul said..."For I have learned, in whatever state I am, in this to be content!" (Philippians 4:11), He also said..."Godliness with contentment is great gain!" (I Timothy 6:6). These scriptures are NOT telling me to find SATISFACTION where I am, but rather, to be humble along the way! Being SANCTIFIED means to be set apart for a specific purpose. When God gave us His word, the Sanctification process had begun! "Sanctify them through thy truth, thy word is truth!" (John 17:17). And because the word is a purifying agent, NONE of us can say, we're always SATISFIED with the refining process! Because let's face it, the TRUTH sometimes hurts! However, it is through this Sanctifying process that we strive for the mastery that is ONLY found in the living word, Christ Jesus! So then, you may not like the journey so much, but you're going to simply adore your final destination! So, let your heart be encouraged today, hang in there, because heaven is worth it! SANCTIFIED doesn't mean you're always SATISFIED... Instead, it's proof you're SAVED! Have a Blessed day, and thanks for allowing me to share the word from a *Pastor's Perspective*...

REFERENCES

Converse, Charles Crozat (1968). *What a friend we have in Jesus.*

Flack, Roberta and Hathaway, Donnie. (1977) *The Closer I Get to You.* Blue Lights in the Basement album.

Hunt, Calvin. (1996). *Mercy Saw Me.*

MercyMe (2001). *I Can Only Imagine.* The Worship Project, USA

REMARKS

"It was a joy to have my son Abram work along side me in the ministry for over 10 years. When God placed it on his heart to write *A Pastor's Perspective,* we prayed that it would one day be published for all the world to read, one day at a time. God Bless you my son in all your accomplishments."
-Senior Pastor Abram Cotton Jr.
Christian Love Bible Church

"A great devo from a fellow pastor and friend. Definitely worth getting his daily thought! "
-Reverend Wayne Hampton

"Wow, Wow, Wow!!! Good word, Amen, Amen & Amen..."
-Luz

"He is able to perform that which He has promised! I believe!!!"
-Ritz

"I love it pastor! What a way to begin each day. Have a glorious day! Love you."
-Tyson Cotton

Made in the USA
Monee, IL
05 August 2020

37654299R10225